Who Killed
TY CONN

LINDEN MacINTYRE
& THERESA BURKE

Penguin Books

PENGUIN BOOKS

Published by the Penguin Group

Penguin Books Canada Ltd, 10 Alcorn Avenue, Toronto, Ontario, Canada M4V 3B2

Penguin Books Ltd, 80 Strand, London WC2R 0RL, England

Penguin Putnam Inc., 375 Hudson Street, New York, New York 10014, U.S.A.

Penguin Books Australia Ltd, Ringwood, Victoria, Australia

Penguin Books (NZ) Ltd, cnr Rosedale and Airborne Roads, Albany, Auckland 1310, New Zealand

Penguin Books Ltd, Registered Offices: Harmondsworth, Middlesex, England

First published in Viking by Penguin Books of Canada Limited, 2000
Published in Penguin Books, 2001

10 9 8 7 6 5 4 3 2 1

Manufactured in Canada.

Text design and typesetting by Laura Brady

NATIONAL LIBRARY OF CANADA CATALOGUING IN PUBLICATION DATA

MacIntyre, Linden, 1943–
  Who killed Ty Conn

Includes index.
ISBN 0-14-029095-8

1. Conn, Ty, 1967–1999. 2. Brigands and robbers – Canada – Biography.
3. Prisoners – Canada – Biography. I. Burke, Theresa, 1956– . II. Title.

HV6653.C66M32 2001   364.15′52′092   C2001-901646-8

Visit Penguin Canada's website at **www.penguin.ca**

PENGUIN BOOKS

WHO KILLED TY CONN

LINDEN MCINTYRE has been a journalist for thirty-six years and has worked on newspapers, radio and television. Since 1990 he has been a host on the CBC flagship public affairs show *the fifth estate*. He has won many awards for his journalism, including six Geminis from the Academy of Canadian Cinema and Television. In addition to his work for the CBC, he has written and presented documentaries for the American Public Broadcasting program *Frontline*. In 1999 he published his first novel, *The Long Stretch* (Stoddart).

THERESA BURKE attended various universities, including the University of Nantes, the University of Alaska and the University of Toronto. She began her career in journalism in 1994 when she became a researcher on *the fifth estate*, where she is now an associate producer.

Dedicated to
Marion Chamberlain

I remember the gleams and glooms that dart
Across the school-boy's brain;
The song and the silence in the heart
That in part are prophecies, and in part
Are longings wild and vain.
And the voice of that fitful song
Sings on, and is never still:
"A boy's will is the wind's will,
And the thoughts of youth are long, long thoughts."

H. W. Longfellow
My Lost Youth

CONTENTS

INTRODUCTION

THE CHANCE AND HURRIED encounter that usually occurs between a reporter and the subject of a story rarely has sufficient impact on either individual to start a friendship. People tend to regard reporters not so much as other people, but as functions. Reporters learn to resist the stirrings of personal feelings when they meet people who are involved in their stories. For one thing, feelings influence perceptions. For another, most of the people reporters meet in the course of their work are profoundly needy in one way or another. And none are needier than the people we meet in "correctional institutions," the positive phrase we've invented to describe prisons.

Friendships with people who have complicated and often tragic lives impose responsibilities few of us have time or the emotional resources to deal with.

Tyrone William Conn became the first exception to that professional axiom. He became a friend.

I met Ty Conn on September 1, 1994, in the Special Handling Unit of the Correction Service of Canada Institution in Prince Albert, Saskatchewan. Prince Albert is an old penitentiary, from an era when prisons favoured high walls of stone or brick. Ordinary people could only try to imagine what went on behind the grim ramparts of a place like Prince Albert or Kingston, Ontario, or Dorchester, New Brunswick. That, of course, was an important part of the deterrent value of imprisonment.

Today's institutions are more transparent. Low buildings squat behind high chain-link security fences topped with coils of razor wire. Drumheller. Millhaven. Springhill. They all have in common the ordered and sterile appearance of an environment that is managed down to the smallest detail, and resolutely controlled. They are hellish places for the people confined in them. And they're only a little less daunting to people who are unlikely to ever live or work inside one of them.

Ty Conn looked more like a high-school student than a dangerous convict when I first set eyes upon him. He was wearing jeans and a sweatshirt and he walked with a cautious, springy step that presented an impression of confidence, but also betrayed his readiness to run. He was twenty-seven years old but seemed much younger. I've met young offenders who were more hardened and more menacing. I had to keep reminding myself that this mild-looking youngster with the steady hazel eyes was working through a cumulative sentence of more than forty-seven years.

He was a bank robber and an escape artist. That, in the perverse prison culture, made him part of the élite. He'd scared the wits out of innocent bank employees throughout eastern Ontario in a few brief and frantic crime sprees. But it became clear before the end of our visit that in the most important aspects of his character and personality he was little more than a confused and curious boy.

How did he get there? He'd grown up in comfortable material circumstances, the adopted son of a prominent psychiatrist. Notwithstanding a willingness to arm himself with lethal weapons to commit robberies, he'd never physically harmed anyone. He had a lot of ironic and sharp observations about society and politics and human nature, and they seemed to be rooted in an unusually old-fashioned sense of justice and fairness. How did he ever stray from what should have been a straight line toward a conventional life of participation in the community to this existence of exclusion from everything he considered to be important and worthwhile?

I didn't know it then, but I would spend a substantial part of the next five years trying to find answers to those questions. And in doing so, I would learn a great deal about Tyrone Conn, and even more about the laws and the institutions that dominated and, ultimately, doomed his life.

Our friendship started with an almost unconscious act. I gave him my business card. I still don't know why. Apart from being intrigued by how this mild-mannered individual ended up in Canada's most secure prison environment, I wasn't much impressed by my morning in the Prince Albert Pen. The interview we recorded was memorable only because of his impressive determination not to tell us anything about himself that might seem dramatic on television.

In one typical exchange I asked him if maybe a lot of his juvenile antics had been to elicit evidence of love from people who controlled his life.

"Yes," he agreed.

I wondered aloud—"Well, why can't you say that?"

He gave the question a bit of uneasy reflection, then replied: "Who knows!"

I was with a television crew preparing a follow-up program after a CBC documentary we'd broadcast earlier in 1994 on the subject of verbal abuse. The original item was a two-hour exploration of the link between juvenile delinquency and the emotional bullying that frequently occurs in a dysfunctional or disintegrating family situation. Among thousands of responses to that program there was a carefully handwritten letter from Prince Albert that disclosed, in the words of Theresa Burke, the associate producer who first read it, that he was "twenty-seven doing forty-seven . . . and never so much as threw a punch."

In the letter, Ty Conn identified strongly with the eleven-year-old boy who had been the focus of our story, a troubled kid named Evan. He knew exactly what Evan's life was about. He'd experienced a lot of the same kind of verbal abuse in an otherwise privileged upbringing. Ty could see Evan starting down the same road he'd travelled.

Unfortunately, when the television camera started rolling, the eloquence that was so impressive in the letter swiftly deserted him. He became reluctant to describe the disturbing childhood experiences he'd hinted at in his letter and in subsequent telephone conversations with Theresa Burke. When he yielded some specific information, after much prodding, he'd swiftly qualify it in order to avoid creating the impression that he was complaining.

In October of 1994, we broadcast our follow-up to the program about Evan. We interviewed a lot of experts in the field of child care and juvenile justice, and a lot of people who told stories of lives imperilled by verbal abuse during childhood. Ty Conn was one of them . . . but he appeared on camera only on condition that we not broadcast his last name. He didn't want to hurt his adoptive father any more than he, presumably, already had by achieving notoriety as a bank robber.

Disclosure started slowly. The first letter he wrote to me was a commentary on the television program in which he'd appeared. He had very little to say about himself, other than that the field producer, Neil Docherty, along with Theresa Burke and me, had helped him to relax "by talking to me like a person rather than a convict and I appreciate that.

"Some of the emotions and feelings that were revealed by other respondents [in the television program] . . . rang true and familiar and although it disturbs me that there were so many, their experiences and behaviour sort of validated my own in a way.

"Even though I'm glad about the attention your program brought to the subject, I'm a pessimist by nature and I can't see people changing their behaviour permanently. I kind of envision people taking notice for a while of their reactions to their kids. But sooner or later will end up reverting to yelling and verbal abuse . . ."

He went on to report that he'd conducted an informal survey among thirty inmates in his section of the special-handling unit and found that fourteen were graduates of juvenile detention facilities. Of that group, twelve had spent time in group homes, foster care or with relatives "while their parents worked out their problems."

His letters were irresistible. I am a lazy letter writer. I've persuaded myself that I have such a high regard for the art and discipline of letter writing that I find myself postponing them until a time when I can give the full measure of attention and thought that a letter deserves. Such an oasis of peace is seldom available in a busy world. So I neglect them for long periods of time. But it was impossible not to answer Ty Conn's letters.

He didn't seem to have any of my reluctance about writing. He had a lot of time on his hands. He read a lot and he watched a lot of television. Ideas and impressions of the outside world scrambled like mice through his busy mind.

One of his early letters, dated April 16, 1995, dealt with the wrongful conviction of Donzell Young (subsequently killed in prison) for murder; the systemic unfairness of the justice system; the cynical way inmates try to capitalize on the disrepute of the justice system by claiming innocence to outsiders "when you'd be hard pressed to find anyone claiming innocence" in prison; a killing he'd witnessed in Millhaven, in which a guard shot a prisoner with a high-powered rifle to stop a fight, but which was really a drug-related murder; the Gerald Regan sexual assault case in Nova Scotia; the new president of the CBC, Perrin Beatty ("How does it feel to have the former head of CSIS at the helm?"); a math course he was taking toward a civil engineering degree; a computer he'd just bought; a book he'd just read and highly recommended (*The Wealthy Barber*).

I confess that for a long time I waited for him to disclose his real motives for writing to someone like me, someone with nothing to offer except, perhaps, the deceptive promise of publicity. I've learned, over the years, that many prison inmates indulge a naïve belief that the media have the moral authority to overrule the work of the justice system by the simple act of telling a story from the offender's point of view.

I've often explained that this flattering notion is true only on rare occasions, and only when there has been a clearly demonstrable miscarriage of justice. And, I have often been tempted to add, it's usually only effective when the victim of such a miscarriage has some personal quality (appearance, charm, intellect) or a social asset (celebrity endorsement) to make him or her attractive to the whimsical "public."

On October 11, 1995, Ty returned to Ontario. He was transferred to the maximum security Millhaven Institution, about ten miles west of Kingston, a place in which he would find no rehabilitative programs, very little peace and no reason to hope for any improvement in his circumstances.

Shortly after his arrival at Millhaven, he asked if I would accept an invitation to attend a family social. He wanted me to meet his mother. I quickly told him I would. He said it would require that I be approved by the corrections system for inclusion on his visitors' list. I consented.

In early May 1996, I drove from Toronto to Millhaven on a rainy Saturday morning. I anticipated a grim day. The family social was from 9:15 a.m. to 3 p.m. I couldn't imagine how one would fill so much time in an environment like that and with someone I knew only from an exchange of letters. But he wanted me to meet his mom, so I went. I deliberately showed up late.

The Millhaven pen is adjacent to the Bath Institution, a medium-security prison, but to the eye of an outsider, there isn't much to distinguish one from the other. There are the same high perimeter fences, the same towers. Inside

Millhaven, I was checked through, then photographed. It was a Polaroid shot which, I was told, would be given to me when I left. It was a precaution to make sure that at the end of the visit some clever inmate, posing as me, would not slip away to freedom. I thought that to be an unlikely scenario, since it would presumably have meant that I'd have agreed to stay behind. Fat chance.

The event was in the Millhaven gymnasium. It was probably as odd a conclave of Canadians as one could find anywhere on that day. There were people of all ages and skin tones. Large men in muscle shirts, their heads shaved and tattooed, gently showed off their toddlers or romped on the floor with their older children. Stressed-looking women watched or huddled in cautious intimacy with their men. Mothers sat with sons at the kind of tables I remember from bingo halls. There was, to my surprise, a warm and festive atmosphere.

I asked Ty Conn a lot of questions, spurred by a deep curiosity about those elusive factors that turn people into criminals. And the more he told me, the more frustration I felt: there was very little about him that matched any of my prior understanding of the criminal mentality, or the origins of deviant behaviour.

I was struck by his unwillingness to recognize that, with a bit of serious help at several junctures in his life, he might be somewhere entirely different now. For him, crime and punishment were the two sides of a common social currency.

I recall, as the hour approached three o'clock and the end of the visit, asking the question: "Have you ever had a decent lawyer to defend you?"

He stared at me with genuine puzzlement and finally responded, "I don't know what you mean."

I explained that I, a layperson, could recognize a lot of extenuating circumstances in his life story, and that I was surprised that a clever lawyer hadn't been able to exploit them to persuade the courts to take a more creative approach to his case than they obviously had.

"Like what?" was his reply.

"How the hell did you end up with a sentence of forty-seven years for a lot of property crimes? Haven't you ever asked yourself that question?"

He then told me bluntly that he'd always had good lawyers and that he'd never been wrongly convicted or, in his view, unfairly sentenced. In truth, he said, he probably got less than he deserved since there were a number of robberies for which he'd never been charged.

"That," I said, "makes you the first guilty convict I've ever talked to."

He seemed genuinely surprised and assured me that almost everybody in the room would, if they were candid, make the same admission. Inmates don't bullshit each other, he said.

I backed away from the subject. He'd obviously failed to grasp my point: that, in justice, guilt and innocence aren't merely about who did what to whom; that a justice system is also supposed to be about circumstances and compassion and mitigating factors. And about rehabilitation, not just incarceration and punishment.

This, I felt, was the wrong place for such a conversation. But, for as far as it went, our chat about his views on justice as it related to his life had disposed of any apprehension I might have had about hidden agendas and secret motives behind his friendliness.

Friendship changes people. Bonds of friendship become conduits through which occur a busy spiritual commerce. Qualities are exchanged. A friend absorbs experience and memory from the other and is changed by the process. In friendship, people grow and are diminished. Lives are altered, and sometimes destroyed. I learned all this from Tyrone Conn.

My initial caution, based on the suspicion that he was cultivating friendship from some base motivation, was mistaken. I don't think he had many long friendships in his life. It was partly because he learned early on that it is dangerous to trust people, and because, as he grew older, he moved around a lot, and finally had to learn to survive within the hard and predatory world of prison. Friendship was a privilege and a virtue, and when he saw an opportunity to form a friendship he responded cautiously.

Friendship, for him, had an intrinsic worth that was of greater value than anything that he could ever steal. You couldn't steal friendship. You had to earn it. For Ty Conn, friendship was a rare place where he could find a little bit of reassurance about the quality of human nature. And it was only with that faith that he could realistically look forward to a day when the circumstances of his life might improve. I think our friendship gave him some of that. But I'm not so certain any more that it gave him enough, or that it was entirely good for him. I believe our friendship changed him, and that the changes ultimately contributed to his death.

In the last year of his life, Ty Conn made choices that I'm not sure he would have made had he not been influenced by the unusual linkage this friendship created with the world outside the prison system. The choices caused him to be incarcerated, in mid-1998, in Kingston Penitentiary, a place that became unbearable to him. In the end, he lost hope of ever getting out of there legitimately. And so he made his own escape in May of 1999, in the fifth year of our friendship.

During two brief weeks of freedom in the spring of '99 Ty Conn achieved something he'd never anticipated: a surprising measure of fame and public affection. People quietly, and sometimes publicly, rooted for this good-looking young hoodlum who'd defeated the legendary security of Kingston Penitentiary and melted into the surrounding countryside. Even the warden, Monty Bourke, made a public appeal that revealed a grudging respect, along with an almost parental concern for the missing inmate.

The sympathetic public response, eventually and unsurprisingly, provoked, if not a backlash, some bitter complaints. Policemen and bankers lamented the public impulse to "romanticize" a coward and a thief. *The National Post* newspaper wrote an editorial under the unsubtle heading "Conn Job." While saying very little of a damning nature about Ty Conn, the editorial sharply rebuked people who thought or had spoken well of him.

Ironically, Ty would have applauded the *Post*'s mean little editorial. It reflected his own lack of sympathy for sentimental notions about crime and criminals. In a letter he wrote to me in February 1996, he commented on a story I'd told on *the fifth estate* about the old bank robber from the fifties era, Edwin Alonzo Boyd.

He knew a lot about Boyd's background and criminal record, and he thought my interview with Eddie Boyd was pretty good.

But he went on to say that it "illustrated in some way how those romantic criminal (heroes?) don't exist any more, nor will they probably ever again.

"I think those characters were a product of [the] newspapers, like your show said. Competition creates strange views and heroes, doesn't it? In some ways those characters and the way they were portrayed are . . . responsible for the creation of people like me. I'm not using that as an excuse but I still remember all those criminals and gangsters that were romanticized for print and film and, no doubt, they had some effect on me."

Ty Conn didn't consult me about his plan to escape from Kingston. He knew what my response would be. I told him many times there was only one successful way to escape from prison, and that was out the front door. Going over or under the wall, I told him, was only to escape into a different kind of prison, the frightened existence of a fugitive. He always seemed to agree with me and I think he genuinely did, until just before the end.

In late April 1999, during a special weekend visit with his mother at Kingston Penitentiary, he turned away from a television documentary about euthanasia and remarked that, should he die during his mother's lifetime, he wanted to be cremated and his ashes to be scattered.

And so, on July 17, 1999, upon instructions from his mother, I delivered the ashes of Tyrone William Conn to the restless waters of the Gulf of St. Lawrence, near a place of exquisite beauty just off the west coast of Cape Breton Island.

According to his mother, he'd always had a profound sense of attachment to the sea and to the Atlantic Provinces. He had written often about his passion for boats. His biological father, of whom he had no memory, had been a Newfoundlander.

The story of the life and death of Ty Conn might have ended there, in that private and symmetrical moment on July 17, 1999. An investigation of police procedures on the night he died concluded there were no serious questions to be pursued about the circumstances of his death. His life, though, left a lot of questions unanswered.

After I'd known him for a couple of years, it became apparent that Ty Conn's story was a case study in failure. Undoubtedly there were a lot of failures by his young parents. And he'd failed miserably when, on a number of occasions, he made choices that profoundly influenced his future. But there were a lot of other and larger failures by individuals and institutions that contributed to the downward spiral of his life.

Late in 1996 I raised the possibility of helping Ty with an autobiographical project. I wanted him to learn more about his life by remembering it and sharing its woeful detail. His first reaction was dismissive: "I find the concept laughable, at best.

"If all the details of my life were laid out in a book, I feel I would be embarrassed, if not ashamed. I may tell great stories about things I've done and these tales are pretty truthful, yet if you look behind the experiences you will see that I'm desperately grasping onto things that prove I wasn't a total idiot!"

But in a subsequent letter, he relented. In November 1997, he advised me that "I will indeed begin to write down my impressions of my early life." It was to be an exercise, at least, in therapy.

From time to time, he shared memories and impressions with me and with Theresa Burke in letters and in longer reflections that sometimes ran to thousands of words. We have interviewed many of the people who intersected his short life at critical moments and who shared enough time and experience with him to know something of his character.

The unfolding tragedy of his life eventually interrupted his part in the telling of it. And then, at about midnight on May 20, 1999, the tragedy and the life ended. Questions, so long deferred, suddenly began to cry out loudly for answers, finally evolving into one.

Who killed him?

In our reconstruction of his story we sometimes enter the difficult realm of internal thought and emotional processes when this is important for understanding the reasons for some of his actions. In each case we have done so with scrupulous attention to the detail he provided in long and intense conversations and the considerable body of correspondence that he undertook for the explicit purpose of telling his extraordinary story.

Linden MacIntyre
Toronto
March 1, 2000

The Beginning
of the End

*Rejoice O young man in thy youth; and let thy heart
cheer thee in the days of thy youth, and walk in the ways
of thine heart, and in the sight of thine eyes; but know
thou that for all these things, God will bring thee into
judgment.*

Ecclesiastes 11.9

THERE WOULD HAVE BEEN A moment, long before the
deathly stillness filled the house at 101 Alberta Avenue, when
he saw with alarming clarity that Toronto had been a huge
mistake.

Toronto is vast, chaotic and fast. You can lose yourself in
Toronto. You can also lose yourself in the forest. You need
particular skills and equipment to survive in the forest.
Without them, the forest will kill you. It's easy to forget that
the same rule applies in the urban wilderness.

In the circumstances of Thursday evening, May 20, 1999,
the silence was a welcome change after the confusion and
weirdness of the previous forty-eight hours. Non-stop

partying and nattering fuelled by a steady supply of drugs and booze. After years in prison it was no surprise that he had trouble keeping up with the others. Now he couldn't stop retching and puking.

He'd been sick on booze a couple of times when he was younger, and back in Kingston Pen heroin had made him deathly ill once. That was when his friend Clint Suzack laid down the law: no more of that shit if you're going to be my friend. It'll kill you. Worse, it'll turn you into the kind of no-class thief who steals from his friends.

He listened then, and laid off the serious drugs. But ever since he showed up at 101 Alberta Avenue two nights before, it would have been difficult not to indulge. He was surrounded there by addicts and crackheads.

Then suddenly everybody was gone. Paulo Teixiera, his acquaintance from Upper G Range in the pen, and Paulo's girlfriend, Sandy, had suddenly vanished. He heard the woman from upstairs, Pam, the lady with the two kids, shouting through the side-door entrance to the basement apartment, first for Paulo and then for Sandy. Then the door slammed and she took off up the street.

It was the first quiet moment since he arrived there, and he was grateful for it. How long ago it seemed. Just two days ago.

His first stop when he got to Toronto had been at Ian's place. Good old Ian had given him refuge back in '89 when he was on the run from Collins Bay. Kept him safe for three weeks. Better than safe, actually. They were three great weeks. Ian was a businessman and well connected. They'd spent a lot of time up north where Ian had a friend with a big sailboat.

Ian recognized him right away on Tuesday evening when he arrived on his doorstep. Ty was wearing ridiculous bright blue contact lenses and a ball cap and his head was shaved, but it wouldn't have fooled anyone who knew him well. Of course it probably helped that his story had been a media sensation for more than a week at that point. You'd have to have been in a coma not to know that Tyrone William Conn, serving forty-seven years for robbery and escaping, had gone over the wall at Kingston Pen and every cop in the country wanted to be the one to put him back.

Which was probably why Ian said no when Ty asked if he could stay there for a while. Unfortunately he didn't have the guts to make it a clear and simple refusal. He made up a lie. He said the cops had already been there looking for him.

That lie changed everything. It meant that the police had somehow cracked the hard drive of his computer and retrieved a complete list of all the people he knew well enough to approach for refuge while he was on the run. It meant that there was no longer any safe place to hide. Not only would he be in danger of being caught, but wherever he went now he'd be endangering whomever he happened to approach.

That didn't leave him with too many options. Only one actually. He had a phone number for Paulo Teixiera, from back on Upper G. That number hadn't been on his list. So the cops wouldn't expect him to approach Paulo.

He was still a bit dubious about Paulo who, after all, had been careless enough to misplace the letter that landed him in the hole for six miserable weeks in January and February. At least he hoped it had been carelessness. Some of the guys on the range weren't that charitable. They were saying Paulo was a rat. He didn't want to believe that. And on Tuesday evening, May 18, he couldn't afford to. Maybe Paulo was unstable. Maybe he had AIDS. Maybe he was addicted to heroin and crack. Maybe he was an informer. But, as they say, any port in a storm.

And so it happened that Paulo was living nearby, shacked up with a stripper who went by the name Sandy Beach. God. His life was turning into pulp fiction. He dialled the number and Paulo told him to come right over. Maybe Paulo wasn't so bad after all. Then he called a cab. Ian asked him if he needed any money. He smiled and pointed to the gym bag he had with him. He had all the money he needed for the time being. Ian understood.

Paulo was waiting on the porch when he arrived. It was a two-storey frame house that looked a bit the worse for wear. Alberta Avenue runs between two busy Toronto thoroughfares, Davenport Road and St. Clair Avenue, near the intersection with Oakwood. Number 101 was known in the neighbourhood as a crack house. Among the frequent visitors to the place were a lot of cops responding to various complaints and disturbances. It was just about the last place a fugitive would pick for a hideout if he had any choices.

Paulo and Sandy lived in the basement, and Ty could see going in that this was a dump. The lock on the door was broken, as was a small pane of glass. The stairway delivered him into a low-ceilinged room that was painted in a gaudy shade of bubble-gum pink. Off to one side there was a small kitchen. In the other direction there were two bedrooms. Paulo and Sandy were obviously sharing the blue one. The other one was full of broken furniture and bags of old clothing. That would be his accommodation for the time being.

And so, two days later, he was sprawled there on an air mattress sick as a dog and wondering what caused it.

He might not have heard the quiet murmur of car engines idling outside, or the soft squish of rubber as the cars fluidly manoeuvred into tactical positions. But soon there would be sounds he could not have missed or mistaken . . . sudden alarming sounds: loud whispering, feet thudding on the ground around the house. Big feet in heavy, thick-soled shoes.

Then he'd know, beyond any doubt: coming to Toronto had been a fatal error. And at that point he would reach out instinctively, past the edge of the mattress to where he'd placed the shotgun, drag its dead weight to his side, pull the hammer back until it clicked. And brace himself for the fatal announcement.

CHAPTER ONE

The Birth and Death
of Ernie Hayes

. . . I ended up in a foster home in the Picton area. The foster family was known to my mother and I think she told me she once visited me there. This is the place that I first recall memories of. I can remember that it was next to either a lake or a river. I remember burying a fish. I know that sounds weird but it is one of my earliest memories. I also recall seeing a car tow an old rusted blue vw bug behind it with a chain. My final recollection of this place is of me sitting on a step, tying up my own shoelace while awaiting the social worker to arrive and take me away. I don't recall being sad at leaving and I'm not exactly certain where I was going, but I remember it quite distinctly.

Ty Conn, 1997

I.

ERNIE HAYES WAS, BY ALL ACCOUNTS, the loveliest child that anyone had ever seen. Bright and cheerful, he seemed to be immune to all the sorrow and confusion that whirled around him from the first moments of his life.

He was the child of children. His mother was sixteen. His father, who was twenty-seven, might have been significantly older in years, but he was small in stature and fine of feature and he seemed more like a boy than a man on the early approaches to his thirties. Whether or not they were ready for marriage, they were clearly unprepared for the responsibilities of parenthood. Marion, entering her teens, had experienced a stormy relationship with her parents and hadn't learned much from them. Jack's mother had died when he was a child, and he'd been raised by an uncle and aunt.

Jack was quiet and he was laid-back. He didn't seem to have a lot of ambition, but he was a good worker with the potential and, it seemed, the intention to be a good provider over the long term. But there was something essential missing there. Jack never had a car when Marion knew him. He later confided it was because of something called "unsatisfied judgment." It was only later that she learned what it meant. He'd been at fault in a car accident once and couldn't have a driver's licence again until he'd paid for it. There was a lot she didn't know about her Jack, and it would bring havoc to her life and to the life of their infant son.

Marion Wood was only fifteen and still living with her parents in Picton, Ontario, when she realized that her relationship with the wiry little Newfoundlander, Jack Hayes, had caused her to become pregnant. It was the summer of 1966. Maybe you had to be there to understand what it was like back then. Pregnancy, but for an act of God, was permanent. Accidents weren't uncommon, but they still left the accident-prone with only two choices: you run away or you get married. Abortion was for people who were amoral enough or wealthy enough to get it done secretly. Abortion was still illegal.

Even when you decided to do the honourable thing, getting married wasn't all that easy if someone was under twenty-one. Parents had to give their formal consent, and while they invariably complied, it was often done grudgingly. Parents confronted with a teenage pregnancy usually expected the worst. Marriage, even when freely chosen, was difficult. A marriage motivated by the coercive and confusing pressures of a social crisis like pregnancy was, to say the least, challenged from day one.

Learning she was pregnant filled Marion Wood with dread. But there was also a sense of anticipation that wasn't all bad. Kids got unexpectedly pregnant in Picton, as they did everywhere. It was just that you seemed more conspicuous in a place like that. Picton was a small Ontario town, with a conservative Loyalist heritage and an insular outlook. Picton is at the centre of Quinte's Isle, just west of Kingston where Lake Ontario filters through a thousand other islands and becomes a part of the St. Lawrence River. John A. Macdonald, who went on to become Canada's first prime minister and "Sir John A.," defended his first criminal case in a courthouse in Picton.

Marion Wood had been aching to get out of Picton for quite some time. The town and the surrounding countryside have the look of prosperity and solid-brick Ontario charm, but she longed for a larger, livelier place, away from the vigilance of her parents. She'd had enough of small-town Ontario, where old eighteenth-century mansions stand in sober disapproval of tacky suburban subdivisions built by people who never intended to live in them. Neither neighbourhood held much attraction for her. Picton was, as Jack Hayes would say about Harbour Grace, where he grew up, a good place to be from. Pregnancy and marriage, whatever else they might bring, would provide a motive for getting out of Picton.

Marion and Jack were married there on September 3, 1966, and moved to Toronto soon afterwards. They found a basement apartment near the Yorkdale Shopping Centre for twenty-seven dollars a week. When Marion celebrated her sixteenth birthday on October 11, 1966, she was happy. Like the boy growing inside her, she was vibrant with curiosity and rebellious impulses. Toronto was the perfect place to be as 1966 drew to a close.

Toronto was a city in which Victorian values informed public order and private behaviour for longer and perhaps more thoroughly than anywhere else in the modern English-speaking world. But by the mid-sixties the place had begun a period of rapid growth and change. Immigrants were turning old British neighbourhoods into microcosms of continental European communities. Hippies and American draft dodgers were transforming the downtown core with their music and outrageous idealism. And the city centre was changing dramatically as new skyscrapers poked upwards into the clouds, assembled by armies of tradesmen and labourers summoned to the big city for their skills and their sweat.

There was growth and work for anybody who wanted it. And on the weekends, the place throbbed with music as the young people unwound and, in doing so, hurried the unwinding of a city that for a long time had taken pride in being Good. These energetic newcomers—from the Maritimes and the Prairies, the north, the outports of Newfoundland, and from abroad—just wanted the city to be good fun.

As Marion's pregnancy neared an end, her baby seemed reluctant to begin the troubled life that awaited him outside the womb. She was in labour for three days. Disoriented and in excruciating pain, she thrashed around so much in the delivery room that a nurse eventually attempted to tie her down. She bit the nurse. Doctors finally delivered the child by Caesarian section. It was January 18 in the year of Canada's centennial celebration, 1967.

Ernie was born at the Toronto General Hospital. His full name was Ernest Bruce Hayes, named after two of his father's siblings who had burned to death in a house fire back in Newfoundland.

In the early days of motherhood, in January 1967, Mrs. Marion Hayes was caught up in the mood of celebration that was developing across the land. Cheerful governments were handing out money for projects and events to mark Canada's one-hundredth birthday. Montreal was preparing to open a lavish international exhibition of the fruits of technology and human skill called Expo '67. Everywhere politicians seemed to be talking about loosening up laws that governed private lives and making good on old predictions that Canada would one day be the world's proudest achievement in the twentieth century. Thanks to a new medicare program, she didn't even have to worry about doctors' bills and all the unexpected medical expenses of having a baby.

Marion Hayes, even though she was only sixteen, felt grown up, a good life with a good man stretching infinitely before her. Infinity turned out to be about eighteen months long.

2.

JACK HAYES NEVER SEEMED TO HAVE a problem getting a job. Fortuitously, he was working in a factory that made baby clothes when Ernie was born. Employee discounts kept the little fellow well and warmly dressed in the first months of his life. Jack then worked at a carpet plant near Eglinton and Birch avenues for a while. Eventually, they moved into an Ontario Housing project in Scarborough, where the rent was based on family income. The marriage soon after began encountering difficulties.

Today Marion figures the big problem was their age difference. It wasn't that he was more mature than she was. Not by a long shot. The problem was mostly that he developed a fondness for partying, and the crowd he liked to hang out with were his age and older and were drinkers. Marion wasn't, and she felt out of place. Eventually, Jack would go off with his friends and she'd stay behind. Gradually, he started behaving as if he thought he was single again. Then one day, when she was seventeen, her husband went to work and never came home. She's never forgotten the feeling.

"That night was pretty scary," she remembers. "I was there and I thought, Oh God, what am I going to do."

After the initial shock, she decided to find out what was going on, and it didn't take her long to discover that there was another woman in the picture. With a bit of digging, she learned that Jack had gone to Victoria, British Columbia. The other woman remained behind, living in the same housing complex as Marion and Ernie.

Marion figured that the other woman would be writing to Jack and so she somehow managed to get in a position to monitor the outgoing mail as it left their apartment building. Before long she had an address for her wayward mate.

By then, deprived of Jack's income, she was living on welfare. With the next welfare cheque she bought a plane ticket and flew to the West Coast. Before she left, she dropped her little boy in Picton with her parents.

In Victoria she tracked Jack down and gave him a long lecture about his marriage and his responsibility and the fact that she and Ernie needed him in their lives. He seemed to be listening. He agreed with her and told her he was sorry and that he was ready to make a fresh start. She believed him, and for a few days Jack squired her around the tidy old town that was so far away and so different from where he'd grown up. Jack could be great company. He'd make you laugh. He'd been born, after all, on April Fool's Day, in 1939. After a bit of a second honeymoon he told Marion that she should return to Toronto and that he'd join her there within a week. He had a few things to clear up in Victoria.

He eventually showed up in Toronto, but not at Marion's place. He went straight to the girlfriend's apartment and moved in. By this time Marion realized that it was all over. He was never coming home. Suddenly the feeling of abandonment was replaced with anger and she did something she's always regretted. She took Ernie and his things and she marched straight over to where Jack was staying with his girlfriend and the girlfriend's two children. She handed over the little boy and told Jack that since he was already helping to look after some stranger's children, he shouldn't mind taking care of his own as well.

She turned on her heel then and marched out the door. A couple of friends were selling their belongings and moving to Alberta for a fresh start. She sold everything she had and went with them.

"I thought I had to get away," she says today. "To go out West just to get away. I wanted a life.

"And when I think back, God how stupid and foolish . . . and I look at these young people nowadays and I think—the mistakes they're making—but I made the same ones. But while you're living in it, you don't see it. You think everything is so rational."

If she thought this "rational" gambit would bring Jack Hayes to his senses, she was wrong. She didn't know her husband very well at all. She wasn't gone for long when she heard that Jack had taken little Ernie out to Picton and handed him over to her parents. They were still raising a couple of kids of their own, a girl about ten and a boy who was nine. Surely, he argued, they could handle one more. The grandparents weren't happy about the arrangement, but they didn't have a lot of choice. The kid's mother had gone. The father didn't want him. They reluctantly consented. Jack signed papers granting them custody and, basically, washed his hands of little Ernie that day.

By all accounts the grandparents did the best they could. And Marion was spending practically all her spare cash on trips back to visit her baby, now a toddler. She could get a flight to Toronto for twenty-five dollars by going standby.

The visits weren't very happy. Whatever joy and reassurance she got from seeing Ernie growing were offset by her parents' view that she was clearly crazy or worse. She would one day in the future, after her mother's death, come across documents in which they—her own parents—were telling social workers and other important people that she was irresponsible and that she didn't deserve to have Ernie because she'd abandoned him. And so on.

It was hurtful but, she would realize much later on in life, it was also kind of true. What else would you expect from someone who had to start coming to terms with motherhood when she was only fifteen? Of course, by the time that grown-up realization dawned it was too late to be of much value to her. And it was of no value to Ernie at all. There would be no turning back. There would be no opportunity to undo what would become bitter reality in the unfolding of time.

3 ·

NOBODY IS VERY CLEAR ON DETAILS any more, but when Ernie was about three his grandparents basically threw in the towel. Ernie was a handsome little kid. He was cheerful and bright, warm and friendly. Descriptions from people who knew him then, including professional people, conjure up images of the kind of kid you see in television commercials or as poster boys on kitschy calendars with puppy dogs and fluffy kittens. It would become one of the more disturbing

perversities in his fate that this infantile beauty would contribute to the beginnings of his destruction.

Marion had worked for a while in Calgary. She'd held a series of tough, often dangerous jobs in factories. Eventually she went to Edmonton. For a spell she worked in a tannery there, spooked by the stink of the place and the hanging cowhides that were a permanent reminder of death. The work was frightening, but at times she was even more terrified of her fellow workers. It was rough work, she figured, for rough people. And at the end of the day you'd go home smelling worse than a cow, reeking of the hides and the chemicals.

On one of her infrequent journeys home to Picton, Marion was surprised to discover Ernie wasn't there. Where was he? she wanted to know. There was a long silence and an exchange of worried glances before her parents told her. They'd decided Ernie would be better off starting his life all over again. They'd handed him over to the Children's Aid Society in Picton. Marion promptly lost what little composure she'd retained throughout the marriage meltdown and the long, lonely trips from Edmonton. All the feelings of desperation and rejection and guilt suddenly transformed into rage. She ranted at them until she realized she was wasting her breath and her energy. Then she stormed out, screaming back at them that she'd never set foot in the place again.

Then, she realized, she had another problem. On her way home, she'd decided not to return to the West. Maybe, she had thought, on the bus trip from Toronto to Picton, her parents might let her stay with them for a while. Maybe spend some time helping out with her little boy. Maybe start again at being a mom. But that was no longer possible. There was no reason for her to stay there. Ernie wasn't with them. But where was he? And more urgently, where was she going to stay now that she'd burned the bridge leading back home? That night, she ended up sleeping in a stairwell.

"I just didn't have any place to go. And I can't remember whether I went back to Toronto or what. I have no idea. You put things in little black boxes and you put them away. And you just don't draw them out very often. Sometimes you never draw them out. But I was so angry . . . angry at my parents. But as I look back now I think . . . they were only trying to do the best for me."

And they probably figured Ernie would be better off too. Of course they couldn't see into the future. Nobody can. Most people can't even see very far into the present. It made sense to expect that handing the little boy over to the care of "the people of Ontario" in those hopeful days would lead to better things for everybody. Wasn't the whole country looking at Ontario as the most blessed part of Canada? Coast to coast, weren't people singing about "a place to stand and a place to grow . . . Ontari-ari-ari-o?"

Yes. It all seemed so obvious. The little boy could only benefit by being delivered out of a situation that was so clearly dysfunctional into the custody of Canada's most functional society. At least that's what they hoped.

With the advantage of hindsight, Ernie, identified by a new name and in circumstances that nobody could ever have anticipated, would one day have cause to spend a lot of time trying to come to terms with his grandparents' decision.

"I can't help but wonder how things would have turned out had I been kept at home with my older aunt and uncle. I wish I could have had the chance to find out.

"Perhaps blame is the wrong word to use but I just can't get the following question out of my head: Why wasn't I kept at my grandparents', especially since they had young children of their own? Was my estrangement from my birth family the result of an attempt to teach my mother a lesson and make her face the responsibility of having and taking care of a child? Or, perhaps my grandparents didn't want me."

4.

SHE WAS STILL ONLY NINETEEN YEARS old and it seemed she'd lived at least twice that long. But as Jack would say, Marion Hayes "had a streak in her" and she wasn't about to give up on her boy just because her parents had. Eventually the Children's Aid Society of Picton confirmed that he was in foster care, being looked after by a young family in a nearby community. They couldn't tell her who or where, but they said they'd consider arranging a visit on neutral territory.

When they finally arranged a visit, the routine was like something out of a spy manual. The foster parents would bring him to town and hand him off to a social worker. Marion would wait in a park behind the CAS office, near the old Royal Hotel in Picton. Then, accompanied by the social worker, Ernie would appear, obviously mystified by all the strange manoeuvrings around him. For a few hours they'd play together, Ernie happily convinced that everything finally seemed to have returned to normal, Marion pretending that it had.

Of course nothing between them was normal. It would have taken a miracle to restore some kind of normalcy to their lives. She actually attempted to make such a miracle happen. She went to Jack and pleaded with him to work with her at reconciling whatever differences there were between them. Just for Ernie. Jack was unmoved.

She attempted to do it on her own. The CAS said they'd give her six months to get her act together. If she could pull together the resources to set up a suitable household, they'd consider giving Ernie back. That period is a blur in her memory, but she remembers hitchhiking back to Edmonton. It took three days. She wasn't afraid, she says. Everybody seemed to be hitchhiking in those days. On the highway outside Wawa, she recalls, the hitchhikers were spaced along the road at intervals for as far as you could see.

In all the rides, nobody once made an improper move. Her favourites were the truck drivers. They'd pay for her meals. They'd go out of their way to drive her into a town when they were at the end of the journey, so as not to leave a little lady stranded in the middle of nowhere. She got back to Edmonton and she got work, but she could never earn enough to make any progress toward her goal—getting her boy back.

"You'd work for a while and then, lo and behold, you'd lose your friggin' job and then it was another setback. So it was just like one setback right after another so you just couldn't seem to accomplish anything."

Eventually she even began to find a rationale for what her parents had done. She returned to Ontario. And she started visiting Picton again.

"I think my parents were trying to teach me responsibility. And to [accept] my responsibilities on that. I had put myself in this position. Like . . . you made your bed, now lie in it. And it just didn't work. It just didn't work because I didn't listen to anybody."

Then she had no choice but to listen. Reading a newspaper one day in the spring of 1970, she saw her name in what appeared to be an official advertisement. It was a public notice to all concerned with Ernie's life that on June 30, 1970, there was to be a hearing at which he would become a legal ward of the Crown. You didn't have to be a lawyer to understand what that meant. Ernie didn't belong to her any more. In a way he belonged to the Queen, a distinction that would entitle him to a quality of care that fell considerably short of royal treatment. It meant, basically, that the Queen, through her principal child-care agency, the Children's Aid Society, was considering launching Ernie Hayes into a new life, with new parents.

Marion, once again, contacted Jack, and they took the bus to Picton and went to court together. It was a big old place on Main Street and she remembers the central stairway that seemed to rise forever before her. The CAS lady briefed her about what was happening. It kind of went in one ear and out the other. She was powerless. Ernie's destiny was beyond her grasp.

Normally, birth parents are given every opportunity to work things out, and the CAS offers a lot of assistance to achieve what all the experts seem to consider to be the best outcome—the return of the child to his natural parents. In Ernie's case, his biological father seemed interested only in getting on with a new life that didn't include Ernie Hayes. His mother just seemed in a state resembling shell shock.

"I don't know why I even went to court that day. Maybe because I had nothing. I had absolutely nothing. I didn't really have an apartment. I think I lived with my uncle and aunt at the time. And so just . . . I guess just to be there because they told me to be there.

"You know. Appear in court this day or whatever . . . and so that's what I did. And it was just like it was all kind of beyond you. I thought they'd know the right thing to do. Like . . . I don't really understand what's going on, but I guess you guys are the ones that know, so I guess . . .

"It wasn't a good time, I'll tell you."

She doesn't remember much about the actual hearing. Records at the Picton CAS confirm that it was a formal hearing to make Ernest Bruce Hayes a ward of the Crown. The presiding judge noted that "there appeared to be no hope for [his parents'] reconciliation" and that "both parents express their agreement with the plan of Crown wardship presented by the society on the basis that they are not able to offer a proper home for this boy."

They cared enough about him to face the brutal facts of their own shortcomings, and they gave him up for adoption, assuming he'd get a better life than they could provide. It is one of the perplexing ironies of the system that had they been stubborn or proud or selfish and refused consent, Ernie would never have been adopted. He'd have bumped around in foster care until one of them could win him back, which, in this case, might well have been preferable to what subsequently transpired.

The next time she saw Ernie was the last time she'd see him for almost fifteen years. This she remembers clearly: She was walking down Main Street in Picton when a car drove by slowly. There were two little boys inside. One of them waved in her direction. It was Ernie. She just stood there and watched the car drive out of sight. She felt numb. Her mind froze on the image. It didn't even occur to her to make a note of the licence plate number. And then he was gone.

5 ·

SOMETIME DURING THE NEXT SEVEN weeks Ernest Bruce Hayes ceased to exist. There is much confusion about that period. Even though he, as an adult with a completely new identity, tried to have the confusion cleared up, the Children's Aid Society of Picton is vague on the details.

Clearly, the plan for Ernie was to get him into a new home as quickly as possible. Get him adopted. Find new parents for him. Burn the bridges to his failed past. Haste was important because at three and a half years old he was already past his prime as a candidate for adoption.

Parents who decide to adopt prefer infants, and the closer they are to the moment of birth the better. Humans begin to acquire psychic and personal baggage even before they leave the womb. The process of character formation, once the actual experience of life in the world begins, is rapid. In three and a half years, one might legitimately assume, a kid would have been marked, perhaps permanently, by the experiences that placed him in the custody of the Crown in the first place. Parenting is challenging enough without having to clean up after the mistakes of the biological family.

The consequences of bad parenting have been grimly observed by psychologists and professional social workers, the police and the keepers of the corrections system. In the bleak view of the Swiss psychoanalyst Alice Miller: "The former practice of physically maiming, exploiting and abusing children seems to have been gradually replaced, in modern times, by a form of mental cruelty that is masked by the honorific term *child rearing*."

People who work for the CAS will usually apply whatever power they have to predict and influence the quality of child rearing in adoptive homes. But, as the boy who was born Ernie Hayes would one day attest, their best intentions don't always translate into wise decisions. Presumably the social workers at the Picton branch of the Children's Aid Society in 1970 were as committed as any individual or agency to the well-being of their wards. How, then, does one come to terms with the transformation of Ernest Bruce Hayes to Tyrone William Conn?

6.

INGRID BATEMAN LOVED HER WORK and she was very good at it. She'd been a psychologist, working with children, since 1951 when she graduated from the University of Toronto with a master's degree. She started out in Toronto, working mostly with problem children, many of whose problems were rooted in learning disabilities.

Eventually she married a lawyer who was building a practice in Belleville, about 125 miles east of Toronto and the closest town of any significant size to Picton. Belleville is mostly about business. A prominent tourist guide once dryly noted "there isn't much for the visitor" here . . . except as a point of orientation for people who want to get to pretty Quinte's Isle to the south, or cheese country to the north on Highway 37.

But, as a hub in the network of highways triangling to Kingston, Ottawa and Toronto, Belleville has prospered into a typical modern marriage of old Ontario brick downtown, and modern strips of suburban commerce fluttering outward in all directions. It was a good place for a law office and, as a service centre for the surrounding farm country and a lot of smaller towns in the region, a good place for a psychologist to start building a practice.

Ingrid Bateman found lots to do in Belleville. Most of her work involved references from the Children's Aid Society and consisted of exploring the psychological mysteries of children about whom the CAS hadn't been able to learn much by way of family background. She had methods and tests that would enable her to assess the mental and emotional condition of kids as young as two months.

So when the local Mental Health Association decided to work on establishing a forty-bed psychiatric unit at the local hospital, one of the first people they got in touch with was Ingrid Bateman. Another person high on their list was a psychiatrist named Dr. E. B. (Bert) Conn. He was working in Windsor and had spent some time employed in a state hospital in Colorado. But he'd grown up in Brighton, not far from Belleville, and people in the local medical establishment knew and respected him. They invited him to return to the area and he was happy to oblige.

Before there was a psych ward at the Belleville Hospital, Ingrid Bateman and Dr. Conn ran a little psychiatric clinic for seven years out of a two-bedroom unit in a brick apartment building in downtown Belleville. After they moved to the hospital, to "the third floor," as the psychiatric unit was known locally despite the fact it was really on the ground floor, they were swamped with work, as doctors and school principals referred scores of troubled kids to them for diagnosis and treatment.

For Bateman, it was a remarkable opportunity to correct a lot of the misinformation and misdiagnosis that created lifelong labels and associated problems for young people.

"They were either slow learners or behaviour problems or put into what in those years were called 'opportunity classes.' And they didn't belong there."

She can't remember an exact date, but one day in the mid-summer of 1970 she received word of a referral from the Children's Aid Society of Prince Edward County in Picton. She was being asked to prepare an assessment of a little boy three and a half years old. He was available for adoption. He was kind of special. They were planning to show him off in a regular newspaper feature called "Today's Child." They didn't tell her very much about him. Before he came to them he'd been living with his grandmother. His name, they said, was Stephen Wannamaker.

7.

MRS. BATEMAN, WHO IS NOW Ingrid Irwin (her lawyer husband died in 1986 and she has remarried), recalls an unusual commotion in the waiting room outside her office in the psychiatric clinic on the day she met the little boy who had been born Ernie Hayes. By then his name was Stephen Wannamaker. Where that name came from remains a mystery, but he didn't have it for long. Shortly after she saw him that day, the psychologist would come to know the little boy as Tyrone William Conn.

"I knew a child was coming and so I opened the door. And I said oh . . . [in] the waiting room . . . people were all surrounding this beautiful child and, you know, down on their hands and knees. I have never seen anything like it. They were so entranced with this child.

"He was chubby, extremely engaging. He had bright blue eyes, blond hair . . . blond curly hair. He was the centre of attention. He felt great. And so I thought he was going to be a good interview and we'll have some fun because he was having so much fun. I didn't think I would have any problems with him whatsoever."

Kids visiting a psychologist usually don't make a distinction between that and other clinical experiences which usually involve physical discomfort, needles and medicine. There's usually an awkward beginning as the adult attempts to reassure the child and help him to relax. But this consultation was exceptional right from the start.

"I had a very interesting room with a lot of fun things around, toys and playhouse, loose sand and rocks even.

"And he was very confident. He, in fact, had verbal, visual and auditory skills . . . [that were] well beyond a three-year-old. And also his expressive language, his use of language and comprehension [were] unreal."

She had a series of devices designed to engage the kid's interest and to test his intellectual potential, creativity and emotional condition. One way was to get him to make up a story, and he promptly obliged with a yarn about chickens. A family of chickens were getting ready for a fair. The mother was doing all the work, but the kids were pitching in.

Nearly thirty years later, the psychologist, who is now retired, still remembers: "It was a story that made sense. They were going out for a picnic and they were going to go on some rides. And, in the end, they went home. It was nothing that would make me suspect that there were any . . . anomalies."

A three-year-old, asked to draw a person, will usually produce a stick figure, and psychologists are able to read a lot into even that. For example, inner turmoil will sometimes be revealed in a figure with detached limbs, or twisted and extraordinary bodies. Little Stephen drew a figure that looked like a snowman.

"It's very unusual for a three-year-old to proceed to draw a circle. You don't expect a six-year-old to be able to draw a round circle, a perfect round circle. So here he goes, he drew a picture of a snowman. I didn't tell him to draw a snowman, just a picture of a person. He drew a snowman."

To the psychologist, the snowman revealed more than the obviously advanced perceptions and drawing skills. There was unusual attention to detail. The snowman had eyes, a nose, buttons on his coat, a broom, an odd mouth with conspicuous teeth.

"He was ready to take on a challenge, but he was angry about something. It was not a happy snowman. But, for a three-year-old, my initial impression was . . . my goodness, this child is bright."

The most telling insights came when she tested him for perceptions of his relationship with a family group. It was clear that he had no fixed notion of a conventional family structure and that he hadn't ever bonded with grown-ups. Presented with a playhouse and family figures, his main impulse was to rearrange the house.

Generally, he was less interested in the testing than he was in just talking.

"He preferred actually to communicate with me not through play but through words, conversation. I asked him a lot of questions and he answered spontaneously and would add something to allow the conversation to move on . . . at three. I wish I had my file."

Her file would, unfortunately, disappear shortly after the examination and become part of the larger mystery that will always cloak the life of the little boy who made such a lasting impression on that day in the summer of 1970.

It might seem unusual that a clinician who has seen and tested thousands of children during a career that spanned more than forty years would retain such particular memories of one session with one small boy. But this kid was so unusual she has never forgotten him.

"I only had two children that tested that high. I have tested gifted children. But these were *gifted* gifted children."

One of her two most gifted clients would overcome excruciating shyness and counterproductive study habits and end up in a Ph.D. program at a major Canadian university. The other had quite a different road ahead of him.

By the end of the session, Mrs. Bateman had a pretty clear idea of where the little boy belonged. He needed a loving family and a stable environment in which he would grow without negative restraints to fill out the apparently vast dimensions of his potential.

"I felt that [he] needed a home in which he would be unconditionally accepted for who he was and not what he did. A home in which there was a lot of love. He needed guidelines because he was self-centred.

"His giftedness needed to be channelled into acceptable . . . ways. And I think [for] a long period [he needed] a relationship between the social worker, the agency and whatever types of people they had working there . . . who could give the home some supervision and guidance in order for this to happen.

"The main thing [he] needed to derive from a home placement was a good feeling about himself. A good feeling of self-realization."

As she finished up with her assessment that day, Ingrid Bateman couldn't help thinking of a young couple who, she knew, would provide a perfect home for the exceptional little boy. They were a professional couple in the area. They couldn't have children of their own because of an accidental injury. It could have been a perfect match.

Mrs. Bateman knew that the couple had a strong marriage and an impeccable home life. Still, they'd be required to undergo what, for many people, would be an intrusive investigation of their circumstances. There would be a home study that would probably go on for six months. Then there would be follow-up visits and a lot of what many people might consider prying and meddling.

But it was all part of the routine that was in place for the protection of kids who'd already experienced enough misery through adult bad luck and mismanagement. As events unfolded, all her expectations turned out to be wrong. Her young couple would never meet the little boy, and the people who did adopt him would do so with minimal fuss and formality.

The next morning, as she prepared for her day's appointments, the secretary, Doreen Lovett, casually informed her that after the commotion attending the little boy's visit to the clinic the day before, Dr. Conn had called her into his office. He wanted to know what was going on. The secretary told him about the handsome little boy and about Mrs. Bateman's glowing report on his intellect and his charm.

Later in the day, Mrs. Bateman briefed a CAS worker on her findings from the assessment the day before. She offered a vivid profile of the boy and his potential for a positive placement. She even went so far as to suggest that she had a family in mind. She didn't mention any names, just that she knew a young married couple who, in her opinion, would provide the boy with just the stable, nurturing environment that he needed.

The social worker appeared to become a bit uncomfortable at that point. Then she told Ingrid Bateman that little Stephen Wannamaker wouldn't be needing a home because arrangements were already underway to give him one. Suddenly, the psychologist was confused. She'd understood the little boy to be a ward of the Crown, available for adoption. That had certainly been her understanding twenty-four hours earlier. Maybe so, but a lot can change in twenty-four hours.

At the end of the previous working day, Ingrid Bateman had gone home high on the satisfaction she got from a stimulating encounter with a child-client. What she couldn't have known was that as she drove blissfully homeward that evening, her professional partner, Dr. Bert Conn, had already launched his own intervention into the child's life. He and his wife had decided that they wanted to adopt him and were already in the process of making it happen.

The precise details of the transaction are shrouded in official secrecy. Picton CAS officials insist that there were three pre-placement visits with the Conn family before the boy moved in with them permanently on August 20, 1970, that there was a home study and that the adoption wasn't finalized until March 29, 1971.

That account contradicts the recollection of the psychologist who assessed him for the CAS, and Dr. Conn's own secretary, who subsequently signed the legal documents relating to his adoption.

They independently recalled, in interviews, that in a period perhaps as short as twenty-four hours Dr. Conn had, for all practical purposes, "adopted" the bright little boy who had been born Ernest Bruce Hayes and who from then on would be known as Tyrone William Conn.

Whatever the precise details of his metamorphosis from Ernie Hayes to Ty Conn, it all happened in a surprisingly short fifty-day period—from the time he became a Crown ward to the day on which he was "placed" with the Conn family. The next eight years would consolidate a life of failure and despair. And in the decades that followed, nobody would come to regret the hasty adoption more than Dr. E. B. Conn himself.

CHAPTER TWO

The Lonely Childhood
of Ty Conn

I remember going out with a couple for a visit of sorts. I do recall that I was aware of the nature and reason for the visit, namely seeing if I got along with the couple, if they got along with me and whether or not the cas would approve an adoption. My recollection of the event was that they were a young couple, childless, and I seem to remember the man telling me he'd take me skiing. I didn't yet know what skiing was, but it sure sounded like fun. I've always wondered what happened to that couple, and whether they were fortunate enough to get a child and once again, that What if? question. Wondering how things would have turned out should I have been adopted by them. I recollect being quite anxious to get adopted and I really wanted to be a member of a family. Once again, strange feelings and memories for such a young fella, eh?

Ty Conn, 1998

I .

LORIS CONN TOLD HER FRIENDS SHE'D always wanted to name somebody Tyrone. She never explained why, exactly. It seemed she just liked the sound of it. And so the new boy in the family was called Tyrone William. Unbeknownst to the Conns, the choice would inadvertently provide a permanent link with the little boy's biological family. His birth father's name had been William John.

Bert Conn would explain to family friends that the adoption made perfect sense. There were two older children, Jeffrey, eleven, and Cairine, nine, and a little girl named Loris Jeanette, who was two. Tyrone, at three and a half, would be a playmate for Loris J., as she was called, and yet, as the third among four children, wouldn't be exposed to the mysterious stresses of middle-child syndrome. He would, in time, however, be exposed to much worse.

Dr. Bert Conn has walled himself off from the disturbing life of his adopted son. He will not talk about him and he refuses to talk to anybody who wants to discuss him. So it is necessary to rely on descriptions from friends and associates to learn anything about his relationship with Tyrone, or about him. And even then, the portrait is full of contradictory elements. He loved his son. He resented his son for being the cause of tensions and, eventually, crisis in his household. Dr. Conn, to those who know him well, is shy, stoic, cold, compassionate, closed-in, self-deluding, a perceptive analyst, quiet, funny, gentle, harsh.

Ty Conn spoke often about his adoptive father, but never critically. The picture he presented was of a physically strong man, about five feet nine, heavy-set, a balding workaholic with a vague facial resemblance to the former Soviet leader Mikhail Gorbachev. His most striking features are a sensual mouth and eyes that are dark brown and full of sorrow and secrets. The boy never knew for sure how much responsibility to assign the man he always called "Dr. Conn" for the misery that became a permanent part of his childhood. And so his feelings always wavered between anger and yearning.

Descriptions of Dr. Conn's first wife, Loris, who became the mother of Tyrone William, are more consistent: paranoid, alcoholic, unstable, suicidal, cruel, manipulative.

By all accounts, Ty brought a brief period of happiness to the Conn family. His first memory of his new parents was of wandering around in a farmers' market in a place that he later found out was Picton. In Ty's remarkable memory, Dr. Conn was wearing a striped shirt.

Because it was summertime, possibly August, they took him straight to their cottage on Oak Lake, not far from Stirling. The cottage was about twenty miles north of Belleville, where they had a comfortable five-bedroom home on Leslie Street, in the city's east end.

According to long-time family friend Anne Boyle, they were thrilled when they got Ty. "They thought he was brilliant . . . I think they were very keen at the time." Another family friend recalls how Mrs. Conn bought the little boy a tiger-striped sleeping bag and pyjamas. They'd call him the little tiger to help him get accustomed to being called Ty.

Ty's memory of his first day at Oak Lake, years later, was brief but vivid: "I can't remember much about my older brother but I remember the oldest sister, Cairine, taking me out to the dock and playing in the water with a metal pot.

"She was about nine at this time, so I expect she was quite anxious to mother her new baby brother. Years later when I had an opportunity to speak to her about this event, she, in fact, confirmed it and told me of how she carried me around on her hip most of the day. I remember being introduced to my new baby sister, Loris J., while she was trapped in her crib. Ironically, the most striking memory of that day is of the diaper bin outside the cottage's screen door."

As the summer drew to an end, so did the idyll at Oak Lake. The family moved back to town, to the big house with the generous backyard on Leslie Street. Considering the course his life had followed up to that point, the little fellow probably tensed up as they drove away from the lake, assuming he was about to go through another cathartic change, in a new place with new people.

But, for him, Leslie Street would leave some good memories, of a developing relationship with his sisters, of a large family room and a neighbourhood teeming with other kids. Perhaps most significantly, it is the only place that left a memory of any affection from his parents and, in particular, from Mrs. Conn. At night he'd climb into bed with the doctor and his wife and sleep there between them. The intimacy wouldn't last for long, however, because it is also where, for the first time, he consciously stole something.

Friends and neighbours have a different recollection of life on Leslie Street. Mrs. Conn was a complex woman, a former psychiatric nurse, who was capable of deep friendship and warmth. But she also suffered from serious delusions that she was in danger from mysterious forces and people who wanted to harm her. The Belleville police would often humour her, listening politely, occasionally offering special protection.

Retired Belleville Detective John Ashley chuckled, many years later, when asked what he remembered about Ty Conn. "I liked the kid," he declared. The boy was friendly and he was bright, and even, much later on when he was causing a lot of trouble, always polite.

The "kid" was about five years old when Ashley first met him. He and his partner, Sam Morgan, and several other police officers were "the kid's babysitters" frequently during the early seventies. Mrs. Conn would become convinced that somebody was stalking her. She'd report mysterious and menacing encounters with strangers. Threatening messages would unaccountably appear around the car or the house. At one point the Belleville police obligingly put the house on Leslie Street under twenty-four-hour surveillance for a period of more than six months. It was widely known in the ranks that Mrs. Conn was paranoid, but because of Dr. Conn's prominence in the community, it became almost department policy to take her complaints seriously.

Doreen Lovett was Dr. Conn's secretary for eighteen years and knew the family well. She witnessed the signing of Ty Conn's adoption papers. Like virtually everyone else who knew the family, she was baffled by the decision to adopt a child when it was obvious to even a casual observer that Mrs. Conn had deep emotional and, perhaps, even mental problems.

"He was the most adorable child with a very high IQ. Why they thought they wanted another child at that stage, I'm not sure. They had three natural children . . . I think the doctor just had him in as an interview and was somehow attached to him."

Whatever demons Mrs. Conn was dealing with, they eventually began to affect the way she dealt with their children and, in particular, their adopted son. Ty wasn't in the household long before people began to notice a disturbing pattern in the way she treated him. Her punishments were frequent and psychologically cruel. He spent a lot of time in his room. She'd speak to him harshly in front of others. Her rebukes would include mocking references to the fact that he was adopted and different from the others.

Friends recall birthday parties from which Ty was excluded as a form of punishment, gifts intercepted before he got them because she claimed he'd misbehaved.

One neighbour, Mary Mulhall, spent years believing that Ty had been found, as an infant, living in a doghouse. Mrs. Conn told her his parents had kept him a virtual prisoner in a kennel until social workers rescued him.

"I believed that for years until Bert set me straight. There was always great drama when Loris was around."

Once Mrs. Mulhall brought her own adopted son, who was still an infant, to the Conns' home. Showing the baby around, she asked Ty if he'd like to hold him. But when she tried to settle the baby on Ty's lap, Mrs. Conn intervened.

"Simon was just five days old when we got him. And Loris wanted Loris J. to hold the baby, but not Ty. She just said he'd been bad. I spoke sharply to her and told her I wanted [Ty] to hold the baby . . . I put the baby into his arms and he was cradling the baby and Loris said, 'He's adopted too . . . does he look like you?' I just took the baby away. What a waste of a life."

Mrs. Mulhall has another memory from Leslie Street.

"There was a birthday for one of the kids. I was there, they had Ty. He was about five. Everybody came to the table. She'd ordered pizza and we were sitting in a little breakfast room. They'd all been playing down in the basement and they started to come up the stairs.

"I hated the way she spoke to him. Ty had a beautiful smile and he was always fighting to get his breath because of the asthma. His little chest would heave and he'd smile with his mouth closed because he could take the air in, but he couldn't push it back out again easily. His hair was thick and blond and blowing in waves to one side. This boy was a picture.

"He was sitting with his hands on the table and she said, 'Is that marker on your hand?' And you would just see the smile go and one little hand came out to cover the other where the marker was. And this was in front of everybody. She said, 'Let me see that. You know what I told you about markers. No pizza for you.' Then she would make him stand on one leg and watch everyone else."

It is significant that in lengthy conversations over the years, and in long reminiscences for friends and psychologists in the corrections system, Ty has mentioned few specific incidents like this. In fact, he never missed an opportunity to caution the listener against "presentism" or retroactive judgment that might be coloured by subsequent events and insights.

Writing once to the authors he commented, "I'm very aware that events unfolding in later years most certainly could've tainted my earliest memories in the Conn household and that my opinions of how I was treated by them is entirely subjective . . .

"This stated, however, I have tried to be as impartial as possible and tried to recall any fond memories of my time with the Conns."

The effort didn't yield much to indicate significant evidence of fondness, on either side.

He had his own bedroom and, at night, wakened by asthmatic distress, dreams or just childish restlessness, he'd set out to explore his new home. On one such expedition he discovered that he had access to the refrigerator, and it was there that he committed his first theft. He stole a prune. His nocturnal raids eventually escalated to include sweets and even an occasional popsicle. He couldn't recall when, precisely, such a pattern began, but he did remember that his pyjama bottoms still came with feet attached. After a couple of close calls, when Dr. Conn would awaken and investigate, he was eventually caught and punished. And to prevent further prowling, they put a hook on the outside of his bedroom door to keep him in at night.

It was his first experience of crime and punishment and imprisonment. It wouldn't be his last.

2.

IN THE SPRING OF 1973, WHEN TY was six, the Conn family bought a hundred-acre hobby farm about ten miles north of the city, near the community of Foxboro. They moved into a huge six-bedroom house alongside Highway 14, just outside the small community on the way to Stirling. Ty again had a room of his own. There was a huge recreation room. There was a two-bedroom bungalow on the property, and it had, apparently, once been servants' quarters. There was a four-bay garage, a large barn, dog kennels and a number of out-buildings for farm machinery. There were sprawling lawns and gardens. And out back, what must have seemed to a boy of six an enchanted wilderness of fields and ponds and scrubland. In fact, Dr. Conn leased out eighty acres to a local dairy farmer.

Ty liked it there at first, but because it was so far from Belleville the move meant that Dr. Conn's already minimal involvement with the family would become even more marginal. When living in town, his working day could extend to fifteen hours. And he was always on call to attend various emergencies at the Belleville General Hospital. Living in the country, the family could never be sure when he'd show up.

Had he spent more time at home, he might have found plenty to engage his professional expertise there. It was perfectly clear to people in their small circle of friends that his wife required a lot of support and perhaps even psychiatric help. It also seemed to visitors that she was projecting a great deal of her own inner torment on the boy they'd adopted. What they couldn't see was that Ty was in danger of developing a few psychoses of his own.

If Dr. and Mrs. Conn had intended the adoption, as many believed, to provide some healthy stimulus for their family life, they'd been seriously mistaken. Like most little boys who are unusually intelligent and curious, Ty was restless and needed a lot of attention. But even beyond that, there seemed to be something about Ty that aggravated Loris Conn. And as she became increasingly unstable, Dr. Conn and the other children began to blame the increasing instability in their home on Ty, the adopted kid. They started convincing themselves and each other that home had been a much more pleasant and normal place before he came—a revisionist perception that is contradicted by family friends and by their own sworn testimony years later when the family, not unexpectedly, fell apart.

Gradually, whatever warmth Ty felt initially from the Conn family was replaced by a complex response that in his mind could only be perceived as hostility.

By the time he was eight, Tyrone had begun to feel a little bit like the Christmas puppy who surprises and disappoints everybody by turning into a dog.

He was escalating the one activity that he had quite by accident discovered to be a source of self-esteem—stealing. It became a way to rebel against the irrational authority that Mrs. Conn had begun to represent. It was a way to get the attention of Dr. Conn in the hope that he'd spend more time at home. Eventually, when that outcome became unlikely, petty theft and mischief was his way of matching wits with Dr. Conn, whom he always believed to be a person of exceptional intelligence. What better way for a bright little boy to make himself feel good than by outsmarting a brilliant adult? Other times he was probably just hungry.

Whatever the cause, once again he was on the prowl most nights, stealing food. And again his parents put a hook on his bedroom door so they could lock him in. Isolation was also a standard form of punishment for real or imagined misdemeanors during the day. Ty spent a lot of time in his room.

It was his physical and emotional isolation that awakened a lifelong love of books. He became an insatiable reader. Books offered escape into the vast, uncharted realms of his imagination. And one morning, while working through one of his brother's Hardy Boys volumes, he discovered a more practical kind of escape mechanism. It was a simple bookmark.

Distracted by an urgent need to go to the bathroom and no longer able to concentrate on the book, he had one of those rare life-altering moments of inspiration. He realized that by standing on a chair and opening the door a crack, he could use the bookmark to lift the hook out of its eyelet. And, better still, when he got back from the bathroom, he was able to lock the door behind him by the same simple process.

With the secret power bestowed by a good bookmark he launched a veritable crime wave in the Conns' kitchen. At first he was content to satisfy normal nocturnal hunger pangs and a child's natural fondness for sweet things. But he could never seem to get enough to quash the deeper cravings that, in all likelihood, had nothing at all to do with his stomach. Soon he was hoarding more than he could ever eat.

There was a large walk-in closet in his room. Dr. and Mrs. Conn stored their surplus clothing in it, and soon the pockets of coats and jackets were stuffed with stolen cookies and tarts and candy.

Even then he had a pessimistic streak and knew he would inevitably be caught. But that knowledge just seemed to compel him to steal more. Maybe it was deliberate recklessness. Maybe he really wanted to be caught and perhaps make them realize that deep and important needs were going unmet.

And he was eventually discovered. Whatever response he'd anticipated, nothing constructive came out of the inevitable showdown. They didn't throw him out and they didn't beat him. They just humiliated him. Years later he remembered the scene clearly. The whole family assembled in his room. And as the various pockets were emptied by his parents, a small heap of goodies grew before their astonished eyes.

If they thought that a dose of humiliation might prove corrective, they were wrong. Somewhere along the way he'd outgrown shame, at least where offences like stealing food were concerned. Standing there with the wrath of his parents and the contempt of his siblings heavy around him, he felt nothing.

His greatest regret was that they had somehow figured out his secret method of escaping from his room. To foil future attempts, they hung a string of bells across the door so that any effort to open it would set off the sound of merry tinkling. He silenced the bells by stuffing them with wads of masking tape, and that worked for a while.

The nocturnal wandering, the innocuous but persistent thefts and the determination to match wits with the adults should have presented a tempting professional challenge for a psychiatrist. The kid was obviously looking for something and it probably wasn't food. Attention? Attachment? A feeling of security? Whatever it was, there is no evidence that Dr. Conn spent a lot of time trying to find out about it.

He left the matter in the unsteady hands of his wife. And her way of dealing with it was old-fashioned punishment: the belt, the wooden spoon, verbal abuse, confinement in his room. And a new lock for the bedroom door.

It was one of those security devices that are commonplace in apartments and hotel rooms. There's a chain with a fitting that slides along a groove in a plate fixed to the doorframe. It allows the door to open slightly, but it's impossible to reach from the wrong side of the door. Usually the chain is for the benefit and safety of whoever is on the inside. In Ty's case, it was on the outside, for the security of the household—protection from him. For all his ingenuity, he couldn't get past this restraint.

Many years later he reflected on the surprising long-term effect of having spent so much time in childhood locked in his room: "I kind of realized that essentially I'd been locked up like a prisoner in his cell since about the age of six. You would think I'd have an aversion to having my door closed or locked because of this but, ironically, even when out [of prison] I have to have my door closed in order to get some sleep."

The locked door came to represent privacy, not imprisonment, and it didn't seem to matter that someone else controlled it. He gradually came to terms with the situation . . . except for one aspect. He couldn't always go to the toilet when he needed to. In one moment of inspired desperation, he discovered that he could dismantle part of a steam radiator in his room and urinate into a pipe. His makeshift urinal was soon discovered, and he was punished. He got a stern lecture. There were grim extrapolations about strange toilet habits.

Unfortunately, the lecture didn't help much when nature called again. Even primitive prison cells provide a bucket. There was no bucket or chamber pot or any appropriate receptacle in his bedroom. But nothing inspires improvisation like a full bladder. So he improvised, using any receptacle he could find. For a long time he got away with using the silo of his Fisher-Price farm set.

It would become a defining feature of Ty Conn's life that small acts of defiance or desperation would carry within them the seeds of great consequences. He would hear again, in the future, about his urine. It would be part of the documentation of his many failures.

3 ·

IN EVERY MEMORY, NO MATTER HOW miserable the life, there are happy moments that rise out of the gloom. Ty

Conn's happiest memory was of summer camp, in 1976, when he was nine. They sent him to Camp Onandaga, near Minden, Ontario, about three hours northwest of Belleville. The camp summer was broken into three semesters, each session three weeks long. People would send their kids for one semester. In the summer of 1976, Ty was there for the entire nine weeks. They just had to get rid of him for a while. Dr. Conn went up to visit once, early in his stay there.

But in Ty's later recollection, the summer of 1976 stood out as an idyllic time. He learned to handle a little Laser sailboat. He learned to swim and to paddle a canoe. He learned rudimentary photography and even tried rock climbing.

As the other kids would come and go, their three weeks completed, Ty became conspicuous for his apparent permanence in the place. If you worked there, you wouldn't be able to avoid wondering: What is it with the Conn kid? Does he have no home to go to? By the third semester, the camp director was taking him along on outings with his own children, for dinner in town or for ice cream. Ty remembered losing his shoes once when a canoe tipped over. The camp director bought him new ones.

Eventually the summer ended. That fall, the problems that until then had been confined to his life at home started cropping up at school. Teachers noticed frequent absences, or late returns after recess or lunchtime. When they investigated, they discovered the delays were caused by visits to nearby stores. When this was reported to his parents, it didn't take them long to realize that the money he was spending in the stores had been pilfered from home.

People who study deviant behaviour have noted a peculiar symbiosis between the badly behaved and their opposites. Without badness, goodness lacks meaning. Whatever the cause of Tyrone Conn's predicament, his life was marked by a perplexing pattern of deviance which seemed to contradict everything else about him. He was intelligent. He was essentially ethical. He had a genuine concern for other people. And yet, his behaviour would, in the long run, prevent him from ever reaching emotional maturity. And as people responded out of frustration or fear or malice to his immaturity, his behaviour would only get worse.

Where did it begin? Did Mrs. Conn find it necessary to shore up her own troubled self-consciousness by attacking his? And where did his "deviance" begin? Perhaps in the deviance that he saw around him: his awareness, at first subconscious but later painfully felt, that everything around him, from the time of birth, was a deviation from the norms of parenting and child care.

Birth parents, grandparents and adoptive parents all deviated from traditional standards of family solidarity and support. Perhaps it was inevitable that the boy would deviate from the rules within the Conn family, as he would, inevitably, from the laws of society.

Was Ty Conn really a thief? Ruth Huffman, who had children of her own, often brought Ty to her place for weekends to give him and the Conns relief from each other. She never believed it.

"I'm in the antique business," she says, "and I used to take him to the fleamarkets and we'd be in a position where there were coins on the tables and things that he could have picked up. For the first while, I watched like a hawk. And I left money lying around my own house and he never stole anything or took anything. He was just not that type of a person. But he was accused of it all the time. She [Mrs. Conn] would put things in his room and then cause trouble and find it and say, 'See, there it is.' I know this is true. I was there."

Eventually, however, Ty became what he was so frequently accused of being. He realized that with money he could buy whatever gratification the stolen food and candy brought. Money, in a way, was easier to steal and to conceal. He started stealing money.

By then the judgment of his parents didn't affect him very much. Whatever respect he had for Dr. Conn was wearing thin. The man was away too much to sustain any serious credibility as a father figure. As for Mrs. Conn, he'd reached the age where he'd become aware that his mother was struggling with a lot of demons of her own and that they probably had little or nothing to do with him.

He'd found a stash of empty liquor bottles hidden in the barn and at first assumed they belonged to his brother, Jeffrey, who, by then, was eighteen years old. But when Jeffrey saw them, he was as mystified as Ty. Ty later overheard Jeffrey and his older sister, Cairine, discussing the bottles and concluding they belonged to Mrs. Conn. Shortly after that Ty found Mrs. Conn comatose on a couch in the family room, and the mystery of the empty booze bottles was solved. At first he thought she was napping. Then he realized her eyelids were partly open, her eyeballs rolled back.

"I thought she was dead, and went and found my older sister who chased me away and, I'm assuming, helped Mrs.

Conn get up. I now know that her battles with alcoholism dated back to just after I was adopted, although it didn't get that bad until I was nine or ten."

The tensions in the home at about this time, perhaps exacerbated by the alcohol, affected the punishments he received. Ty Conn went to great lengths, whenever he spoke of his life with the Conns, to stress that he was never physically abused, except for the conventional spankings by Mrs. Conn and a rare slap up the head from his father.

But Loris Conn seemed to have a remarkable streak of creativity when it came to psychological punishment. There were taunts and accusations that he somehow expected preferential treatment because he was adopted. The first time that happened, he was about six years old.

"I didn't even know what it meant, so how could I have thought that I was special because of it? I recall this very discussion and accusation being levelled at me on several occasions and I tend to believe that Mrs. Conn was drunk . . . as I recall slurred speech, a symptom that I didn't associate with alcohol until years later."

And the punishments for theft sometimes bordered on the bizarre. Because he stole mostly sweet things, she'd force him to eat a mixture of sugar and vinegar, or pudding and pepper, presumably to teach him a lesson of some kind.

Standing in the corner became such a common part of his life that she had to invent embellishments to make it feel like punishment. He'd be forced to stand on one foot, or stand on his toes. It often went on, he later remembered, for hours. Once when Mrs. Conn observed that he was no longer standing on his toes, she held a paring knife under his heels as an incentive to keep them well up off the floor.

It was, perhaps, relatively innocuous compared to the abuses suffered by many children in institutions and in families, adopted or otherwise. But in the larger context of conflict in the family and his own belief that he was, somehow, the cause of all the distress and unhappiness he saw around him, it would have a lasting effect.

4 ·

TY CONN HAD HIS FIRST EXPERIENCE with a "tactical assault" when he was ten. It happened in school. Suddenly one day he was surrounded by teachers demanding to search his desk and his locker. He complied. In a subsequent interrogation which seemed to go on for hours, he learned that a diamond ring and necklace had gone missing at home and that he was the prime suspect.

He told them he didn't know what they were talking about and he stoutly denied that he'd been involved in any way with the disappearance of the jewellery. But his denials didn't carry a lot of weight, given his track record as a proven thief. The effort to extract a confession from him went on for weeks.

Dr. and Mrs. Conn told him they were certain that he'd buried the ring and necklace somewhere on the property. So he was handed a shovel and told to start digging. His protests had no effect, and so he did as he was told. He dug up flower beds and gardens and lawns. Each day after school, he'd get the shovel, or a rake, and go off again on his pointless search. His parents calculated that, sooner or later, he'd grow weary of the work and confess. It didn't seem to occur to them that maybe this time he was telling the truth. He just kept digging and, gradually, began to derive perverse pleasure from the calculated destruction of their landscaping.

Then, one afternoon as he was digging, he felt a frightening constriction in his chest. Suddenly, it took every ounce of strength just to breathe. He dropped the shovel and headed for the house. Halfway up the stairs from the basement to the main floor he collapsed and tumbled to the bottom. His parents found him there and bundled him off to the hospital, where it was confirmed that he'd had a severe asthma attack.

The digging stopped then. There was no further mention of the missing jewellery after that, "except when I was accused of stealing something else."

For the rest of his life he remained convinced that Mrs. Conn had attempted to frame him, and it wouldn't be the last time he'd have to deal with a wrongful accusation of a serious theft in the Conn household. Perhaps, it occurred to him, it was her way of trying to get rid of him. Maybe the nine weeks he'd spent at Minden had raised in his mother's mind the tantalizing prospect of getting him out of the household once and for all.

"It may seem very paranoid or conspiratorial thinking, but taking her alcoholism, mental problems and particular animosity toward me into account, I think I have a case."

His assessment of his adoptive mother was echoed in comments later by a friend of the Conn family. Near the end of her life, Loris Conn would designate Anne Boyle her next of kin.

"I always felt sorry for her," said Mrs. Boyle. "She was a woman with a lot of potential. She was very bright and she knew a lot about caring for people as a nurse, but she was all twisted up by drinking or another mental problem, whatever it was. Whether it was a mental illness or the drinking, she was quite manic a lot of the time. No label was ever put on anything. She was not a well person. She was in her own world."

Shortly after the asthma attack, which was probably brought on by the stress and the digging, somebody found the ring and necklace in the house. They were in a bookcase in the family room. But nobody told the accused culprit for another ten years, by which time his belated exoneration didn't mean much to him or anybody else.

5.

WHEN HOME BECOMES UNPLEASANT, you start looking for ways to avoid going there. When you're ten and living out in the country, there aren't many alternatives available. There are no gangs to join, no easily accessible hang-outs. There aren't many organized activities for young people. There is only school.

Ty wasn't particularly fond of school, but he found that as the end of the day approached, he'd feel a profound sense of dread at the thought of going home. So he got into sports. He joined the cross-country running team. He played soccer. Anything that gave him an excuse to stay away from the big unhappy house that he shared with the Conn family.

Running would become a passion that stayed with him for the rest of his days. No other experience gave him the sense of release he felt jogging through the dry autumn country-side of Hastings County. With the fresh cool air pressing his face, he'd imagine he was travelling with the wedge of geese he'd hear croaking through the dull sky overhead. This was what freedom was supposed to feel like. Freedom, that abstract quality that people were always celebrating or dying for in the books he read. Something he wanted to grow toward.

In games like soccer, he was nimble and competitive and a good team player. His chronic asthma, however, got in the way of any serious athletic ambitions he might have entertained. And inevitably, the run would bring him back to where he started, or the game would end. And he'd be on his way back home again.

Books offered an unrestricted source of fantasy. Escape fantasies. Imagined flight. Redemption by adventure. Through reading, he could participate in schemes that challenged his busy brain. The characters in books made him welcome in their fantastic worlds, made him part of their noble and heroic exploits. He'd spend long periods of detention in his room on secret missions with people of intelligence and quality, people who accepted him because he was really and truly and organically one of them. Not some whimsical add-on.

Escape, as a means for acquiring freedom, becomes an obsession for a prisoner or for a child who is chronically unhappy. No matter how impossible the escape might really be, it takes on the purity of an ideal. It becomes a project, compelling as any dream and as addictive as ambition. And once experienced, with its contradictory sensations of fear and uncertainty and elation, it can never be forgotten.

His first experience of the sensation happened unexpect-edly one night. He must have been only about six years old at the time. He later remembered that he was still wearing those pyjamas with the feet. He'd been caught late at night standing on the kitchen counter, rifling through a cupboard in search of food.

Dr. and Mrs. Conn weren't sure what to do about it and retired from the room to discuss an appropriate form of punishment. There was a sunroom that wasn't used much in the winter. With no particular plan in mind, he wandered in that direction. As the jury deliberation dragged on, he began to contemplate the door. He turned the knob and pulled. The door swung open. Freedom, a great black void, cold, unwelcoming, and heavy with all the menace of the world, stood silently before him. He had only to walk into it. And he did.

He soon realized that he couldn't stay outside for long because there was snow on the ground. So he headed for the barn. Once inside he realized that the uncertainty of his predicament was almost offset by a rare sensation of free-dom. And, inadvertently, he'd put his parents to a crucial test: If they cared at all, they'd come and find him. If not . . . nothing really mattered anyway. He waited for half an hour, it seemed. Then he saw Dr. Conn making his way toward the barn, following the little footprints in the fresh snow. They cared after all.

Without further ado, he turned himself in. There was no more discussion of punishment. He'd made his point, recorded a small victory. But he had also discovered some-thing new: the intoxicating feeling of escape, the infinity of possibility in the unknown.

6.

RUNNING AWAY. ESCAPE. LIBERATION. It fills up the consciousness. And when it's motivated by anger and resentment, it becomes difficult to keep inside. There are moments when the secret sensations swell up and almost release the private obsession just to shock or frighten or hurt. One day, unthinking, he did it to Mrs. Conn.

"I'm going to run away," he blurted.

The declaration was followed by an ominous silence. There were three of them in the room, he remembered forever after. Himself, his mother and his little sister, Loris J., who was eight or nine at the time.

All reality seemed to be frozen around them and he found himself growing uneasy, even frightened, at the ambiguity in Mrs. Conn's expression. What he saw there in her face wasn't what he would have expected. It certainly wasn't shock or pain.

"Well," she said finally, "is that so."

He recalled a long moment of contemplation, then words to the effect that if this was his plan it was fine with her. But he'd go the way he came, with nothing. Then she made him strip.

It was on that day, it seemed, that a new condition entered their relationship. Whatever they started out with had eroded steadily almost from day one. Eventually it had become irritation, then resentment, and finally hostility. Now, at least on his part, there was hatred.

Standing there in his nakedness, clothes piled around him, painfully conscious of the disbelieving stares of his sister, he heard his mother telling him: Now you can go.

Taunting then, she urged him toward the door and out-side. She left him there for what she thought, presumably, was long enough to get the point: that he needed them a lot more than they needed him and that without the family he was nothing.

Ty Conn never denied that he presented a challenge to the household with his complicated needs and the deep-seated impulses that led to wandering and theft. And, at a certain point, as often happens in a deteriorating relation-ship, he would consciously set out to do things to aggravate his adoptive mother and siblings. But near the end of their relationship the conflict became so dark and frightening that it could only be explained as being one of the consequences of crumbling sanity.

Apparently, Ty wasn't the only one who noticed the erratic behaviour of Mrs. Conn. Dr. Conn, increasingly concerned about his wife's condition, asked at least one family friend to make written notes on anything unusual or bizarre. Many in their social circle had noticed disturbing changes in the once warm and gregarious Mrs. Conn during the seventies. And some of them agreed to keep an eye on her.

"We'd all try to figure out what we could do to help," said Anne Boyle. "But there really wasn't anything you could do because Loris was in denial. It's anybody's guess what went on in the home with the children. But I don't see how it could have been very good."

Doreen Lovett would occasionally take care of the Conn children and recalled in a later interview that "Ty was treated worse than the other kids but it was bad for all of them."

According to former family friends, Dr. Conn increas-ingly leaned on them for comfort and support in coping with the problems at home and would often appear spontaneously for a chat or "just to laugh." The state of his home life became an open secret among his confidants, but it was contained within the sealed world of Belleville's social and professional upper crust. Gradually, friends who had initially been sympathetic to Mrs. Conn transferred their support to her husband.

The notes prepared by one family friend, who continued to see Mrs. Conn, make depressing reading. She had gone from being "a tall, slender, attractive girl with a very positive personality" to someone who was a heavy drinker and "loud and rude."

"Since I have had the opportunity to observe manic behaviour at close range," the friend wrote in notes prepared for Dr. Conn, "I thought that she was manic. She was hostile. A kind of turbulence took over. Since we were still having lunches together . . . I could observe that her tolerance for martinis was considerable and I decided that her behaviour must be due to alcohol.

"Her phone calls were strange. She seemed to have many different moods—aggressive and hostile to her husband and children, hilariously loud and boisterous, aggressively positive, hysterically funny or convincingly warm and cozy. It was almost as if one was speaking to different people."

That note was written in 1977 and, according to the person who wrote it for the eyes of Dr. Conn, it was motivated by "deep concern for my friend Mrs. L. Conn."

Clearly by then the Conn marriage was deteriorating. Mrs. Conn obviously needed professional help. Instead, she got surveillance. Her children obviously needed help too, but Dr. Conn would later assert that he wasn't aware of the unhealthy environment they were living in until much later, by which time he was divorcing his unfortunate wife.

In perhaps their worst confrontation, Ty told Mrs. Conn he hated her. It was one of those moments when the voice, unbidden, comes from nowhere and everywhere at the same time. The words rise from some limbic zone as if spoken by a stranger. As the awful words hung there between them in the suddenly still room, Ty marvelled at that interior stranger and admired him. And he wondered what was going to happen next.

"Well," his mother said calmly, "if that's the case, why don't you kill me?"

And then, as if in growing awareness of some compelling logic or even beauty in the idea, she fetched a small paring knife and placed it in his hand. She turned her back to him, urging him to do it. It wouldn't take much, she assured him. She was a nurse. She told him that even a small stab wound, as little as an inch deep, could be fatal. It would be so easy. Just do it.

Ty just stood there, studying her back, the little kitchen knife in his hand, tempted. Years later he acknowledged that the unbidden voice that disclosed to her his hatred also instructed him to comply with her irrational suggestion. Just do it. Kill her. Of course he didn't, but later, possibly lamenting the lost opportunity, he conceived a murder plan that had the attraction of being less messy. But it was also ridiculous.

He sabotaged her cigarettes. He knew that rubbing alcohol was poisonous and it occurred to him that if he soaked one of her cigarettes in it, she'd inhale toxic fumes and react the same as if she drank the stuff. She'd go blind. She'd suffer. She'd die.

"She used to smoke those long brown cigarettes, and I soaked one in alcohol for a moment or two, then carefully inserted it back in the package. A couple of hours later, noticing that she wasn't laid out on the floor anywhere, I decided to take a look to see why she hadn't smoked my cigarette yet. I opened the package to discover a cigarette which appeared to have been eaten away [as if] it had been burned. The thing must have gone up like a Roman candle when she lit it. I guess she didn't have any reason to believe that it was anything but a defective cigarette."

By the time he was ten, the idea of running away was almost constant, idling in the back of his mind like a getaway car, revving up every time there was trouble. Eventually he ran. There was no plan. It was an impulsive decision. He came home from school one day and sensed immediately that he was about to face another harangue for some real or imagined offence. He was told, first, to feed the dog. Then to appear before Mrs. Conn for a discussion on some other matter.

He couldn't imagine what it was, but the thought of another confrontation was too much for him. He went out and did what he'd been instructed to do. And when the dog was fed, he just walked away.

He walked about a mile until he came to the intersection with Highway 62, then along that road until he arrived at the home of some friends from school. They played together for a couple of hours. They rode bikes and gabbed about everything and nothing as young boys are inclined to do. He decided not to tell them that he'd become a runaway or that, in all likelihood, he wouldn't be seeing them again. When his friends returned to their homes, he just walked on, heading nowhere in particular.

In boys' adventure books, the wanderer never goes far before coming to a friendly brook where he finds fresh, sweet water, or a stalwart stranger with cheese and meat and bread to share, or an inviting cottage with a warm hearth fire glowing in the windows. If there's no cottage, he invariably finds a soft and sheltered place and falls quickly into an enchanted sleep under a protective canopy of stars. Then he goes on to find his fortune.

Reality is different. Trudging along the highway, the cold night settling in, the first thing the runaway begins to notice is a gnawing hunger. Then thirst. Then the natural uneasiness that comes from disorientation. After all, he doesn't know where he's going and soon won't even know where he is. And then the feet grow sore.

The first car that came along, he did what anyone would do in the circumstances. He put up his thumb and the car stopped. He got in, sized up the big friendly fellow in a suit who was driving and decided to say as little as possible. The driver asked where he was going, but before he could reply he noticed a small plastic garbage bag hanging from the knob on the ashtray. Inscribed on the bag he saw the Ontario provincial crest, and the initials OPP. Ontario Provincial Police.

Wonderful, he thought. First car I flag down in my new liberated existence is a cop car.

He stole a sideways glance at the driver who, at that moment, pulled a small leather wallet from his inside pocket and flipped it open to reveal a badge. Ty considered jumping out, but the car was going too fast. And he didn't have to think very hard to guess where it was headed for.

The policeman told him he'd done a terrible thing. His parents were frantic with concern. How could he have been so thoughtless? The whole countryside was mobilized, he said, at that very moment scouring the surrounding farmland and woods, anticipating the worst.

Sure, he said to himself, his spirits plummeting at the thought of returning to the Conns. I just bet they are. They're probably celebrating.

But as they approached his home he was astonished to see the vehicles, at least thirty of them, lining the road in front of the house, and the slow sweep of red emergency lights swathing the front yard as dozens of people swarmed around. There was even a command centre in a white cube van. His fears vanished, replaced by a feeling of awe that "the Conns would put up such a fuss over me."

A police officer questioned him at some length about why he'd run away. He was noncommittal, still a bit overwhelmed by the startling notion that maybe, just maybe, they cared about him after all. They certainly went to a lot of trouble to get him back. Maybe this was a turning point, he thought. And he was right. But the turn wasn't in the direction he was hoping for.

7.

THINGS SEEMED TO SETTLE DOWN, at least for him. Mrs. Conn was a different story. Her distress deepened to the point where she didn't seem to notice him much any more. He was nearing his eleventh birthday. Perhaps she'd given up on him. Perhaps she'd given up on everything.

He'd been aware before of marital problems between her and Dr. Conn. Once she actually told him that she and her husband were planning to separate. Whom, she wanted to know, would he prefer to live with? His answer was swift and sincere. He wanted to live with Dr. Conn.

He felt a loyalty to his adoptive father and it survived for a long time, even longer than the doctor wanted it or the persistent neediness that seemed to go along with it. The doctor's absences at least prevented a lot of outright conflict with Ty. There were minor eruptions, probably out of frustration with both his wife and the boy. Once, Ty remembered, the doctor threatened to throw him out through a large picture window. Mrs. Conn's response was that Ty would probably lay criminal charges if he did. But, with his adoptive father, there was little evidence of the toxic feelings that undermined his relationship with Loris Conn. Years later, he'd continue to reach out to Dr. Conn. He was, after all, the only father Ty had ever really known.

Early in 1978, Ty was surprised one morning as he was getting ready for school to find Dr. Conn sleeping in the family room. He stood for a moment, watching his father as he slept, wondering why he was there. Dr. Conn suddenly awoke. Without any explanation, he asked Ty to go to the master bedroom to see if his mother was okay. Okay? Why wouldn't she be okay?

Then the boy became alarmed. On the way to the master bedroom he noticed small random drops of blood on the floor. Just outside the bedroom, he saw a crude smear of what seemed to be fresh blood on the doorframe. Even after the disturbing encounter with the paring knife, it didn't cross his mind that she might have harmed herself.

He opened the door slightly and peered in. The room was dark, but he could see her. She was on the bed, curled up in the fetal position, her back toward him. She seemed to be asleep, breathing gently.

He reported to Dr. Conn that, from what he'd been able to see, she was fine. Then he asked about the blood spots and the smudge outside the bedroom door. Dr. Conn became immediately alert. He and the older children went to investigate, warning Ty and Loris J. to stay in the family room. Nobody ever specifically told them what was going on, but from the quick escalation of panic among their older siblings and the doctor, they realized that something serious had occurred. Jeffrey, the Conn's older son, then took Ty and the little girl outside and away from the house. Recalling the events of that unhappy day, he wasn't clear about just where they went.

As he remembered the day much later, the details were all scrambled and distorted by conflicting emotional responses to what was happening then and later on. He remembered that when he and his younger sister returned to the house, there was an ambulance there. And he remembered that Mrs. Conn was absent for weeks thereafter.

She had attempted suicide. As he heard it explained later, she slit both wrists and made such a mess of the right one that the nerves were damaged. Her doctors had serious doubts that she'd ever fully recover the use of that hand. She was hospitalized for a while in a psychiatric facility in Toronto. Dr. Conn told friends that psychiatrists there were making the absurd suggestion that he, her devoted husband, was partly to blame for her condition.

8.

IN ABOUT FEBRUARY OF 1978, JUST after his eleventh birthday, Ty started hearing family discussions about another move. The novelty of country life was pretty well exhausted. Driving back and forth to town had become a burden to the doctor. Now, after what seemed to be a fairly serious suicide attempt, it was obvious that he should be closer to home. Perhaps Mrs. Conn, who'd never seemed all that enthusiastic about country living in the first place, would be happier in town where at least she'd be closer to her friends.

And, in any case, they no longer needed such a large house. Both Jeffrey and Cairine were going off to private schools, leaving only the two younger kids at home. So the big house in the country went up for sale, and the Conns began to look at houses back in Belleville.

Jeffrey Conn was attending Trinity School in Port Hope then, and Ty got the impression there was a plan afoot to send him to Trinity also. Somebody actually made the suggestion that he should skip ahead a grade, take the admission tests and start there later that year. He was so bright he shouldn't have a lot of difficulty getting in. The idea appealed to him, though he wondered how the family was going to manage the considerable burden of tuition and boarding costs for three of them.

"I was intrigued with the idea of going there," he said later. "I knew my brother loved it there and I would've loved

being away from home. The independence I could experien.
there probably would've been a good thing for me. I might
have been thieving there, but perhaps the school environment
would have curtailed those activities."

The kind of punishment he faced at home for his misde-
meanours no longer had any effect, other than to increase his
anger and his contempt for Mrs. Conn. The threat of social
ostracism in a new environment—an environment he
enjoyed and wanted to succeed in—might have given him an
incentive to curb his worst impulses and, perhaps, to con-
form. But this is all conjecture. The pleasant prospect of
boarding school was to remain beyond his grasp.

He actually went to Trinity for interviews, wrote the
entrance tests and felt pretty confident he'd been accepted.
And as the summer of 1978 approached, his spirits soared
for another reason. There was serious discussion of sending
him back to Camp Onandaga, near Minden. This time, it
seemed, it would be for a briefer stay. He looked forward to
the swimming and sailing and canoeing. Mostly, he looked
forward to a brief holiday from home.

Years later, he'd remember feeling fairly upbeat in the
spring of 1978. At eleven and a half years of age he could
already feel the onset of his teens. One more year and he'd
be on the threshold of that glorious period in life when
independence begins to grow quickly, spreading the bounty
of its options before you. Once he became a teenager he,
like his older brother, could begin to disengage from home.
He'd gradually withdraw from the dark mysteries that troubled the lives of his parents. He'd turn his face outward and
begin to make a plan to execute a better life than theirs.

Life, however, is never entirely predictable. As the summer
of 1978 began and he dreamed hopefully of camp and private

schools, the adults in his life were engaged in discussions that would lead, in early July of that year, to a decision that would dispatch him on an entirely different course.

By July 13, they had moved out of the big house near Foxboro and into a smaller place in the east end of Belleville. Ty was in his bedroom reading that day when he was asked to come downstairs to meet somebody. He couldn't imagine whom. There was no reason to expect anything out of the ordinary.

There was a stranger there. He was a tall, friendly looking fellow with a bushy brown beard. His name, Ty was told, was Jared Campbell. He was from the Children's Aid Society of Belleville.

After some small talk, Ty learned the reason for the visit: the Conns had decided to send him to a group home for the summer. They thought he'd like that. It would give everybody a little break. He shrugged. He'd have been happier going to Camp Onandaga, but anywhere would be an improvement over where he was. At least that's what he thought.

Had he been able to see just a few months into the future, he might not have felt so cheerful. He was about to be dumped again. It would be, by his own count, the third rejection. His natural mother had handed him over to his biological father, who dumped him on the doorstep of his grandparents, who turned him over to "the Crown." Now it was Dr. Conn's turn.

As he left the Conn household on a hot July day in 1978, he couldn't have known he'd never be a part of it again . . . if, in fact, he ever had been. And if Mrs. Conn took any satisfaction from his abrupt departure, it was because she didn't know that she too would soon have to face her own day of expulsion.

CHAPTER THREE

Out of the Snowball

Although the situation was totally alien to me I quickly realized the set-up of your average group home run by a couple. The Benches had numerous children of their own, some their natural children and many adopted. I think their kids numbered about seven, but two lived on their own. Then there were five kids from the CAS, including myself. At times this number of CAS kids varied. Occasionally some were mildly mentally and physically challenged. Some of them were thieves like me, but most were victims of bad families. The very day I arrived, I noticed where they stored their popsicles. Later that night I raided the freezer . . .

Ty Conn, 1997

I think it all began with the problem of wanting to belong and I guess it was like a snowball coming down a mountain. The avalanche came out of the snowball.

Leonard Coen, Group Home Parent

1 .

THE FIRST THING HE DID ON THE DAY he left the Conns'
was pack a suitcase. Then he gathered up whatever spare
change he could find lying around and filled up a little blue
cloth bag that had once contained a bottle of Crown Royal
rye whisky. He tossed the bag of loot in with his clothing
and sat down to await the return of Jared Campbell of the
Belleville CAS.

Soon he could hear the whine of Campbell's Volkswagen
Beetle approaching on the street and turning into the driveway, and he went out to meet him. He was actually looking
forward to a change of scene and to meeting some new
friends. There was no doubt in his mind that he'd be back
with the Conns in time to start the new school year.

He was going to stay at the home of James and Gail
Bench and their blended family of about ten kids, some of
whom they'd adopted and some of whom had been referred
by the CAS. Mr. Bench was in the military, at CFB Trenton,
and the home was about a mile from the air force base.
Shortly after Ty got there, they moved to a larger house near
Foxboro, not far from where he'd lived with the Conns.

Life with the Bench family would soon present a vivid
contrast to what he remembered from the Conn household.
They were staunch Baptists, active in their church. With as
many as a dozen kids around at any given time there was
always the potential for chaos. Mr. and Mrs. Bench relied on
strict rules and firm enforcement to maintain order. Mrs.
Bench could issue a reasonable verbal reprimand which
would affect him in a way that Mrs. Conn never could with

her often hysterical criticisms and bizarre punishments. Mr. Bench, he discovered early on, was a firm believer in corporal punishment.

As the summer crept by he worked hard for Mr. and Mrs. Bench. They had just moved to a small farm property with hayfields, a gravel pit and a horse barn. They kept the older children busy building fences. Ty liked the work even though he disapproved, in principle, of people using foster children for "indentured servitude."

He also disapproved of physical punishment. Spanking. Like most kids he regarded the prospect of a spanking by Mr. Bench with justified alarm. Another CAS kid, Lorraine, had been caught stealing a couple of dollars from the Bench kids' grandmother. Ty could hear her screaming in the basement. Later, when Ty asked Lorraine what had happened, she took him under the deck and slipped her shorts down to reveal the black and blue bruises on her buttocks.

He was not impressed. He realized that, even though he was enjoying his time in the Bench establishment at one level, he'd be glad to return home at the end of the summer. Even after just a couple of weeks away, he was feeling a lot closer to the Conns. Absence, believe it or not, was making his heart grow fonder. He even dared to think that, maybe, his absence would have the same positive effect on them.

A group home is, by its nature, not a place where a kid ever feels settled. You're there because of some breakdown in your life and you're waiting for somebody to fix it. And you just assume that somebody will do so while you're gone. "Home," for a group-home kid, is always somewhere else. There's no incentive to form a lasting bond with the people who run the place or with the other kids. In fact, it's more natural to transform the confusion and insecurities you brought from your real home into a sullen resentment of the group home and the people in it.

In the summer of '78 Ty Conn was pretty typical of the kids that James and Gail Bench saw coming and going through their group home. He thought of himself as a problem and a thief, but Mrs. Bench recalls nothing extraordinary about him other than the fact that he was obviously "very, very intelligent."

Gradually, he began to feel a sensation that just weeks earlier would have been unimaginable. He started feeling homesick for the Conn family. Even though the sojourn at the group home was only for the summer, it was beginning to look like this was going to be one very long summer.

By September he was desperate to get back to the Conns', no matter what he might have to face there. CAS workers in Belleville still felt they could "reintegrate Ty into his family following a period of family counselling." But there were some serious obstacles standing in the way and they weren't all his fault.

For one thing, Dr. and Mrs. Conn didn't want him any more. His presence in the house coincided with the near-complete collapse of Mrs. Conn's personality. Just as in 1970 Dr. Conn had somehow believed that Ty's arrival might be therapeutic for the family, in 1978 he seems to have prescribed that the cure for the family's considerable misery was to get rid of him. CAS documents offer a different opinion.

"Basically, Ty is a pleasant youngster to have around," a CAS report dated October 10, 1978, observed. "He can be open, verbal, honest and co-operative with peers and adults and for the most part has been like that."

They mentioned some "aberrant" behaviour by Ty, and it would have come as no surprise to anybody, including him, that it involved thefts of money and food. Significantly, it also included urinating in the wrong places . . . an aberration he might easily have explained for them if he'd been asked about it. But it obviously wasn't worth serious discussion.

"Our assessment of him is that he is not a seriously emotionally disturbed boy and given appropriate handling, he can function reasonably well," the social worker assigned to his file noted. "There is no question that he could return to his home, but Dr. and Mrs. Conn will have to alter some of their own ways of reacting to Ty as well as make some changes in lifestyle."

Reading the CAS reports today, it's difficult to reconcile the concerns of the workers in 1978 with the circumstances of Ty Conn's adoption eight years earlier. The picture they present of him is consistent with what the psychologist Ingrid Bateman saw in the little boy just before Dr. Conn adopted him. It is in their belated assessment of the family situation that one finds glaring inconsistency.

A case worker noted that there "appear to be significant stresses in this family, some of which are the result of the long hours of work and absences from the home of Dr. Conn." And there was some evidence that "Mrs. Conn has a drinking problem and has attempted suicide on a couple of occasions."

And then this: "It is probably fair to say that Ty has been miscast in his role and not afforded the kind of individuality he required, as well as being the scapegoat in a shaky, unsatisfying marriage."

It was a startling and disturbing observation by CAS workers in Belleville, considering the haste with which another branch of the CAS, in Picton, just eight years earlier, had approved the home for an adoption. Was the marriage shaky and unsatisfying in 1970, or did it only get that way after three-year-old Tyrone arrived? If it was shaky in 1970, how come nobody at the Picton office of the CAS noticed? And what happened when child-care workers from a different CAS office discovered eight years later that the adoption wasn't working out?

In September Ty was enrolled in a new school, clear evidence that the "temporary" absence from the Conn household was becoming permanent. Then in early November a social worker told him that he was to be allowed to return to the Conns', but just for a visit. He was thrilled. That was all he needed. They warned him not to get his hopes up, but he couldn't suppress his excitement. He was optimistic. He even bought a gift for Mrs. Conn.

And from his point of view, the visit went extremely well. After a history of sibling rivalry with his younger sister, Loris J., he found that they now seemed to get along well. She showed him around the new neighbourhood in Belleville and introduced him to some of her friends. It felt like a whole new beginning.

But it wasn't long before he was back at square one with Dr. and Mrs. Conn. He and Loris J. were busted with a package of Export Lights. And since he was only there for a visit and was presumably immune from prosecution, he did the gallant thing and took the rap. He said the cigarettes were his.

The consequences followed quickly. They sent him back to the group home a day early. And it wasn't long before he was informed that there would be further repercussions. There would be no more visits to the Conns'. Whatever hope there had been for reconciliation seemed to be dissipating before his eyes like the smoke from those wretched cigarettes.

And Mrs. Bench soon broke some news that was even worse than that: Mrs. Conn had made a serious new allegation. A valuable coin collection was missing from a safe. He was the prime suspect.

Him? From a safe? Ty Conn took a certain irrational pride in the fact that nothing could make him cry. But he cried that night. He never forgot the hopelessness he felt as he wept uncontrollably on Gail Bench's shoulder.

He convinced himself that, as had happened with the missing diamonds, the adults would eventually come to realize his innocence. But, improbable though the accusation was, it didn't go away. It got worse. Near the end of November he had a visit from Jared Campbell of the Belleville CAS. Campbell was sad and he was uncomfortable because he was delivering more bad news. There was to be a hearing in the family court in Belleville.

Court?

Not about the theft. This would be a different kind of hearing. Dr. Conn was going to ask a judge to transfer custody to the CAS indefinitely.

Custody?

Ty didn't know what that meant. Custody of what? Him?

He, of course, couldn't have remembered the last time it had happened to him, back in 1970 when he was three. He was to become a ward of the Crown once again.

He would remain, legally, a part of the Conn family. But they were no longer to be responsible for him. He would even become available for adoption by somebody else, if anybody wanted him. Fat chance. He knew from his time in the group home that the likelihood of another adoption was remote. The place was full of big kids like him. Nobody adopted eleven-year-olds.

Far in the future Ty Conn would one day be asked to recall the unhappiest day of his life. He only had to reflect for a moment. It was December 27, 1978. On that day a social worker drove him to the CAS offices in Belleville. As he waited there, Dr. Conn and the CAS worker appeared before a family-court judge to finalize his status. The Conn family were to be rid of him once and for all, and with hardly any more effort than it took to acquire him in the first place.

"I didn't actually have to appear before the judge myself and I was supposed to have a meeting with Dr. Conn before going home. He [Dr. Conn] couldn't make it, however, and Mr. Campbell told me he was pretty shaken up about the hearing. I thought that was touching, considering that it was he that was going to court to get rid of me.

"I guess he and the Conns felt guilty . . . because I was presented with a bag containing Christmas gifts."

He seemed to realize that these would be the last gifts he'd ever get from any of them. Mrs. Bench found the packages later, still wrapped, in the garbage. She quietly retrieved them and put them on his bed. There was a puzzle and a toy and a sweater. He gave the toy and the puzzle away to a young friend in the group home. He saved the sweater until he returned to school after the Christmas holidays. Then he tossed it in one of the school trash bins and nobody ever saw it again.

Mrs. Bench, who always kept a careful inventory of all her kids' clothing and was quick to raise questions when anything disappeared, never mentioned the missing Christmas sweater.

There was an appalling symmetry about the date of Dr. Conn's appearance before the courts in Picton to relieve himself of responsibility for his adopted son . . . December 27, 1978. It was on that same date, December 27, that the boy's grandparents had appeared before the same court to give him up to the care of the Crown in 1969.

2.
———

EARLY IN 1979 TY TOOK A HARD AND unsympathetic look at himself and decided that he had some serious work to do to improve his own behaviour, and he hoped this might lead to improvements in his lot in life. Practically from infancy he'd been stealing. Food. Candy. Small change.

He had no moral view on theft. Stealing was simply exploitation of an opportunity. The act of taking something that belonged to someone else without their permission was the same as getting a gift or a payment. Opportunities happen. We are supposed to "seize" opportunities, aren't we?

Religious people told him stealing was a sin and that sin was bad for you. But he didn't believe that. The only aspect of theft that was bad for you was getting caught. The abstract notion that one is always "caught" because "God knows everything" and because of the inevitability of "divine justice" meant nothing to him. Religious instruction hadn't been a big part of his upbringing until then. The only moral deterrent he knew was the prospect of immediate and painful punishment.

But at just about the time he became twelve years old, it occurred to him that his problems with the Conns, which had now taken on life-altering dimensions, were somehow a punishment for stealing. Maybe religious people, like the Baptist Bench family, were on to something. Maybe theft was a bad idea after all, just because God said so. Maybe there was something intrinsically wrong with theft. Maybe, even when you thought you were getting away with it, you weren't. Could it be that there was, out "there" somewhere, a cosmic all-seeing and all-knowing police officer who, for lack of a better description, was known as God? He decided then and there to get religion.

"I decided to accept Christ into my life. I got down on my knees in my bedroom and prayed for God to make me a good boy. I saw my thieving as the major cause of my estrangement from the Conns and I thought that if I was a well-behaved kid I might get another shot at going home, despite the pessimistic outlook.

"Interestingly enough, it seemed to work. I stopped thieving and for all practical purposes was a normal kid for once. The Benches noticed the difference and gave me some positive reinforcement by praising me and extending a bit more trust in me. It wasn't so much that I believed in God or anything, but instead I was sort of using religion to keep my nose clean."

Of course, it couldn't last. His objective was not to make a favourable impression on God or the Bench family. What he really wanted was feedback from Dr. Conn. But the Conn family were far away and couldn't have known about Ty's conversion experience, even if they were slightly interested. In any case they had embarked on a different project. They wanted him out of their lives. He could become a saint if he wanted to. He could wear sackcloth and fast and pray until Judgment Day. As far as they were concerned, Tyrone William Conn was history.

Early in the new year, 1979, he got another bit of news. Mrs. Conn's coin collection had reappeared as mysteriously as it had gone missing.

One bit of news he didn't get was that Dr. Conn had made a dramatic career change. He had become a civil servant in New Brunswick, a senior administrator in the mental health branch of the provincial department of health. The Conns were moving.

It only took Dr. Conn a few months to grow bored with the new job and to decide that he wanted to move back to Ontario. But an interlude of a few months was long enough to complete the family's psychological separation from the troubled little boy who had shared their lives for eight years.

3 ·

THE CROWN WARDSHIP PROCESS JUST after Christmas in 1978 was the second major turn in the course of Ty Conn's life. It would always be a reference point for perplexing questions. How much of his later life can be explained by the ambiguity of his status in the Conn family? How much of his behaviour, there and later, was a reaction to his own belief that he didn't really belong in the Conn family? Why did he feel that way? Was it the complexity of his needs because of the instability around him during infancy? His rejection by his biological family? Was it because of what the CAS would come to regard as the Conns' "shaky, unsatisfying marriage"? Was it the influence of a mother figure who appeared to be dedicated to self-destruction? Was it the ineffectiveness of the two men who were his fathers?

Ty Conn never achieved a sense of personal security because he never really belonged anywhere. He never really owned anything. What possessions he had were invariably controlled by the authorities who had overall responsibility for piloting his life. From the age of three he was a "case," a file with a number and, only occasionally, for the handful of people who were touched by his charismatic personality or his tragic plight, a person. He was an adult before he learned that someone loved him. Even his obvious physical assets as a well-formed and attractive child were compromised by persistent asthma, the symptoms of which seemed to be aggravated by emotional stress. And his young life was rarely free of stress.

It was, perhaps, to achieve the feeling of security that comes from being liked, or noticed, or seeming clever that Ty Conn became a thief.

Dr. Bert Conn must have had a colleague or a book or a case summary in his files that could have told him there would be unpredictable and probably tragic consequences from that dry legal process on December 27, 1978. But on that day, going by the recollections of his friends, it would have been difficult to imagine what was on his mind.

One family friend, Ruth Huffman, reported that there was a consensus around Belleville at the time that Bert "did it" because of his wife.

"I honestly believe that Bert thought that it would be best for that boy to be put back into a foster home where he'd get more love and better treatment than he was getting at home. I don't know if he was right."

According to Mrs. Huffman, "he sat and he cried like a baby" after the court appearance.

Anne Boyle was a friend of Dr. Conn's at the time and reports that he was "quite heartbroken.

"I think he really loved Ty and he thought he wasn't safe at home. His wife was erratic, eccentric, she tended to drink a lot and he thought he [Ty] wasn't safe at home. The woman was so unusual I think anything could have happened there."

Mrs. Boyle describes Dr. Conn as "a very kind man . . . very compassionate," but her sister, Mary Mulhall, offered a different picture of the day Dr. Conn handed his son back to the Crown.

"Bert would come to our house by himself often. He came the day he'd gone to court to give Ty up. And all Harry [her late husband] said when he left was 'Chilling, isn't it?' His coldness about it and his strange attitude about it."

The Mulhalls had adopted a son who, like Ty, would encounter problems growing up and eventually run afoul of the law. Dr. Conn would confidently assure them he knew from his own experience how they should respond.

"He thought we should use the Crown wardship process to give him up. It's funny, we know three people in Belleville who have done this. It's like, if they don't fit into the scheme of things . . .

"It revolts me."

4 ·

IT IS UNCLEAR HOW LONG TY CONN continued to hope that his family would take him back. He seemed, somehow, to always know where they were, despite the fact that they moved around a lot for a few years. He found out that they hadn't remained in New Brunswick for long and were soon back in Belleville. That discovery was about all it took to stir the embers of his unlikely obsession—to belong to a home in which he had known so much unhappiness.

As spring approached, his piety was becoming tiresome and, he figured, futile. He started thinking of escape. His group-home parents had obviously factored escape fantasies into their household security arrangements, for when the kids went to bed they locked the bedroom doors. The kids had to leave their shoes outside in the hallway. This did not deter Ty and a friend named Todd. They decided to make a run for freedom anyway.

Flight. Running away. It is an act with potential for pure creativity. It is, at once, an end and a new beginning. It's easy to overlook the fact that, like any creative act, escape requires preparation. Especially if you're eleven. Ty Conn was never good at preparation. He was clever enough. But he wasn't practical.

So, on the night of the great escape from the Bench group home, Ty and Todd, dressed only in their pyjamas, bundled their clothing and a few personal belongings into a wool blanket and went out their ground-level bedroom window.

It was March and there was still snow on the ground. As they crept away from the house a dog began to bark furiously and they saw a light go on in the bedroom where they knew Mr. and Mrs. Bench slept. They started to run and, in the panic, lost the blanket and their clothes.

They travelled about a mile in stocking feet before the cold and the damp forced them to take refuge in a building that was part of a riding school. After a brief rest, they were off again in the general direction of the small town of Stirling. Before long they had to take shelter again, this time in the back seat of a car. They soon fell asleep there.

They were eventually discovered by the car owner, and after he took them into his house and fed them some toast and Cheerios, he drove them back to the group home. There was, to their surprise, no punishment. But there were consequences. Before long he'd be moving to a new home.

In early summer, Mr. and Mrs. Bench told him they were planning some summer activities that didn't include him or any of the CAS kids in their care. They'd be going to foster homes for the summer. It was to be a temporary arrangement.

It was true, but like all the other temporary arrangements in his life, it didn't take long to become part of his permanent feeling of alienation.

5.

AFTER A FEW WEEKS AWAY, STAYING with some friends of the Bench family, he was assigned to a new group home. The social workers told him this too would be temporary. It was a large chicken farm owned by a Dutch-Canadian couple, Marion and Anne Vreugdenhill, who had a large family, including four kids who were adopted. They got along well, and after a couple of weeks he asked if he could stay. The family didn't hesitate

"I said, 'Boy, he just fits in. He's the perfect kid,'" Mrs. Vreugdenhill recalled years later. "He seemed happy."

"In those days we didn't know what we do now. We didn't know how badly these children are damaged from their early years."

As far as Ty was concerned, he was ready for a change, but he soon found that he'd become part of another home with strenuous religious beliefs. The Vreugdenhills belonged to the Dutch Reformed Church, and when it came to piety they made the Baptist Bench family look pagan. They went to church twice on Sunday. Ty had to join a Christian cadet corps. He had catechism every Wednesday night. And he went to a Christian school where religious indoctrination was a big part of the curriculum. They weren't even allowed to watch television cartoons on Saturday mornings.

In retrospect, all the prayer and religious instruction didn't have much effect on him. It did nothing at all to offset what had become a permanent feeling of rejection or to prevent the emergence in his character of a deep cynicism. As had happened before, the alienation and the cynicism soon began to express themselves through a compulsion to steal.

It wasn't that he needed money. He never passed up a chance to earn an honest wage, even at work that would be considered hard by adult standards. At the Vreugdenhills', and at a neighbouring farm owned by their in-laws, the Vanderlaans, he earned more than he needed helping with the chicken farming. In addition, they were all encouraged to go out through the countryside seeking odd jobs, cutting grass, shovelling snow, babysitting. Everybody seemed to have a bank account, and it wasn't long before Ty had substantial savings of his own, all earned honestly.

He even liked the work and the feeling of achievement that came with a hard day in the Vreugdenhills' massive chicken barn.

"I enjoyed the sense of accomplishment and of feeling tired at the end of the day. It's a damn shame this sense abandoned me in later years. It probably could've prevented a lot of the bullshit . . . to come."

He couldn't seem to resist the temptation to explore, gradually working up the nerve to invade the privacy of homes in the neighbourhood. An unlocked door was an invitation to enter. An empty room, or house, was a world full of revelation.

In one of his first raids on a house near his new home, he stole marijuana, cigarettes and a Van Halen record album. He was only twelve and he didn't smoke tobacco or pot, and he certainly had enough money to buy his own records. Perhaps significantly, he later reported experiencing enormous gratification in giving away the dope and the cigarettes. He kept the record.

He was developing a reputation among other kids for generosity at the candy store and the local go-cart track. He always seemed to have money to burn. Then, over dinner one evening, Mrs. Vreugdenhill reported that the police had been around that day investigating a neighbourhood break-in, and their only clue was a set of bicycle tracks. She wanted to know if any of her kids had been in the area of the house that had been burgled.

Ty knew that this wasn't one of his crimes, but there was something in the tone of voice that indicated a strong suspicion among the adults that he was a thief.

It wasn't anything specific, but he suddenly felt transparent, with all his evil needs and impulses exposed to everybody at the table. He just knew that, sooner or later, he was going to be busted for something, guilty or not.

And sure enough, Mr. Vreugdenhill announced one evening shortly after that a much-prized coin set had gone missing. He wasn't accusing anybody, but he offered a ten-dollar reward for its return. Ty felt trapped. He knew he hadn't stolen the coins. But for some reason, he seemed to be the prime suspect. The feeling left him paralyzed. He was afraid to help look for the missing coins because he believed that it would be just his bad luck to find them, which would only confirm that he'd stolen them in the first place. At the same time he knew that by not helping in the search he was just inflating the suspicion that he was the culprit. His instincts were prophetic, but they didn't curtail his activities for long.

A few weeks later he stole a stopwatch from the school. He just couldn't help himself. It was one of those new digital models and it would be easy to sell to one of the other kids. Mrs. Vreugdenhill caught him when he tried.

She was a large woman and physically strong from farm work. After she slapped him, he thought for a moment that his head was gone. She sent him to his room then to await the judgment of her husband and, sitting there, he started to speculate on what that was going to feel like. Mr. Vreugdenhill, it seemed to him, was massive. He must have stood at least six foot four, and he was powerful. You could tell just by watching him working around the farm. Ty couldn't even begin to imagine how he was going to survive when Mr. Vreugdenhill got his big hands on him.

Short of a miracle, there was only one way out of this. And because he wasn't accustomed to beneficial miracles, he concluded he was going to have to save himself. He got permission to go to the bathroom and then exited through a small window, mounted his bicycle and was gone.

He headed for Belleville, nearly twenty-five miles away. The Conns, he knew, were back from New Brunswick. Maybe he could find them. Maybe in these life-and-death circumstances, they'd find mercy in their hearts and take him in. It was a long shot, but it was all he could think of at the time.

6.

STANDING IN FRONT OF THE DOOR of the last home he'd lived in with the Conns, reality was suddenly whirling through his head. These were the people who had treated him like a leper for all the time he could remember. These were the people who had, when the going got rough, sent him packing the way you'd return a faulty product to the manufacturer. Except in his case they didn't even know who the manufacturer was. So they sent him back to a kind of warehouse. What on earth would they think when they saw him again? Did they even live here any more? How would they react to him if they did? And if they weren't living here, or if they just slammed the door in his face, what would he do? He was a long way from the Vreugdenhills' farm and he didn't have a plan.

The door opened and he was suddenly staring into the eyes of Loris Conn. There was a moment in which she didn't seem to know who he was. It had been almost two years since she'd seen him. He'd been gone since July 1978. Kids grow quickly and change a lot in two years. He'd begun to look like a teenager. Then she smiled.

"Hello, Ty," she said. "Where did you come from?"

He was stunned. There she stood. And she smiled. And she was just like a mother was supposed to be. He was speechless.

Finally, he asked: "Is Jeffrey home?"

For some reason he felt that if anybody was going to understand what he was feeling and what he needed, it would be his big brother. Of course Jeffrey wasn't home. And, in any case, Mrs. Conn was actually behaving as if she was glad to see him. She invited him in. She asked if he was hungry. He sure was. She fed him. Then he told her that he'd run away from the foster home in which he'd been living.

It was one surprise after another. She smiled. She let him in. She fed him. She seemed to be genuinely interested in him. Then she told him that she was going to a swimming class. She was giving swimming lessons at Albert College. Loris J. was going with her. How would he like to go swimming with them? He'd love to, he said.

When Dr. Conn came home that evening, he was driving a brand-new Cadillac. He had it out for a trial run because he was considering buying it. They had a civil and almost sympathetic conversation about Ty's current status, after which Dr. Conn called the CAS. And then he called the

Vreugdenhills to report that Ty was okay. Then they drove him back to the Vreugdenhills' farm in the Cadillac.

It was all very confusing. He'd expected rejection by the Conns, but instead was welcomed as a guest. He expected to be punished by the Vreugdenhills. They just sent him to his room. There was even talk of future visits with the Conns.

7.

A COUPLE OF DAYS WENT BY AND there were no apparent repercussions in the aftermath of the sudden flight to the Conns'. There hadn't been any further talk about the stolen stopwatch or the missing coin collection. He was starting to think his problems had blown over. He was wrong. One evening shortly after, Mr. Vreugdenhill invited him out to the barn for a private discussion, and it didn't take long to realize that he was facing summary justice there.

After an exchange of pointed accusations and robust denials about recent thefts, along with strong suggestions that he was the prime suspect in the case of the missing coin collection, Mr. Vreugdenhill removed the long leather belt he wore around his substantial girth. There was a buckle on one end and a metal tip on the other. Ty was told to drop his trousers and to lean over a platform that was normally used for milking goats.

The thrashing left him bruised and sore, and for a long time afterwards he couldn't wear shorts in gym class for fear of having to explain the marks on his legs and rear end. The metal tip of the belt left a pattern of small crescent-shaped

cuts on the inside of his thighs. Exiled to his room afterward, he brooded over a plan to run away again.

The only thing that stopped him was the prospect of
another visit to the Conns'. He knew that any further contact
with the family, and certainly any faint hope for a reconciliation, would depend on exemplary behaviour in the coming
weeks.

And his forbearance seemed to be rewarded. There was a
visit. First they said it was going to happen. Then, miraculously, it happened. It was uneventful and, mercifully, free of
any conflict with either his younger sister or his mother.

They scheduled a second visit, but this one didn't go as
well, and consequently it was his last. At some point during
the second trial visit he'd unwittingly provoked a fierce verbal attack from Mrs. Conn. She accused him of snooping. He
didn't know what she was talking about. He'd stumbled on
a photograph of himself and, with it, a number of ribbons
and awards he'd won at summer camp three years earlier.
He'd assumed they'd been lost. He was thrilled to find them,
sitting out in the open in the laundry room. Just sitting there
where he couldn't avoid spotting them. He wasn't snooping
at all. He thought his parents would be as thrilled as he was
that they'd turned up. They weren't.

He was an incurable snoop, she said. Always meddling
with other people's things. Always, the implication was clear,
looking for opportunities to steal stuff. It was a bum rap as
far as he was concerned. He, in fact, had been bending over
backwards to avoid any hint of the kind of behaviour he
knew to be provocative. But he had failed.

After the bogus snooping charges he knew it was over
with the Conns as a family. His future contacts would be

with Dr. Conn alone, and they would be brief and, for the most part, superficial. There was also, after that visit, a sharp deterioration in the relationship between Ty and the Vreugdenhills. And, in his own subsequent recounting of the next few months, there was a marked increase in delinquent activity. In retrospect, it is clear that the seeds of adult failures and perceived injustices were beginning to germinate.

That summer the Vreugdenhills sent Ty and an older foster child, a girl, to the town of Frankford to work for a family friend named Gerald Suurdt. He owned a company called Consumer's Carpet and Lumber.

Ty was thirteen. He worked hard at odd jobs for the Suurdts. He earned plenty of money, but he never missed an opportunity to steal anything that wasn't nailed down. He stole from the Suurdts and from the automobiles and homes of strangers. It was at about this time that he claims to have started taking a perverse pride in his outlaw status. His early thieving may well have been to get attention. Now he was determined to avoid being noticed.

"I've had many opportunities to speak with young men like myself whose criminal careers date from pretty much the same stage in life," he said years later. "They all had one thing in common despite whatever had happened to them since. Those early years seemed to build confidence in their own impunity."

He also began to learn bitterly that impunity for a thief is an illusion and, at best, it doesn't last for long.

Near the end of the summer of 1980, there was a minor incident that would eventually provide a rationale for a later and rapid escalation in criminal behaviour. He was driving a lawn mower, and while backing up he noticed, too late to react, that one of the younger Suurdt boys had dropped a bicycle in his path. He swerved, but still ran over the front wheel. The boy said he'd done it deliberately. His denials had no impact against the credibility of his accuser.

While continuing to protest his innocence, he agreed to fix the bike. He even paid for a new tire and tube out of his own earnings, but that wasn't good enough. When he left the Suurdts' at the end of the summer to return to the Vreugdenhills', they kept his last two weeks' pay, a total of eighty dollars. He felt he was being robbed, but as he said later, using prison slang, he decided to "take it dry." And he vowed to take revenge.

"As the summer ended, I was an increasingly bitter kid. I hated the Vreugdenhills. I hated the Suurdts. I hated the church that I was forced to go to and I hated the CAS that had placed me there."

He was generally unhappy. The summer, he concluded, had been a failure.

8.

THE THEFTS ESCALATED. HE WAS shoplifting clothes, wrist watches, cigarettes and cassette tapes and usually getting away with it. He'd discovered that people who ran foster homes and group homes got paid. It seemed to come as a startling revelation that they weren't just taking in kids out of altruism. It was another example of adult greed in action.

It was becoming clear that he wasn't going to be at the Vreugdenhills' home much longer. So he broke into a neighbour's house where there was an air rifle that he coveted. He took it and stashed it for the day when he'd be leaving there . . . a day he knew by then to be inevitable.

The breakdown had become obvious to the Vreugdenhills.

"The stealing started after the honeymoon was over," Mrs. Vreugdenhill would recall. "He was stealing from us and we found out much later that he was also stealing from friends of ours. It wasn't anything that I was prepared for. I couldn't believe it at first, and then he was caught. Other things came out too—other theft incidents. It was much worse than I thought.

"We reacted by confronting him with it and he responded by denying it. Total denial. Till he couldn't deny it. Till it was proven. And then he would shut down. Shrug his shoulders. In the end we decided we couldn't deal with it any more. That it was escalating. From school . . . I think one of the neighbourhood kids was involved too. To be honest, it's very painful. I just couldn't seem to reach him. He would just look right through me. I just couldn't reach him. I felt bad because we had never given up on a child before."

When it was time to leave the Vreugdenhills', he didn't get a lot of notice. He had money, from his earnings, in the bank. He'd bought a goat, an investment which, by the time he left, was worth one hundred and fifty dollars. He had a decent bicycle and about one hundred dollars' worth of fishing tackle. He had to leave it all behind because it wouldn't fit in the social worker's car. He did manage to find room for the stolen air rifle.

Mr. Vreugdenhill said he'd sell the goat for him and forward the money and other items later. After about two months he got a cheque for seventy-five dollars. And some-

body else's fishing rod. He never got his bike. He was
outraged.

9.

HIS NEW HOME WAS IN MARMORA, about an hour away
from the Vreugdenhills' farm. He'd be living with Leonard
and Sharon Coen, who had three children of their own, all
of them close to his own age.

The Coens have a positive memory of his arrival. "He was
a very likeable person," Sharon Coen remembers. "Very
happy. We kind of got the feeling that it must have been an
adoption breakdown because he was a nice kid."

His own memory was shaped by the anger that was eating
at him then. Besides the three Coen kids, there were three
others like himself, wards of the CAS. The "group-home kids"
quickly briefed him on the lay of the land: it was, basically,
another two-tier society, with the birth children on the top
level and the rest in a second-class status.

Certain areas were off limits to the kids who weren't part
of the biological family.

As Leonard Coen explained it years later: "The kids were
told that we were a family. But yet within this family there
was another family of our own and sometimes the lads really
wanted to belong to that inner circle. But we had to draw a
boundary around some of the things we did, so we had some
activities we only did with our kids."

It might have been a sensible and necessary arrangement,
but all the "group-home kids" could see was that they were

somehow lesser people than the biologically correct children in the house. That there were clearly defined no-go areas for them—family rooms that were out of bounds, activities from which they were deliberately excluded—created an atmosphere of suppressed tension most of the time.

As for Ty Conn, notwithstanding his usually pleasant disposition, he represented the kind of influence from which most responsible parents would instinctively try to protect their own children. The Coens seemed to realize from the start that there was something deep and dangerous lurking within him.

Leonard Coen was never able to put his finger on any single factor that might explain Ty's problems, and nobody at the CAS seemed willing to tell them much about his background.

"It's hard to say what his problems stemmed from. [But] I think it all began with the problem of wanting to belong and I guess it was like a snowball coming down a mountain. The avalanche came out of the snowball."

10.

THE NEED TO BELONG IS ALMOST AS persistent as the need to survive. In Ty Conn's case, it seemed to grow stronger with each rejection or exclusion. For years his main focus was to belong to the troubled household that had adopted him when he was three and a half years old. For a long time he maintained a powerful desire to patch things up, at least with Dr. Conn. He wrote a lot of letters and made a lot of phone calls, just to keep his hope alive.

According to a CAS review dated March 24, 1981: "Before entering into the Coens' group home in December 1980, Ty and Dr. Conn were expressing a desire to see each other occasionally. Ty has had frequent contact by telephone and letters with his father. During this period [December 1/80 to March 1/81] Ty and Dr. Conn had two visits together over dinner. Both visits were satisfactory according to Ty and Dr. Conn. Although Ty would like more frequent visits, Dr. Conn finds it difficult to find the time to see him more often."

The CAS notes reflect growing concern about Ty's behaviour. Ty "has not accepted the Coens' group home." Ty has not accepted that "he will not be able to reintegrate into the Conn family." He'd been coerced into playing hockey by the Coens, and he clearly didn't like it. He was unhappy about being made to spend two hundred dollars of his own hard-earned money on hockey gear. He was skipping classes at school. And he was getting caught for stealing.

As usual, a lot of the thefts were to get approval: cigarettes for his friends, chocolate bars. In one case, it was a deliberate act of revenge. In Frankford one evening for a hockey game, he broke into the Suurdts' carpet and lumber store and stole forty dollars. He told himself it was a partial settling of accounts for the incident involving the bicycle and his confiscated eighty dollars. Whatever the motive might have been, Gerald Suurdt would be a frequent target for Ty Conn's acts of anger and vengeance against a world that he believed rejected him.

It was a crucial moment in his life. He was at an age when people start making choices for which they'll be held accountable. Usually there's a lot of structure and advice available from people who've already gone through the maturing process and that's how you avoid a lot of mistakes. Ty Conn missed out on that structure and that guidance. People were "looking after" him, but nobody cared enough or had the time to provide what he might normally have learned from a parent.

It is symbolic, if not significant, that at about this time he lost his virginity in an encounter with somebody named Roxanne. It was, all in all, about the only pleasant memory he carried away from this period of his life. They were schoolmates, in the same shop class. Working under an engine one day they just started fooling around. One thing led to another. And so they consummated their curiosity in an empty church.

He was in frequent conflict with his foster parents. They discovered that the air rifle he'd brought with him from the Vreugdenhills' had been stolen. It led to his first serious encounter with the police, and his first appearance in court. With that behind him, he had turned another corner. He was now "known to the police." He'd received a suspended sentence for theft. He was, officially, a thief.

Policemen tend to work on the assumption that in any given population of children, there are only a few thieves. Once identified and labelled, they will automatically be a part of any future investigation. Ty Conn acquired that status near the end of 1980.

He also seems to have deepened his capacity for cynicism. He noted that bad behaviour got the attention of CAS workers . . . and Dr. Conn. They met just before Christmas in 1980 for dinner in a restaurant.

Then in January 1981, they met again, in another restaurant. Their birthdays, both in January, were only a few days apart. A social worker drove him to Belleville for the joint celebration. He bought his father a coffee mug as a birthday gift. His father bought him lunch. It doesn't seem to have been a particularly warm encounter and it didn't last very long. Dr. Conn gave him five dollars as he was leaving.

The trip to Belleville gave him a chance to visit a Canadian Tire Store, where he stole a cheap camera and a battery charger. He later told his social worker that Dr. Conn had given him thirty dollars and he'd used it to buy the items. Whatever the motive for the stealing and the lie, the truth would not take long to emerge. And it marked the beginning of the end in his relationship with the CAS workers.

CAS documents now began to reflect a sense of despair. It seemed that nothing short of a miracle was going to help him. And the only miracle that would help would be some dramatic change in the Conn family that would open a way back in for him.

Whatever Dr. Conn was telling Ty during their lunches, he was leaving no doubt in the minds of people at the CAS: there was no room in their lives for the boy and nothing was going to change that. Not even a miracle.

It's unclear just what Dr. Conn was telling Ty during their encounters, but months later, another psychiatrist would observe that Ty became "aggressive, evasive and tearful" whenever talk moved into the realm of his failed family life.

As an adult, he would remember this period with a lot of bravado and cynicism. He liked to think of it as a time when he left a lot of bullshit behind and began to come to terms with the truth of his existence. He was bad. Whatever had caused him to be bad was a mystery to him. But if he had to be bad, he was going to be good at it. That's how he saw it in retrospect. But his actions at the time were those of a little boy working hard to destroy the fears and inhibitions that were preventing him from taking charge of his pathetic life.

I I .

BY LATE FEBRUARY, TY HAD PRETTY well concluded that there was only one course of action left for him. He decided to run away. And this time he wouldn't be running in his pyjamas and he wouldn't be on some sentimental futile trip into his pitiful past.

On February 25, when he was getting ready to go to school, he packed a gym bag with extra clothes. Leonard Coen, by then in the habit of monitoring his every move, checked it and unpacked it, but said nothing. Ty was halfway to school when he realized he'd been tricked. But he took off anyway, with another boy from a different foster home. That night, after walking and hitchhiking all day, they arrived at the Ontario mecca for youthful strays and runaways, the corner of Yonge and Dundas in Toronto.

It was a whole new world. Eaton Centre teemed with kids who seemed to be just like them. The noise and the lights of the street and the video arcades and the swarm of young people had an intoxicating effect. He would forever associate the hallucinogenic images of that night with a sense of liberation.

The small question of where they were to sleep that night seemed to be answered by an older man who invited them to stay with him in a hotel room. He said he'd buy some booze and they'd have a little party. Ty was uneasy, but his buddy, Steve, was older and wiser, and he winked and said not to worry. The old guy would get drunk and then they'd bop him and roll him and run with his money. People did it all the time. No problem.

They went along with the old guy, who, true to his word, bought a bottle and led them to a seedy hotel room where he proceeded to drink enough to get brazen enough to make his move. And when he did, they grabbed him. Steve whacked him, but the old guy was so freaked out that he got away before they could relieve him of his money, and he ran screaming bloody murder into the lurid city night.

They took what was left of his booze and drank it and wandered around the city all night, finally and foolishly setting off on foot northward on Highway 400. Ty's friend knew people in Barrie, sixty-two miles away.

For Ty, the whole world was now kind of like Barrie . . . just out there, distant but waiting. Full of stuff to be had. You just had to get there. And around every bend in the road, there would be new adventure and gales of new sensations that would propel you into the next discovery. It was wild.

Reality pulled up in front of them, signal light flashing, as they trudged along the highway, not really noticing that it was 2 a.m. It was an OPP officer and he was curious. Just where the hell did they think they were going at that hour? They had no visible means of support and no rational answer to the question, so he drove them to a hostel . . . from which they promptly escaped.

At some point the next day, after a couple of more futile attempts to flee, Ty Conn was back at the Coens' home. All he had to show for his initiative were blisters on his feet.

There was a lot of ominous silence. Everybody knew it was just a matter of time before he'd be gone again, and gone for good.

Three weeks later he ran away again. He headed for Frankford and, once again, broke into the Suurdt's business, the Consumer's Carpet and Lumber store. Then he set off to look up some friends in the Marmora area. He knew some kids in a large family in the poor section of town. He knew them from school. There was a sixteen-year-old named Georgina, and he just couldn't get her off his mind. She was gorgeous. And he had a condom in his pocket, just in case.

He never did hook up with Georgina, but her sister Norma, who was married, let him stay at her place overnight. The next morning they had a grown-up chat over coffee and Norma persuaded him that the smart thing for him to do was to go back to the Coens'. Try to make a fresh start. Reluctantly, he agreed. She called the police, then gave him a warm hug and sent him on his way.

When he and the policeman arrived at the Coen farm, Leonard met them at the door and informed Ty that he didn't live there any more.

As bad as he thought it was, it had been home. Now it wasn't. The Coens had their bellies full of him. There were too many kids out there who needed and appreciated and benefited from what a foster home like theirs tried to provide. They didn't need this rebellion and this grief.

CHAPTER FOUR

A Boy Falling
out of the Sky

> ...and the expensive delicate ship that must have seen
> something amazing, a boy falling out of the sky,
> Had somewhere to get to and sailed calmly on.

W. H. Auden, Musée des Beaux Arts

*Ty is a sad boy showing a degree of depression that is
related to his unsettled life experience and his continuing
lack of attachment to a family or a suitable substitute. He is
able to relate well to the examiner and to talk satisfactorily
on many topics, but becomes aggressive, evasive and tearful
when anything of a personal nature is introduced. He is
lacking in positive self-esteem and does not even dare to
think about good things for himself and the future. He can
relieve his negative feelings by taking drugs and possibly by
the excitement of running away and getting into mischief. Ty
has positive things to say about many of his family members
and is interested in having clarified what their intentions
are towards him.*

D. P. Harris, M.D.
Letter to Belleville CAS, May 29, 1981

I .
_____

TY CONN'S LIFE LACKED THE BENEFIT of the most essential and natural and elusive condition of human existence: belonging. There are dozens of words for it. But it is most effectively described by a common word for its absence: alienation. It is a paradox of belonging that for many people it only has meaning in the despair created by its loss.

For those who have never belonged, there is a hole in the centre of existence. In Ty Conn's childhood, the hole at the centre of his life was filled with confusion. In adolescence, the confusion turned into bitterness. The despair and desperation came later.

Ty Conn never belonged and so his life was shapeless, like something accidentally spilled, flowing into the emptiness around him, a blot on the social fabric. The unconventional shape it eventually acquired came from the crude, deforming instruments of punishment. When he eventually adopted a code for the regulation of his attitudes and actions, most of it came from the perverse norms of the misfits who embraced him and destroyed him.

Leaving the Coen farmhouse on the morning of March 18, 1981, Ty Conn wasn't at all sure where he'd be stopping next. And he didn't really care. He'd never accepted the Coens as a family. Perhaps it was the domestic apartheid that reserved important sections of the home for their biological family. The largest factor would have been, however, that his stay with the Coens coincided exactly with the end of any hope that he could ever, in any circumstances, live with the Conns.

At the age of fourteen he was leaving childhood behind without ever having bonded with a conventional "family." He might, at that point, have been vaguely aware that it had become highly unlikely that he ever would. He'd run out of "family" opportunities. From now on life would revolve around institutions.

The Countryview Observation and Detention Home was a large house operated by Countryview Inc. in Corbyville, just north of Belleville. Corbyville is a sedate old Ontario village with an air of prosperity that it probably owes to the whisky distillery that shares the Corby family name. His new home was close enough to the distillery that he could often smell the mash.

He wasn't there more than a few hours when a pair of older boys decided to clarify the domestic pecking order by roughing him up. But he fought back, an instinct he'd honed in his three previous group homes, and they decided to leave him alone after his brief resistance.

He was, at this point, a full-fledged juvenile delinquent, facing five charges for theft and possession of stolen property as a result of his flights from the Coens' group home. For the adults at Corbyville, it was hard to reconcile the charges and the bumpy history of failure in his file with what they saw in front of them. A Countryview supervisor wrote to the court that in his first week there "Ty has related well with staff and has presented very few problems."

He was, she reported, "co-operative and he appeared to accept authority with little hesitation." His behaviour, she said in summary, was "quite good . . . he seemed to adjust to the program and was able to follow our routine with little difficulty."

The endorsement must have made a favourable impression on the judge. He remanded Ty to the custody of Countryview until further notice, presumably to let social workers monitor his progress there.

The social workers were clearly running low on patience. And he soon began to observe what seemed like a new strategy in the way the CAS people were dealing with him. They were still friendly. But they were making a deliberate effort to scare him, presumably to awaken within him, finally, a fear of the consequences of his delinquent behaviour. One of the possible consequences they talked about was a trip to a training school.

In the mythologies of boyhood, the frightening images of "reform" school, the archaic label for the friendlier-sounding "training" school, stand out among all the bogeymen that adults invoke to influence behaviour and inspire conformity. Ty Conn's various connections with other boys, many more troubled than he, had persuaded him that one of the places he never wanted to end up was training school. In his fertile imagination, it was a place where beating and rape became routines in a bad boy's existence.

And yet, whatever prophylactic effect the Victorian images of training school might have had, he seemed determined to rebel. The social workers might paint all the grim pictures they could imagine, but they were hardly going to reverse the tide of delinquency that had carried him this far.

As a young adult reflecting on a life of failure, he would come to regard the efforts of the social workers in 1981 as "a noble attempt" and he would sincerely regret their failure. But failure was inevitable.

"I wish it had worked," he lamented. "But instead it made me more rebellious and angry at those that seemed to be constantly controlling my life. This seemed to be a constant theme in my life. Someone always telling me what to do and I was more than experienced at defying authority."

It never seemed to sink in, even later in a more reflective stage of his life, that being constantly told what to do is part of the transaction of growing up in a structured environment. Of course the other part of the transaction is supposed to be the kind of feedback that gives the kid a sense of his intrinsic worth and the awareness that all the instruction and control—even punishment—are an investment of effort to increase his already considerable value. Maybe that was the problem: feedback.

Ty Conn got a different diet of feedback: That he was a bastard and a foundling, a reject and a troublesome thief; that he was on a course heading straight for destruction and it was up to him to change that, to wake up and smell the rich aroma of the opportunities around him, opportunities just screaming at him to come forward, with all his gifts, and fulfil his promise. It was the eighties, for God's sake. It was Ontario. The sky was the limit.

But Ty Conn's understanding of his worth as a human being never progressed much beyond a twisted sense of the value of his own intelligence. Brains, he believed, were his secret weapon, and he found perverse pleasure in trying to outsmart people who, he thought, considered him bad and stupid.

In his own simplistic view of the world, and in his determination to take a hand in his own destiny, he decided not to await the pleasure of the child-care and justice systems. They could take their care and their justice and stick it.

Memories of that sensation of liberty he experienced in track-and-field returned and he started jogging. The people at Countryview seemed to think it was a healthy sign. And so they'd let him take a run each evening, down the length of laneway to the road and back again. It was about a mile in all. One evening before setting out on his daily run, he dropped an Adidas gym bag full of clothes out a window. As soon as he left the house, he picked it up and started running for real. At the railway tracks, he turned south. He was planning to head for Trenton. He didn't stop running until he came to the community of Cannifton, three miles away. Here he ransacked an empty house in search of money. He found a collection of silver dollars. A coin collection? Why not? he thought. His life had gone to hell over false allegations concerning a coin collection. This was fate doing him a small favour.

That night, he checked into a seedy motel at an interchange on Highway 401, not far from Trenton. He'd run away perhaps four times previously. He knew this was different. The other escapes had been desperate gestures, calculated mostly to get attention or to make a point. Shock therapy for Dr. Conn. None had lasted more than forty-eight hours.

He no longer had anything to prove or anyone he cared to impress. He could go to the moon and the Conns wouldn't care. He could arrive at their place in a limousine and they'd still send him packing. That was all behind him. He was on his own. He was beginning his own life at the precarious age of fourteen.

In another era he'd have run away to sea, or joined the circus or the French Foreign Legion. But it was the early spring in 1981, and there were no such worthy adventures to be had.

So he dyed his hair black and headed for Toronto, drawn again to the noise and the glitter and the sleaze of Yonge Street.

He arrived there late in the day and alone. On his previous trip he'd been with the tough streetwise Steve who had looked after both of them. Now Ty was on his own. He remembered they had seen a hostel, not far from Eaton Centre. Steve had pointed it out to him. A place for losers. You had to be sixteen to get in. Fortunately, the guy on the front desk wasn't very observant, or didn't care, or figured that, rules notwithstanding, it would probably be best to let this greenhorn in out of the menacing city night.

Once inside he knew he was safely off the street, but he didn't feel very secure. He had entered the world of the homeless. He was now on the margins of society, among people for whom life had bottomed out in mistakes, failures, illness. There were noisy drunks and washed-up addicts. The hostel had the stench of struggle between powerful antiseptic cleaners and the rank pungency of human defeat. For a kid who had grown up in an environment that, for all its troubles, had been hygienic—the home of a doctor and a nurse—this place was shocking and scary and disgusting.

He wanted to take a shower but was restrained by adolescent phobias about the perversions of strangers. He took a chance on it anyway and survived. Nobody even noticed. He climbed into a bunk, finally feeling clean and safe at least from any danger of discovery. Nobody from Countryview was going to come looking for him here.

In the next bunk over there was a fellow who seemed to be in his mid-twenties. He had scraggly, wispy hair and a scruffy beard. He was staring in Ty's direction. He seemed to have something on his mind. Ty didn't care to dwell upon what that might be. Finally the stranger spoke.

"Your shoes," he said.

"What about them?" Ty replied.

He had carefully placed them beneath the bunk, side by side. The fact that there were no shoes under the other bunks didn't register. You don't expect neatness in a place like this.

"You plan to leave them there?" his neighbour asked.

"Why not?"

The guy shrugged and yawned.

"Because," he said, "they'll be gone by morning. You can bet on it."

For Ty Conn, thief, this was a notion almost too bizarre to comprehend. You steal candy. You steal cigarettes. You steal money. You steal things that you can sell to get money or candy or cigarettes. But shoes? He almost laughed.

Shoes, his neighbour told him briefly, are the most important possessions among the sparse chattels of the homeless. You live in your shoes. Your life is as comfortable or as painful as your shoes. Good shoes can make the difference between contentment and misery. With a good pair of shoes you can keep on moving, and as long as you can keep on moving, you can survive. People steal shoes. His shoes, probably, were worth more than he was.

That made sense. As a matter of fact, it made particularly good sense in his case. He wasn't just homeless. He was on the run. And you couldn't expect to run very far without your shoes.

And so, that night, in a smelly hostel on Yonge Street in Toronto, he slept with his shoes under his pillow, the laces tied together and wound tightly around his wrist. And it was a good thing too, for he slept very soundly. At some point, as he drifted off to sleep, he vowed that he would stay out of this world of homeless losers by whatever means available, and for as long as he could. He had the brains and he had the balls and he was going to use them to get a life. And it was going to be a better life than this.

2.

HE SPENT THE NEXT DAY WANDERING the ten blocks of the Yonge Street strip running north and south from Eaton Centre. You could feel all the possibilities of spring in the air. Soon you wouldn't have to worry about the weather when looking for a place to sleep. Only safety. And that didn't seem to be such a large problem. The street, it seemed, was full of kids just like him.

Yonge Street was like a free zone for kids. Obviously more than a few of them were on the run. At least, they had that look. Whether it was real or contrived didn't matter. It created a comfort zone, and he could easily forget that somewhere, not far away, a lot of people were looking for him. And that their plans for when they caught up with him weren't exactly friendly.

It was a good day to be fourteen and free, not answerable to anyone but yourself. For the entire day he wandered in and out of the video arcades and the head shops and stores, meeting people and forming friendships that would last maybe a few hours. It was a warm and fluid day. He even did a bit of shoplifting, just to see how alert the Yonge Street proprietors were. Big-city theft actually seemed easier.

Then as the day began to fade, he realized he hadn't made a plan. Making plans was never Ty Conn's strength. All his life people had been doing the planning for him. Even when he was just dropped into the middle of something, like a social agency, his presence would set off a series of responses that would sweep him up and carry him off to . . . somewhere. He was kind of like driftwood, out on one tide, back on the next. Between tides you just rolled around, waiting. There was always a tide coming or going. You don't develop much of an instinct for making plans like that.

What to do. The sun was vanishing behind the towers on Bay Street, one block west. The population of the street had changed, and with it, the character of the place. It didn't seem as friendly or safe. Most of the kids like him had gone away, probably back to their homes in the suburbs where they'd tell their parents lies about how they spent the day. They were being replaced on the corners and in the doorways by a different crowd, guys and women with eyes that looked right past you, or right through you. These were people on the make, and he wasn't anxious to be made. He wasn't sure about the kids, like him, who'd stayed behind. A lot of them looked like they were up to something and, whatever it was, he didn't want to be a part of it.

The thought of the shelter where he'd spent the previous night worrying about his footwear didn't appeal to him at all. So inevitably and irresistibly he started thinking about the only place that had ever seemed like home, the Conns'. But there could be no going there. It would be like the last time he went there when he was on the run. Some fake smiles, a sandwich if he was lucky, then back to the CAS.

That's how he came to think of Jeff. His older brother. Jeffrey Conn was working in Smiths Falls. He was at a radio station there. A disc jockey or something neat like that. Get in touch with Jeff. There couldn't be that many Jeff Conns in Smiths Falls. It seemed like a great idea. He'd never been close to Jeff, but by the same token, had never had a problem with him either.

First, he took a bus to Belleville. Then he looked up Jeff's number and phoned him. His brother sounded surprised but also glad to hear from him. So he poured out his predicament: living in a secure home in Corbyville; lots of charges outstanding; ran away; don't want to go back. Want to go visit in Smiths Falls.

Right on, said Jeff. Jump on the next bus and come on down. Call from the terminal just before the bus leaves. Jeff was going to meet him at the other end. Ty was elated. Right away he went out to a mall and spent almost all the money he had left, after getting his bus ticket, on a gift for his brother. Near departure time, he wandered back to the terminal to place the call, as he'd been instructed to do. Jeff's friendliness on the phone had opened up a whole new array of possibilities.

He only noticed the guy who was standing by the pay phone when it was obvious that the man was pointing at him. Then he realized who it was. It was his social worker, no more than twenty feet away. Just standing there with a determined look on his face, beckoning. Come over here. Shit, he thought, this is either an extraordinary coincidence or I've been sold out. He could never be sure—but he suspected his brother.

Ty did the natural thing. He wheeled and ran. He ran like the wind, down streets and alleyways, over fences and through backyards, not even checking to see if he was being pursued. Finally, fatigued, he slumped down and reflected on his predicament. He was broke. He'd been hoping for help from the one person left in the world he felt he could trust. He was out of options. Except for one.

After a brief rest he started hitchhiking to Frankford. That was the little town, ten miles north of Trenton, where he'd spent a summer working for the friends of the Vreugdenhill family. The Suurdts. It was quite a distance away, but he knew a place there where he could probably find what he needed to survive for the next few days: the Suurdts' business, Consumer's Carpet and Lumber. Mr. Suurdt, he figured, still owed him some back pay.

He'd broken in there twice before. This time he went through the same door and headed straight to where he knew they'd have left small amounts of money. But this time he didn't just take cash. Mr. Suurdt had another little business on the side. He had a small used-car lot called Penny Pincher Motors. Ty spotted a set of car keys just hanging there on a nail and figured it was time he learned to drive.

The keys were for a Dodge Aspen station wagon. He knew the theory about how cars worked and how to drive them from shop classes in school. But once behind the wheel he began to discover that driving was more complicated than the theory. You needed a lot of specific skills and they didn't come naturally. Hand-eye co-ordination. Hand-*foot* co-ordination. Ability to judge distances and to control speed accordingly. As with many other life skills, he soon realized driving a car requires competent instruction and a lot of supervised experience before the first solo expedition. But it was too late for that.

Highway 4, from Frankford to the 401, is little more than a country road. Funny how he'd never before noticed how close the Trent River was to the road. One wrong turn of the wheel and splash. Hanging on to the steering wheel for dear life, he learned about all the mistakes novice drivers make while driving too fast and at night. He over-steered and kept hitting the shoulder of the road, then over-corrected and almost spun out many times. He just couldn't find a comfortable speed. He was always, it seemed, going too fast.

It started to rain just as he was hitting the 401, probably Canada's busiest highway. Funny how, in all the times he'd been a passenger in cars and trucks on the 401, he never before noticed the number and the size of those eighteen-wheelers. He'd never noticed how close the semis were when they roared past and how they created air pockets that either sucked you in or pushed you away, or both, and how they made you almost lose control. It was like they were trying to kill him.

He was heading east and, finally, near Belleville he was starting to get the hang of driving. It was well after midnight by then and, feeling in a mood to celebrate, he broke into a restaurant. The place was perilously close to Countryview. But he'd been gone by then for more than the usual forty-eight hours and he had wheels. He was beginning to feel kind of untouchable.

He stole some cigarettes and liquor, then got back in the car and headed up Highway 14 towards Marmora. It was a good thirty miles away, but what the hell. He was driving. And he knew a drugstore there where he'd be able to break in and find some food to tide him over the next few days.

He hid the stolen car, then threw a rock through the glass front door of the drugstore and waited to see if anyone would react to the noise. A trick he'd learned from some other delinquents. You never know with those small-town shops. They often had somebody living in a back room or apartment. The last thing you wanted was to walk into some old-age pensioner carrying a shotgun.

He waited a few minutes and there was no sign of life inside. But before he had a chance to enter, he saw a police cruiser drive by and decided to abandon that plan.

Racing back down Highway 14, he fell asleep at the wheel and wiped out.

Never having been in a car accident before, he wasn't sure at first what had happened. Then he noticed that the station wagon was stopped and pointing in a direction that was 180 degrees opposite to where he'd been heading before he dozed off. He managed to start the engine, but the car wouldn't move. It was only when he tried to get out that he realized that he'd been knocked around quite a bit and was bruised and sore all over. But the car was in worse shape. He'd been crossing a small concrete bridge when he lost control and all the spinning and bouncing around had more or less demolished the Aspen.

He was still about a mile from Stirling and so he started walking toward town. Passing the local Co-op store, he realized he was going to need some new clothing sooner or later and this was as good a time as any to see what the Co-op had available. He was vaguely familiar with the place. There was a little office at the back and, if he remembered correctly, there was a window that might provide an entry. It never crossed his mind that the place might have an alarm system.

Once inside, he found some cash and a fine selection of warm clothing and footwear. He was trying on a stylish insulated vest when he heard a car arrive in front.

Silently, he fled back toward the office. Then he heard somebody knocking loudly on the store's front door. This was strange. Somebody knocking? To be let in? He stopped and turned, and peered through the darkness. As his myopic eyes focused, he could see the familiar outline of a uniformed policeman.

He bolted into the office and was squirming out through a rear window when he noticed a lot of other people standing around. They were all cops and they were all watching him in what seemed to be a state of collective amusement. And they all had guns in their hands. And all the guns were pointing at him.

3 ·

BACK AT COUNTRYVIEW THERE WAS no end to the hilarity over the dyed black hair. But it wasn't mockery. It was the kind of ribbing you give the guy who's pulled off something you just can't help admiring. He'd actually escaped from the place. He did it without a lot of fuss and bullshit. Just went, alone, like a real solid guy. He was nabbed and back and facing four new charges, but the attention felt fine.

And he stole a car? Damn! Arrested at gunpoint?

Of course the people who ran Countryview weren't very impressed. In fact, they informed him, he'd be moving on in a day or so. They were sending him to a place in Kingston, and he'd find a few changes in his circumstances when he was there. He wouldn't run away from there so easily.

The St. Lawrence Court Home was an ancient place, carved out of that distinctive Kingston limestone that you see in a lot of the institutions in the area. Queen's University. Kingston Pen. Collins Bay Institution. Places like that.

The Court Home had once been part of the Kingston railway station and, contrary to his original expectations, he found he liked it better than Countryview. You were treated more like a grown-up. You were allowed five cigarettes a day, and you could earn more if you behaved yourself. And Kingston was a city. The home even had bicycles, and depending on your behaviour, a resident could borrow one and drive downtown and hang out for hours. Even him. Ty Conn, the one-kid crime wave.

The people there took an instant liking to him. After a week, Tom Brzezicki of the St. Lawrence Youth Association was describing him as "a mild-mannered and likeable boy with a good sense of humour." He was "pleasant and co-operative with staff," and while he sometimes "questioned the utility of certain rules, particularly if they required some physical exertion on his part," he was a model kid.

"He has followed our program well, attended school regularly and presented few behavioural problems," Brzezicki wrote.

It must have been difficult to square first impressions of this pleasant and curious and funny kid with his most recent string of offences, which now included car theft. What on earth was bugging him anyway?

They sent him to a place called Beechgrove Children's Centre for a psychiatric assessment, but it didn't yield much. Perhaps, having lived for eight years in Dr. Conn's household, he was impervious to psychiatry. His resistance to the process didn't go unnoticed, and a social worker told him after his first session that he might have to stay at Beechgrove for as long as it took to figure him out.

It was a depressing prospect, equated in his vivid imagination with an indefinite prison sentence or confinement in a
mental institution.

In fact, the psychiatrist who examined him at Beechgrove
had concluded that young Ty Conn probably needed some
form of institutional confinement and a lot of work to correct his obvious anti-social tendencies.

"My opinion," Dr. D. P. Harris told Belleville CAS officials
on May 29 that year, "is that Ty requires a stable long-term
placement in order to control his behaviour and give him a
suitable opportunity to grow and develop in a socialized
direction, to learn in a manner appropriate to his age and
hence prepare himself for adult life.

"Over the past four years it has been shown that a series
of foster homes and group homes has not been able to hold
him and see that he behaves properly. He therefore needs a
placement which will be able to put a stop to his anti-social
behaviour and hence make possible socialization, learning,
and growth and development."

All in all, it was a stern but realistic observation. After
fourteen years of bouncing around from home to home,
never really being part of any of them, Tyrone Conn
definitely needed some firm direction if he was ever to
achieve socialization. His sense of rules and rights and
responsibilities was a jumble of inconsistency. But the struc-
turing wasn't going to work unless Ty somehow came to
believe that the process was really aimed at improving his life
and not just sparing society further grief from his anger.
One thing he did know was that the anger and the pessimism
and the bitterness were the spawn of circumstances that

weren't all his fault. That "society" had a few failures of its own to explain.

As the day of his appearance in court approached, he sensed that the social workers around him were more concerned than he was about what was going to happen to him. They were working hard to get him one more shot at something resembling a home life. They wanted him to be optimistic, but he refused.

He'd later recall: "A theme that would follow me for many years was one where I consciously made efforts to be a pessimist when thinking of what could happen. Rather than be optimistic and then suffer disappointment, I chose to look at the worst-case scenario, and then prepare myself for that eventuality. The theory being that, if prepared, I would adapt to these events more easily."

Of course it rarely worked out that way. Optimism might well make some people vulnerable to disappointment. But pessimism often leads to something worse—despair. And it would become a defining feature in the life of Ty Conn that despair would inevitably lead quickly to desperation followed by impulsive acts of self-destruction.

4 ·

LOOKED AT AS A WHOLE, TY CONN's life had a clear and consistent shape, as if set by a tragic inevitability. But there were a few particular moments when it might have veered onto a different and happier course. One such moment arrived in June of 1981. It was, however, doomed by his self-defeating pessimism and circumstances, which were at once ludicrous and pathetic.

He was, according to a social worker, to get one more chance at living in a family setting, and the one they had in mind seemed perfect. A young couple in Tweed, about thirty miles north of Belleville, had one small child and were interested in providing a home for somebody like Ty. The social worker actually seemed excited giving him the news.

And, he admitted years later, it probably was perfect. On an introductory weekend visit he instantly felt comfortable. He really liked the young couple who kind of reminded him of what he thought "hippies" were like. Easygoing and genuine.

They seemed to want to take him in because it would be good for *him*. Not as a distraction for some other kids or as an income supplement. He just knew in his gut that this would be a place he'd like. But it was too late. He had already set his own destiny in motion and there could be no turning back.

He had a girlfriend. Her name was Leanne and she was fifteen, and he was about as completely in love as you can be at fourteen. Leanne was also a resident at the St. Lawrence Court Home in Kingston and had demons of her own to sort out. But, like Ty, she had a penchant for flight and they had secretly cooked up a bizarre escape plan. They were going to break out, steal a motor home and go touring in the United States.

In fact, the plan was to have been executed on the very weekend that the social worker had arranged for his visit to the prospective new home in Tweed.

Over dinner it crossed his mind briefly that he should seriously reconsider his options. But he felt committed to

Leanne and she had already alerted her pal, Yvonne, who had decided to run with them.

And so, after the family went to bed on the first night of his visit, he lowered himself out his bedroom window using a bed sheet. He then hitchhiked to Belleville. He never did have much luck in Belleville and probably wasn't surprised when he found himself stranded there. And so he walked for thirty miles, eastward, until he got another drive near Napanee.

He discovered when he arrived in Kingston that the girls had run away the night before. He had a hunch they'd headed for Trenton, where they had mutual friends, and that, eventually, was where he found them.

The plan was to head for Frankford where, yet again, he would burglarize Gerald Suurdt's store, but the scheme promptly fell apart when Yvonne, who was conspicuously large for her age, was spotted by a policeman. And, predictably, it wasn't long thereafter before all three were back in custody. The drive back to Kingston was, as he'd later remember it, "solemn."

His circumstances were now entirely predictable. The staff at the home kept him under close observation during the following days. He was forbidden to have anything to do with Leanne except for a brief farewell just before they took him to court on June 9 where he was to face assorted charges incurred during his flight from the Countryview Home in Corbyville.

Life-altering experiences sometimes don't last very long. He recalled years later that the appearance in court was over quickly. His Honour Judge W. J. Pickett found that Ty Conn's persistent delinquencies were "an affront to the community," that the CAS clearly wasn't capable of controlling him, and that the circumstances called for a stretch in custody. The judge then prescribed a term in the Brookside Training School in Cobourg. For the rest of his life, Ty Conn would regard June 9, 1981, as a turning point.

Years later he wrote that "it seemed to be one of those cataclysmic moments that separates the first part of your life from everything else that follows.

"My experiences in training school would change me forever. I choose to believe for the worse. I'm not blaming anyone for future behaviour or attempting to avoid my own responsibility for my actions.

"I'd certainly left authorities in charge of me with very few options. But in retrospect, sending me to Brookside was a mistake and it shaped my life in a way that was to condemn me to many more years of imprisonment."

CHAPTER FIVE

The Rod of Correction

This act shall be liberally construed to the end that its pur-
pose may be carried out to wit: That the care and custody
and discipline of a juvenile delinquent shall approximate as
nearly as may be that which should be given by its parent,
and that as far as practicable, every juvenile delinquent
shall be treated, not as a criminal, but as a misdirected and
misguided child, and one needing aid, encouragement, help
and assistance.

Section 31, Juvenile Delinquents Act, 1908

Mr. Conn is a young man 16 years of age, before the adult
courts for the third time in six months. The needs of the
community appear to be the overwhelming concern in this
case . . . .

Our service has had no positive effect on Mr. Conn
since May 1983 and we will probably experience the same
situation again. . . .

Warren Fredericks, Probation & Parole Officer,
November 4, 1983

Foolishness is bound in the heart of a child; but the rod of
correction shall drive it far from him.

Proverbs, 22.15

I.
_____

THAT DAY, JUNE 9, 1981, AS TY CONN walked through the massive white front door of what had become his new home, his original sense of foreboding slowly diminished to be replaced by an expanding curiosity and also by a strange kind of optimism.

He'd felt he was going to jail and this was clearly more of a prison than a foster home. The place had a buttoned-down feel to it, unlike the glorified hostels, Countryview and the Court Home, where he'd been allowed to go jogging down the road or cycling around Kingston.

Still, Brookside had no towers or walls or perimeter fences. There was a cluster of small buildings and a few larger ones that seemed to be for programs and administration and the like. Overall, it looked to be a piece of cake to someone who had achieved some experience at running away from places he didn't like. Right away he started feeling sure that he wouldn't be there for the five months he understood to be the average stay in Brookside. And he was right in that. He would, in fact, be there for almost two years.

This, of course, he couldn't have known as he bid farewell to the friendly older couple who had escorted him to Cobourg from the court. He actually felt warm toward them as they wished him well. He was glad that he hadn't complicated their lives by escaping from them en route. There'd be lots of time later for planning a proper escape.

But as soon as they were gone, something about the place changed subtly. It looked the same, obviously. It just *felt* more prison-like. Maybe the biggest security factor was the attitude of staff. They weren't particularly friendly. They didn't treat him like a kid. They treated him like a con. He sensed it when the staff guy who'd met him at the front door and signed him in slipped his hand into the waistband of his trousers, gathered a fistful of the material and told him to start walking. The voice was as impersonal and firm as that hand at the small of his back. They were off, he was told, to get some new clothes.

It wasn't far, but obviously to reduce the chances that he might try to sprint away from his escort, they were going to drive in an old police car that was parked in front. A police car? Yes, and it even had a security cage in the back. Perhaps there was a lot more to this joint than met the eye. He was actually anticipating being made to wear a drab green prison uniform. But the new clothes turned out to be blue jeans, T-shirts and the like. Only the footwear dismayed him. Cheap five-and-dime-store sneakers, totally unsuitable for a runner.

Then there were the accommodations. The security might not have been conspicuous, but it was inherent in every part of the place and in everything they did.

There were six residential buildings, four for boys, two for girls. Two of the boys' residences and one of the girls' were "closed." And, he quickly learned, "closed" meant secure. The doors were locked solidly twenty-four hours a day. All activities happened in your residence behind those locked doors, except recreation. For that, there was a large enclosure with twenty-foot-high chain-link fences. You got to the recreation yard through a caged-in passageway leading from the back door of the residence.

Cripes, he thought, as they showed him the yard. You wouldn't even be able to scramble up the fence if you wanted to. You'd get up sixteen feet on the conventional wire, then you'd hit a four-foot expanse of mesh screening so fine you couldn't get a grip with fingers or toes. They'd thought of everything. His only hope was to get into an open residence.

That was everybody's objective. Nobody wanted to be in the closed houses, named Martin and Thompson after some famous Canadians. Closed was like maximum security and, as in the adult prison system, maximum security was a sort of limbo. It would only be in medium or minimum security—or, at Brookside, in an open residence—that the offender could make any real progress. But he was about to learn that you had to earn your way out of closed accommodations by behaving and showing a properly positive attitude, some contrition and some evidence that you really intended to stay there and get it over with.

In other words, he had to earn the right to earn the right to rejoin society.

Once in an open residence, he'd get to eat in a separate dining hall and to attend a relatively normal school. Even recreation would be in a more open playground. Open residence presented unlimited opportunities for personal growth, they said. Getting from "closed" to "open" could take a couple of months, if he followed the rules. He could hardly wait. In his mind, open residence would present unlimited opportunities for flight.

One thing that puzzled him was the fact that the judge hadn't really spelled out the precise duration of the time he was to spend there. Was it an oversight? People who knew the place said five or six months, and that sounded reasonable. But it was strange that the judge hadn't confirmed a specific time.

Once settled in, however, he realized that it was a bit like university. He'd be there for as much time as necessary to work his way out of it. He'd have to pass through specific levels toward graduation. The speed at which he got through would be, theoretically, up to him. Once past grade four, they'd be trying to put him back into the community. Getting to grade four would prove to be more difficult than he could have imagined.

2.

HE NEVER FORGOT THE SCENE. IT was near the end of his first day at Brookside. He was standing in front of two staff members outside the office in Thompson House, one of the secure residences, where he'd be living until further notice. One of the staff guys was laying out a long list of rules.

They had their backs to the office door. Ty was facing it. To his astonishment, one of the residents slipped along the wall behind the staff and, like a cat, through the open door of the office. With Ty watching and struggling to keep his face expressionless, the kid snatched a gym bag belonging to a staff member and rifled through it until he found what he wanted. A pack of cigarettes. He quickly opened it, plucked two, closed the package and shoved it back in the gym bag. Then he slipped out of the office with all the poise and indifference of someone who was invisible.

As a reward for being a marginal part of the cigarette raid, Ty got to puff on one of the smokes later in the bathroom. He was warned that there was a strict policy against smoking at Brookside. You could get in big trouble for it. It seemed that there were a lot of things that could get you in big trouble in Brookside. But the most important discovery was that he was in the company of guys for whom that didn't matter much. These were guys with a sense of daring and defiance that was worthy of respect. From that point on he was listening and paying attention and beginning to recognize the norms of a society in which he might feel, for the first time, a genuine sense of belonging.

3.

LIFE IN BROOKSIDE WAS ALL ABOUT earning points. Everybody had chores and it was the chores that earned the priceless points. The way the system worked, the points also determined the chores. The person with the highest number of points got to pick his weekly chore. Which didn't necessarily mean that by getting a lot of points, you got cushy chores. Cushy chores didn't earn many points. And so the highest number of points usually went to those highly motivated people who would do the worst jobs well, then opt to keep doing the worst jobs just to keep piling up the points.

Points became precious. Access to showers was on the basis of points. Status, in the eyes of staff, depended upon points. Freedom, ultimately, depended on the point system. The smallest things depended on points. At the end of each week, residents were awarded "tuck," what for ordinary kids in ordinary circumstances would be called treats. Candy bars, soft drinks, potato chips. People with the highest point aggregate could qualify for two bars, two bags of chips and two pops. Somebody who had messed up or just been a pain in the ass all week would end up with little or nothing. In the Spartan world of Brookside, tuck was one of the few bright spots in the weekly routine.

Life there wasn't complicated, he discovered. It was as simple as tuck. You got tuck by earning points, and you got points by working hard, and you kept them by conforming to the rules and by being nice and avoiding conflict with staff and your fellows. And then they let you out.

The problem was that for most of the kids in Brookside, conformity and being nice to people didn't come easily. Which meant that, for most of them, the quality of life depended upon either learning or faking attitudes and behaviour that had, for one reason or another, been impossible for them to achieve on the outside. For somebody like Ty Conn, who had long ago defined himself in totally negative terms (bastard, liar, thief), winning points would be a daunting prospect.

Earning his way out of Brookside would be so difficult that he could see himself growing old in there.

That just left running away. His history of running away hadn't been any more impressive than any other part of his biography, but it seemed like his only option. It would become a matter of endless speculation to find out why everything seemed so black and white to him on that summer day in 1981. But that's how it was, and how he'd always see things during the important moments of his life. His fundamental worthlessness made complex situations seem hopeless. There's a pure simplicity in hopelessness. For most people, hopelessness is an excuse for doing nothing, but there was something in Ty Conn's nature that wouldn't permit him to be passive. His responses to hopelessness would usually result in some wild and desperate decisions. Like running away.

Of course he knew the consequences of trying to run away. Nothing good ever happened after an escape attempt, and this place wouldn't be any different. On day one it became quite clear that the most serious offence imaginable was trying to run away. An escape attempt—and he was told emphatically that there were *only* attempts, there was *no such thing* as escape—would mean a return to square one. Grade one. Day one. *Minute* one of his incarceration. The message was clear: Don't even think about it for a nanosecond.

But within a few weeks, living in a closed residence with only two hours of outdoor activity allowed each day and the whole outside world basking in the hot sweet summer of 1981, Brookside had become a bit too much for a fourteen-year-old to bear. He became obsessed with the thought of escape.

He was living in a small bare room in Thompson House. The furnishings consisted of a narrow bed and a desk that ran along one wall. There was no dresser. The kids kept their clothing and shoes in a common change room. It was another device to reduce the possibility of flight. But it didn't daunt Ty Conn. It wouldn't be the first time he ran away in his pyjamas.

In the wall above his desk was a window. It opened easily enough. But there was a heavy screen bolted to the outside wall. The first thing he did when he arrived was to stand on his desk and try a few strong kicks against the screen. It didn't budge. There was a story going around that a fireman had once attempted to break through one of those screens with his axe and had failed. Ty didn't believe it. Just another institutional myth. Part of the security.

Escape, he figured, would be as simple as cutting through the screen. All he needed was a tool, and the opportunity to get one came easily.

He frequently needed an inhaler to help him breathe when his asthma was acting up. The staff kept his inhaler in a cabinet in the office. It was the same cabinet where they stored the cutlery. On one of his trips to the office to use his inhaler, he stole a stainless-steel table knife. His plan was to saw through the screen using the serrated edge of the knife blade.

He smuggled the knife out of the office in the waistband of his pyjamas. He didn't want to raise suspicion by going straight from the office to his room, so he ducked into the bathroom and hid the knife there, inside a radiator. He didn't realize that another resident, sitting in a toilet stall, saw him do it. The witness, out of curiosity, decided to take a look when Ty had gone; and while he stood there with the table knife in his hand, a staff member walked in and caught him. He quickly reported that the knife belonged to the new guy. Ty Conn.

Punishment for such a serious offence meant a trip to the "digger." That was the Brookside term for a few small rooms that were used for solitary confinement. Ty was shocked the first time he saw the digger. They put him in a tiny cell-like space that was cool and airless and about six feet square. There was no bed or furnishing of any kind. The walls and floor were of ceramic tiles. The door was of heavy metal,

solid except for a small plastic viewing window with a sliding plate which, closed, left him in total isolation.

The first time the digger door closed behind him, the
sterile coldness struck him like a slap. There was no place to
lie or to sit. He paced the six feet of space until he became
tired. He was wearing only pyjama bottoms. Eventually he
had no choice but to lie on the chilly floor. Curled up there,
he couldn't help wondering why there was carpeting on the
wall and not on the floor. It ran from the floor up the wall to
a height of maybe four feet. It had no practical purpose that
he could think of, except, perhaps to torture kids by making
them imagine how comfortable it would be if it were only
on the floor where carpets belonged.

It was only much later that he discovered the real purpose
of the wall carpet. After a couple of days in the digger, some
kids became agitated and responded by pounding their heads
against the walls. The carpet was to prevent them from
doing damage to themselves . . . at least those who were
under four feet tall.

Ty Conn, in two years at Brookside, would get to know
the digger well.

4.

FOR HIS ENTIRE STAY AT BROOKSIDE he just couldn't stop
thinking about running away. And, to the great dismay of the
staff there, he couldn't seem to resist trying. At least seven
times he actually made it past the perimeter. Once he got
about twenty-five miles to the east, past Brighton, heading

toward Trenton where he'd once lived. His mistake was to stop at the Vreugdenhills' farm, his former foster home. He broke into their garage and stole a bicycle. It was a bike he'd bought from one of the Vreugdenhill kids for seventy-five dollars soon after he'd gone there. They'd kept it when he left, along with some of his other stuff. Obviously, he never forgot. So he stole it back. He also stole a couple of rifles.

When he was, inevitably, caught, he only had the bike. He'd stashed the rifles somewhere and the police never found them. The Vreugdenhills didn't even know they were missing until long afterwards. He was charged with stealing the bicycle, but when he explained the situation to the cops, and he was even able to produce the original receipt proving that he'd bought and paid for it, and that the Vreugdenhills had ripped him off in the first place, they dropped the charges. But there would be no talking his way out of the digger at Brookside. It was the digger and day one all over again, as it would be every time he tried to run away. And yet he just couldn't stop trying.

The longer he stayed there, it seemed, the farther away "graduation" got. It was the beginning of a pattern that would define his life: a growing restlessness in confinement, a longing to be part of the real world, depression, an irresistible urge to run, escape, capture, and a new measure of punishment that extended the term of confinement even farther into the future.

Gerald Suurdt's family still talks about that Sunday in September 1982, when they were celebrating the baptism of their youngest daughter. September nineteenth. A policeman called and asked Gerald if he'd come down to the shop. They were investigating yet another break-in at Consumer's Carpet and

Lumber. Even the cops were starting to treat the break-ins as some kind of a joke. Gerald Suurdt didn't find it very funny.

On the way to church that morning he'd noticed something different about the place and realized that there was a car missing from his used-car lot. Plus, on closer inspection it was obvious that somebody had broken into the store. And it was also obvious who had done it.

On the day before, while away from Brookside on a school excursion, Ty Conn went AWOL. As usual, he needed money and transportation, and the first place he thought of was Frankford. Consumer's Carpet and Lumber and Penny Pincher Motors had, in the past, provided him with both necessities.

They found the car in Belleville, undamaged, where he'd dropped it. What they didn't know was that he'd then broken into a shop there and stolen a bicycle and cycled all the way back to Frankford, a good twenty miles. He was actually hiding in a cube van on the lot as the cops were investigating the earlier break-in. You had to give him something for gall.

The last thing Gerald did, when the cops left, was to padlock the chain across the entrance to the lot. Not that anything was going to happen twice in the same day. Right? Wrong. He was hardly home, celebrating the baby's baptism, when a neighbour called. You know that chain you have across the entrance to the lot? Yes. Well, it's lying on the ground.

He'd hack-sawed through it . . . and stolen the cube van!

Of course, being fifteen and stupid about vehicles, Ty hadn't realized there was hardly any fuel in it, and he soon had to abandon his second stolen vehicle of the day down on MacMaster Road, near Highway 2, maybe ten miles away. They also found the bike. The next day, they found him and brought him back to Brookside.

It shouldn't have taken a lot of thought by a bright mind to arrive at the conclusion that this didn't make sense. Like the gambler on a bad night who keeps trying to get back in the black by doubling his bets, Ty Conn should have realized that he was running the risk of mortgaging his future to such an extent that he'd no longer have any equity left in it. He should have known that at the rate he was going he would eventually encumber his entire life. But when you're fourteen or fifteen such notions are almost too large to comprehend.

Brookside was the formal beginning of his criminalization. More than a dozen years later, when he was in more trouble than his malleable fourteen-year-old mind could have imagined in 1981, he confided to a psychologist in a federal prison in Saskatchewan that Brookside was where he "began to learn about crime . . . namely serious crime."

In Brookside, when he wasn't hanging out in the playgrounds or the lounges and common rooms listening to descriptions of advanced methods for hot-wiring cars, break and entry, disposal of stolen property, evading cops and scamming straight folks, he was watching television programs and reading books that glamorized all those activities.

"Romantic notions of a criminal lifestyle and the realization that it could provide me with money, notoriety and, most of all, a sense of self-worth, convinced me that this might be my thing to pursue," he told the psychologist.

Later in the same confessional he declared that when "surrounded by like-minded individuals I began to flourish in this environment. Feelings of self-respect and pride flooded through me as opposed to the feelings of self-doubt and shame I had felt as a result of being ostracized for my activities among a straight and normal society."

He just couldn't wait to get back on the street and start living out what, locked up in Brookside, was just a fantasy as far-fetched as his old boyhood dreams of running away to great romantic adventures. Crime became a vocation. He made no moral value judgments about it. He never believed that society owed him anything, or that his background justified anger or an impulse to take revenge on the people and institutions that had fumbled his life. For as long as he lived he would never tolerate any such suggestion. Pity, self-generated or external, was the most degrading sentiment he could imagine.

His calling to crime was nothing more than the dawning of an awareness of opportunity. Crime would be, he thought, a simple matter of using his wits and his gifts to get stuff that would enable him to live as fully as possible. He would draw the line at hurting people. The possibility of accidents didn't enter his mind. Nor did the inevitable consequences for his own safety and liberty. When he wasn't plotting escapes or dreaming about them, he was avidly absorbing the experiences and the techniques and the lore of the young criminals around him in Brookside.

Reform school became the opposite of its institutional purpose. His time there, in spite of all the high-minded and optimistic mission statements of people in the systems of justice and community welfare, became a period of vocational training in the criminal crafts.

5 ·

TY CONN COULD HARDLY HAVE PICKED a worse time to embark on a criminal career. As the decade of the eighties began there was a growing public perception that youth crime was increasing and that it was time for stern new approaches to the problem. Thanks to perceptions like those, there were legal changes coming to a head at exactly the wrong time for him.

Sitting around at Brookside, fantasizing about criminal glamour, he wouldn't have been paying a lot of attention to trends in the justice system. He couldn't have known that society was in the middle of a philosophical shift away from a Victorian view, enshrined in the Juvenile Delinquents Act since 1908, that people like him and his fellow Brookside inmates were just "misdirected and misguided children." The new attitude was that, children or not, they were criminals and should be treated as such in a new law.

The Young Offenders Act would come into force in 1984. It gave a lot more emphasis than the old legislation to the responsibilities and legal accountability of young people. By 1986, it would include anybody under the age of eighteen. It would also, by the time it was fully in force with its hard edges smoothed and modified, reflect the need for balance between the needs of society and the special circumstances of young people in trouble. But none of the good aspects of the new law would matter to Ty Conn.

By the time he turned seventeen, in January 1984, the only relevant change for him would be those negative attitudes that caused the lawmakers and the courts to take a more punitive approach to his misdeeds. People in the justice system would be less inclined to look for the extenuating circumstances in his background that might explain his anti-social behaviour. And, in any case, the new law wouldn't extend to seventeen-year-olds until 1986.

In the long run, he would suffer from the hard-line attitudes that led to a new law, without benefiting from any of
the specific safeguards that the new law would eventually
spell out.

6.
———

EVENTUALLY HE GOT OUT OF BROOKSIDE but not because
he graduated. He just outgrew it. Or they just grew tired of
him. Or both. He turned sixteen on January 18, 1983. He'd
been there three times longer than the usual stay. It was clear
to everyone that he wasn't going to settle down and earn his
way out. And, in any case, once he became seventeen he
would no longer be a "juvenile." Next stop for Mr. Conn was
the adult system. On March 28, 1983, they told him he was
leaving. It was to another place in the juvenile system. And
the place he was going to would be even farther away from
where he wanted to be.

He was, he reported later, shocked at the news. They'd
led him to believe that he'd be leaving Brookside as a free
person. But obviously he hadn't reformed much there and
his keepers doubted that he was ready for freedom. He felt
betrayed and angry.

March 28 was the beginning of Easter Week that year, a
time of mystical dreariness when winter is worn out and
spring still full of ambiguity. The day started with sunshine,
but it had grown overcast as he walked to the car that would
take him away. The enveloping gloom was only partly the
fault of the weather. Ty Conn would enter the records as an

institutional failure. Institutions hate failure. Nobody was happy that day.

He wasn't sure where exactly he was going and became mildly curious as the car turned west on Highway 401. Curiosity turned to anxiety an hour later as they sped through the frantic corridor of commerce just north of Toronto. By then it was raining. Everything familiar to him lay far to the east—Trenton, Frankford, Belleville. The Conns and the Benches, the Vreugdenhills and the Coens. Countryview in Corbyville and the Court Home in Kingston, Brookside. Oh well. At sixteen, perhaps it was time for some new experience.

They were an hour west of Toronto, passing Kitchener-Waterloo, when they finally turned off the expressway and headed into the flat countryside of southwestern Ontario. Smooth brown fields fell away toward the horizons, like pictures he'd seen of the prairies. Then, near the small town of Petersburg, they pulled into a driveway and stopped in front of a large house.

After twenty-two months at Brookside it didn't take him long to realize that he was moving to another institution for delinquent youth. It was a large red-brick country house with room for eight. It had a big fireplace in the living room and, he was told, was classified as "open." This one had a more inspiring name: Hope Manor Group Home. But the old Ontario country elegance of the place didn't fool him. It was just another institution. His world seemed to have become a series of institutions.

Hope Manor, they called it. He might have wondered, What hope? Hope for whom? Considering what happened next, it is, however, most likely that he simply looked at his new surroundings and said: "Screw this!" Because, within forty-eight hours, he was gone.

They never had time to get used to him or to learn his pattern of brooding, restlessness and flight. On March 29 people were paying more attention to the weather and to the holiday approaching at the end of the week. There would be reflection in the churches on reconciliation, resurrection and redemption. But such hopeful concepts were a long way from the mind of sixteen-year-old Ty Conn. He was plotting a personal course toward damnation.

Since the day before, the temperature had dropped sharply and there was a brisk wind. It was at least minus 10 outside. It was the kind of a day that made staff and residents alike just want to stay inside, close to the warmth.

But that night the new guy, Tyrone Conn, stole a van and disappeared.

They found the van a couple of days later, abandoned in St. Catharines. Shortly after that, he was picked up not far from Kitchener, possibly trying to make his way back to home turf in the Belleville area.

This time there would be no digger, no institutional punishment or loss of tuck. This time they threw him in a grown-up jail and left him there until May 19 when he appeared in court to faces charges relating to his flight from Hope Manor.

The judge gave him eighteen months' probation on the condition that he stay out of trouble and live in another group home called the House of Concord, just outside London, Ontario. A court worker drove him there afterward and checked him in. He stayed less than twenty-four hours.

The next day, May 20, 1983, police picked him up in Sarnia and charged him with a break and enter there. A week later, back in Kitchener, a judge handed him a three-month jail sentence. It would become four months when, in mid-July, his initial eighteen-month probation was converted to four months in jail, to be served concurrently with the three months. There would be no running away this time.

At the end of July his long relationship with the Children's Aid Society officially ended. The CAS went to court and terminated the Crown wardship invoked by Dr. Conn just after Christmas in 1978. Tyrone William Conn would go down in their records as a singular failure. His adoption had broken down, foster homes and group homes had only heightened his feeling of being an outcast. He'd become an angry little outlaw. From the age of fourteen he'd been confined to a training school and now, at sixteen, he was in an adult jail.

What now? He was, at that point, responsible for himself . . . unless, of course, his adoptive father was willing to take another stab at parenting.

7.

ON SEPTEMBER 18, 1983, HE WAS out of jail and back in Belleville. The Ty Conn who returned was changed fundamentally from the sad boy who'd waited impotently in late December 1978 as his adoptive father and a social worker went through the motions of making him a public responsibility. Now he was an ex-convict.

The first thing he did, back in Belleville, was get on the phone to Dr. Conn. He actually got through to him and the doctor seemed pleased to hear from him. They met. He never discussed what they spoke about, and Dr. Conn refuses to discuss Ty in any way, shape or form. Ty would later admit that when they met he harboured a faint hope that he'd be invited to make a fresh start in the Conn family. It's unlikely that he would have directly expressed that longing.

All we know about that meeting is that when it ended they went to a pharmacy where Dr. Conn bought him an inhaler to help relieve symptoms of his asthma. Then they went to a low-end motel where Dr. Conn checked him in, gave him sixty dollars and left.

Ty Conn didn't stay in that motel for long in September of '83. Within a day or so, he was back in a group home where he lived uneventfully for a short while. Then he started collecting welfare and moved into his own apartment, unit 6, at 148 Front Street in Belleville. His apprenticeship for a career in crime was over. He was ready for the real thing.

CHAPTER SIX

The Detestable Solution

We are aware of all the inconveniences of prison, and that it is dangerous when it is not useless. And yet one cannot "see" how to replace it. It is the detestable solution, which one seems unable to do without.

Michel Foucault
Discipline and Punish, The Birth of the Prison

Belleville, Ont. (cp) — Two Ottawa youths were arrested Monday afternoon at the Belleville CNR station and charged with robbery shortly after the first robbery of a financial institution in Belleville for about 10 years.

Police recovered a sum of money and a handgun while arresting Tyrone William Conn and Richard Mel DeHaan, both 16.

Canadian Press, March 13, 1984

I.
___

TY CONN DIDN'T GET TO ENJOY THAT new apartment at 148 Front Street in Belleville for very long after he moved there late in September 1983. On October 17 he was in court again, charged with two counts of possession of stolen property. On October 6, finding himself flat broke, he stole a '77 Chrysler Cordoba and once again looted an establishment that he was getting to know all too well: Consumer's Carpet and Lumber in Frankford.

He was picked up that same day in the stolen car along with another young fellow, Kenny Sager, who seems to have been sharing his digs on Front Street. They were both charged for the car theft (Sager was later acquitted). Ty was also charged for having, besides the car, a lot of stuff that didn't belong to him, to wit, "a quantity of tools, tool box and radio, of a value exceeding two hundred dollars, knowing that all of the property was obtained by the commission of . . ." etc., etc.

It's tempting to speculate that his failure to make any meaningful connection with his father, Dr. Bert Conn, when he returned to Belleville from southwestern Ontario triggered an angry and frustrated response that translated into a criminal act. He admitted in a later interview with a journalist that he'd made contact with the Conn family on his return to Belleville after he got out of the Kitchener jail, "sort of hoping they'd invite me to stay." Instead, Dr. Conn gave him some money and checked him into a motel.

It must have been a crushing disappointment. But in his interview with a probation officer in early November, he wasn't making any excuses. His only explanation for the theft that had led to the most recent charges, and which he readily admitted, was that he needed money.

In a pre-sentence report dated November 4, 1983, probation officer Warren Hendricks was unsympathetic.

Summing up, Mr. Hendricks commented: "One has the feeling that 'help' for Mr. Conn is providing him with substantial amounts of money while he chooses the residence that he wants to live in and few demands are placed on him. This writer is obviously concerned about his actions when he will be released again. He will not stay at a group home or any structured residence and he seems to be unable to live off the receipts of welfare. He seems totally unprepared for the struggles and efforts involved in coping in our present day society."

It was a fairly safe and probably accurate conclusion. You hardly needed a lot of schooling in social work or the law to figure out that someone who was sixteen years old, who for the past five months had lived in an adult jail and who, for the two years before that, lived in a facility for juvenile delinquents would be "totally unprepared" for life on his own in a complex world.

Mr. Hendricks was quite justifiably concerned about what would happen if young Ty Conn were to be dumped back onto the streets of Belleville. After all, he'd been reaching out and crying out and lashing out for almost five years to get the attention of the family that had wanted him so badly when he was three years old and pretty and intelligent. What had changed their minds? He seemed desperate to get their attention and an answer to that question. It was not unlikely that he'd lash out again.

The one deficiency in Mr. Hendricks's report, which faithfully spelled out the miserable chronology of Ty Conn's short life, was that it didn't have any constructive suggestions for how to proceed from that day, November 4, 1983. There was no evidence even of curiosity: How does somebody so young get so screwed up? Why was he "unprepared for the struggles and efforts" of society? What did he really want? Or, perhaps more to the point, what did he *need?* Maybe some answers then would have saved society and Ty Conn a lot of future trouble and expense and tragedy.

The probation officer actually admitted defeat when he observed that "our service has had no positive effect on Mr. Conn since May, 1983, and we will probably experience the same situation again."

The only solution was to lock him up again. And the only place to lock him up was in the adult system. On November 10, 1983, the court sentenced Tyrone William Conn, sixteen, to five months in "common gaol," to be followed by eighteen months' probation. And so, for the next three months, he cooled his heels in the Rideau Correctional and Treatment Centre at Burrett's Rapids, not far from Smiths Falls.

2.

THE NEXT FEW MONTHS WERE A black hole in his life, and it's difficult to reconstruct what was going on inside. After serving the required two-thirds before mandatory release, he left Burrett's Rapids on February 18, 1984, and vanished into the criminal underbrush of central and eastern Ontario for a few weeks. He didn't surface again until March 12, when he showed up at a trust-company office in Belleville with a gun in his hand.

He probably spent most of those few weeks in the Ottawa area. He had concluded while still in Brookside that, if he was to make a living as a criminal, robbery was the most promising vocation to pursue. And Ottawa seemed like a perfect place to learn the basics.

He felt he needed a place to practise before trying a job closer to home, in Belleville. Montreal and Toronto were, by all accounts, far too dangerous for a beginner. There were established and well-organized criminal groups in both places, and they weren't hospitable to newcomers or free-lancers. And he wasn't a joiner or a gang type anyway. His preference was to work either alone or in short-term alliances. And it wasn't just the gangsters you had to worry about. It was also a well-known fact that the big cities were full of dangerous cops. The holdup squads in Montreal and Toronto were considered to be even more brutal than the crooks.

Ottawa, on the other hand, was a smaller market, disorganized and affluent. There was a thriving criminal culture there and, as the hoods liked to joke, there was a lot of crime down below Parliament Hill as well. There were 115 chartered banks in Ottawa and in 1983 one in five was a victim of robbery. Gas bars and convenience stores were also frequent targets.

February 18, 1984, the day they let Ty Conn out of jail, the *Ottawa Citizen* had a front-page story reporting that there had been a 20 per cent increase in robberies at convenience stores in 1983. Of twenty stores visited by the reporter, fifteen had been robbed.

Not surprisingly, the storekeepers were fed up. Fourteen of the twenty in the informal *Citizen* survey said they had weapons and were prepared to use them. Ty Conn obviously wasn't reading the newspapers very carefully then, because the first time he tried to rob an Ottawa convenience store, armed with a handgun, he was surprised when the store owner pulled a knife on him.

"I couldn't believe it," he related, smiling at the memory. "He was Lebanese. I pointed the gun at him and asked for his money. He reached down as if he was going for the cash register. And when his hand came up, he was holding one of those big knives they have over there [in Lebanon]. And he started climbing over the counter. And I said, 'Hey man, I've got a gun here.' And he said, 'I don't give a fuck what you've got. I'm sick and tired of you guys.' And he just kept coming. So I ran."

After that, Ty resolved, he was just going to rob banks. He would make one or two future exceptions out of dire necessity, but for the most part, he stuck to that policy. Banks, he knew, advised employees to co-operate. And banks were symbolic, in his mind, of the power and the wealth that he'd come to loathe in the years after he left the Conn home.

The Conns, while far from rich, had been comfortably middle class. In his new value system, they represented a class of people he wanted to avoid, in some ways the enemies of the people he chose to hang out with while he was living in group homes and foster homes. Poor people, or those on the margins of society, were always less judgmental and were easier to get along with than people like the Conns, he'd say. And for a while he believed that criminals were morally superior to almost everybody else in society.

As he in his adolescent innocence saw it, they lied and stole for a living. But they didn't steal from each other and they didn't lie to themselves. This romantic notion, of course, was bound to change.

Robbing banks was always scary and unpredictable, but it was easy. He became part of a phenomenon that was described at the time as "beggar bandits." That was how the Canadian Bankers' Association referred to a wave of new-style holdup men who appeared on the scene in the early eighties. Typically they were young, inexperienced and nervous. They'd walk into the bank and get in line with the regular customers. When their turn came they'd hand a note to the teller, asking for whatever cash he or she had handy. They'd invariably have one hand concealed suggestively in a jacket pocket, but were usually without weapons.

That was how Ty Conn learned to do it, but he quickly found that you didn't get very much money that way. You'd go through all the preparation and the stress and the fear for a few hundred dollars. Then you'd have to do it all over again in a day or so, or perhaps even on the same day. And that just jacked up the odds of getting caught.

Eventually he adopted more sophisticated and, for bank employees, more terrifying techniques.

3 ·

PEOPLE IN BELLEVILLE GOING ABOUT their Monday business at the Central Guaranty Trust Co. branch office in Century Place at about noon March 12, 1984, would probably have assumed the gruff demand for money was a prank. This was just before society decreed that jokes about violence aren't funny, especially in banks and airports.

There would have been several reasons for their disbelief. Perhaps the strongest was that robberies simply didn't happen in Belleville, Ontario. Bank robberies *always* happened in Montreal and were becoming alarmingly common in Toronto and Vancouver. But there hadn't been a bank robbery in Belleville for as long as anybody could easily remember. And you wouldn't have expected serious hold-up men to pick a little trust-company operation like this one. You'd expect them to hit a branch of a major chartered bank, like the Bank of Montreal on the corner just across Bridge Street, or the Scotiabank or the Royal Bank, a stone's throw away.

Then again, most people there didn't even know it was happening. The guy asking for the money was relying mostly on a crude note. And even if people did hear him when he spoke, he didn't look much like a serious holdup man. Kind of pimple-faced and unsure of what he was doing.

Anita Dixon, the teller, might have laughed at the absurdity of it, except she'd just been on a course for bank employees. It was a workshop to instruct them how to respond when confronted by a robber.

It couldn't have been more timely because he was suddenly in her face, overwhelming and underwhelming at the same time. It was like looking at a moving picture that suddenly froze. Later it would be a big surprise that nobody else seemed to have noticed what was happening. Not even the other tellers. If she hadn't been on the course, even she might not have known that this was the real thing.

Actually, he looked to be somewhere between fifteen and seventeen. Assume That They Are Armed, she'd been taught. So she did, even though she couldn't see a weapon. Later, she heard that there had been some kind of sawed-down long-barrel .22 and that another kid, on lookout at the door, was carrying it.

She would later learn that he was Dr. Bert Conn's boy, Tyrone. Dr. Conn was the well-known local psychiatrist. People said that Tyrone had always seemed like a nice young kid. Adopted. Polite to people. There was a story afterwards that he'd even suggested to a lady who had been on her way in that she might want to consider doing her banking "somewhere else today." He was almost pleasant about it. The customer caught on right away and did a quick U-turn out of there.

The gun would have been the biggest clue that even if they were kids and amateurs, they were serious. And that's when the whole scene would have become scary. All the evidence of their youthfulness and their nervousness would have added to the sense of instability and peril in the moment. Youth was no longer reassuring. Youth was additional cause to be terrified because it suddenly became clear that, because of it, there was nothing controlling the situation, no steady hand of experience guiding this moment carefully toward a resolution that would take account of everybody's interests.

Experienced bank robbers only want money. They get no satisfaction from harming people. But things go awry when people are panicky or doped up or psycho or young. And bank robbers are usually at least one of the above.

Bank employees just want it to end quickly and quietly. Anita Dixon remembered from her course that you are supposed to give them the money as quickly as you can. And you are supposed to make sure they get the "bait money." That's a special pile of marked bills which, if they're really dumb or greedy, will later tie them to the robbery.

Fresh off a course on how to be robbed, Ms. Dixon did everything by the book that day, March 12, 1984. But that didn't help her get over the way she felt afterwards. Bank employees admit that they are changed at the core by a robbery. In the more stressful robberies the first thing they notice is something as simple as noise. Hurrying footsteps and loud voices. The robbers are in a hurry. When you work in a bank you aren't accustomed to loud voices and people running around. Banks are like libraries and churches.

So, first, you are startled. Then the reality crashes down on you because they want it to. They want you to focus quickly and fully on them so that you will be completely under their power and will efficiently do what they want you to do. Then you go numb. It's only afterwards that you feel sick. And for years you feel a miserable combination of fear and anger whenever you are startled excessively and unnecessarily by an unfamiliar sound. Somebody raises his voice in a disagreement with an assistant manager or customer-service rep, and you break out in a sweat.

It's simpler for customers. They don't have to be there every day. And, in the event, they just have to try to avoid being singled out. The most important rule for a bystander to follow is to become invisible. If that isn't possible, just Shut Up. Don't make eye contact. Don't move. Forget about trying to slide that purse or briefcase out of sight, unless you are 110 per cent sure you can get away with it. The moment you're noticed you become part of the project. Your ring or watch or wallet, part of the assignment. In an extreme case your ass becomes a hostage.

In this particular case, with a couple of frightened and inexperienced kids running the show, the greatest danger was that somebody who didn't even know what was going on was going to get shot by that gun in that unsteady hand.

Fear is the common denominator in an armed robbery. Everybody is afraid. Ty Conn did it, he figured, about twenty-five times and he was always terrified. You never outgrew it, and when you finally realized that fear was the factor that caused the danger, and because you never stopped being afraid the job would never stop being dangerous, you quit. If you were lucky enough to survive long enough to become that wise.

That's what he said once, just before his last job.

March 12, 1984, was one of his first, and the adrenaline factor was still dominant. After a successful robbery there is a sense of release and satisfaction that sounds, the way it's described by some robbers, as being almost post-coital. You're usually in a room with a bed and the money spread out on it and it's all yours. There is no lovelier sight. Sure, there are more important things than money, but money buys them. And there's the feeling. It's like a drug effect. You have taken on the system and beaten it and survived. Someday you will probably be caught, or worse, but it didn't happen today, and right now "someday" means absolutely nothing. It's about as far-fetched as your own grave.

He'd entered the whirlpool and there would be no escape.

4.

AFTER THEY LEFT THE CENTRAL Guaranty Trust office, the two young robbers walked briskly through the unsuspecting noon-hour crowd in the Century Place mall, then dashed out through a back exit from the mall to the sidewalk where they flagged a passing taxi. They jumped into the back seat and instructed the driver to take them to the railway station.

Back inside, the branch manager, Robert Lee, was already on the telephone to the Belleville police to report that there had just been a robbery. A what? Yes, he told the shocked officer, a holdup. An armed robbery. And that the guys who did it had just walked outside and jumped in a taxi and fled.

It might have been ten years since the last robbery, but you didn't have to be Sherlock Holmes to figure out the appropriate responses to this one. First you start tracking the taxicab to find out where they went. If they were planning to leave town it was entirely possible, though perhaps kind of weird, that they intended to leave by bus or by train. So the police dispatcher sent units to both the bus terminal and to the train station.

Sure enough, standing on the platform in broad daylight were a couple of lads who fit the descriptions provided by the teller Anita Dixon.

They were just kids. They offered no resistance. They still had the money, including the marked bait money, and before they knew it they were twiddling their thumbs in the Belleville jail while the cops did the unfamiliar paperwork for charges of robbery, use of a firearm and accessory to armed robbery. At that point, young Tyrone Conn was the only one to know that the cops were just scratching the surface. He'd been a busy boy in the previous few weeks.

It was March 12, 1984. Tyrone William Conn, who until just about seven months earlier had been a child and a ward of the Crown, was in an adult jail for the third time in less than a year and he would never, in any significant way, be free again during his lifetime.

5 ·

MARION CHAMBERLAIN DOESN'T remember now whether or not she was aware of what had happened at the Central Guaranty Trust on March 12, 1984. And even if she had known who was involved, the name wouldn't have meant anything to her anyway. The last time she saw her little boy his name had been Ernie Hayes. The name Conn meant nothing. She didn't need psychiatrists and her social circle didn't include people who were that important. She knew Ernie had been adopted and had a new name but she never had a clue what it was.

It was her understanding that Ernie had gone to a good home and was with "professional people." That had been a big comfort to her and had allowed her to get on with her own life. But she had never forgotten a couple of promises she made to herself years before, watching her little boy driving away with strangers, waving at her uncertainly from the back seat of a strange car.

She'd resolved that day to let him go, to give his new parents a chance to make him a part of their lives, no strings attached. She knew that this was more important than her own feelings of loss and guilt. Ernie's first few years had been unpromising. She was going to give his new parents whatever slack they needed to make it up to him.

But she set a time limit. Fifteen years, max. And she promised herself that one day fifteen years down the road she was going to go looking for him, and she was going to find him and explain things and perhaps even establish some kind of relationship. She set a date: January 18, 1985. That was her target. It was the day on which he'd turn eighteen.

He would be an adult and would presumably have acquired the maturity for a good adult conversation with his biological mother. He would, after all, be two years older than she was when he was born.

She'd changed a lot since then. She'd been rebellious before she had her baby, then impetuous and immature for quite a while afterwards. Made quite a few mistakes, but then her life slowly started to take on shape and stability. To meet her today, mature, devout and contentedly middle-aged, it's difficult to imagine that she was ever anything but a solid and sensible woman.

She married her husband, Max Chamberlain, in the early seventies. She still wasn't very old—just twenty-two—for somebody who was making a fresh start in life. She and Max got along well, and when Max Jr. was born, in August of 1974, she figured that finally she was ready for motherhood. She had clearly learned a lot in the hard years since she gave birth the first time. It was as if she'd lived a whole life already.

They moved around a lot in the years after she and Max got together. He was mostly self-employed on subcontracts in construction. He was a bricklayer. They lived in New Brunswick for a couple of years. Then they moved back to the Belleville area. She had long since been divorced from Jack Hayes, Ernie's father, but in 1984 she decided to try to have her first marriage annulled by the Roman Catholic Church so she and Max could have their union blessed.

A helpful Catholic priest agreed to work with them, but after some preliminary inquiries he reported to Marion that the annulment wouldn't be necessary. Jack was dead. He'd recently passed away at the age of forty-five.

Jack's untimely death, though sad, simplified her life. She and Max were able to have a church marriage. They decided to tell young Max that she'd been married to someone before she was married to his father. So, he wanted to know, who were you married to? Her first husband, she told him was dead. Young Max seemed shocked and there was a long and awkward silence before Marion realized that the boy was sitting there thinking that big Max had killed the other man. They reassured him: Jack Hayes had died of other causes. Then they told young Max that he had a brother. Somewhere.

Most significantly, news of Jack's death reminded her of her commitment to finding Ernie. And it also reminded her that they were only months away from his eighteenth birthday.

She told a few close friends that she was planning to start looking for her first-born, and a lot of people told her they thought she was making a big mistake. She was risking her own emotional health and peace of mind stirring up the dark, cold ashes of past misfortune. And she probably wasn't doing the boy any favours either. She had to presume that he was a lot better off than if she'd kept him and that she should leave whatever peace and comfort he'd found in his new life undisturbed. And, in any case, they told her, the government and the social agencies made it extremely difficult to locate kids after they'd been adopted into new families.

Her mother was more direct. She told Marion that she should be careful "not to ruin any more lives" through her stubbornness. Her mother died shortly after that.

But Marion had a lot of encouragement from her husband, and when her best friend advised her to go for it, there was no changing her mind. She contacted a Toronto-based organization that helped reunite parents with their birth children, and she started learning the formalities and the techniques for tracking down a child who had gone missing in the walled-off world of adoptions.

It would take a year to find him, and when she did, a lot of the warnings of her friends and her mother would come back to haunt her.

6.

IT TOOK ALMOST TWO MONTHS for the wheels of the justice system to arrive at the case of Tyrone William Conn, bank robber, in the spring of 1984, but it didn't take long to dispose of it. He offered no defence. In his own mind he was guilty as charged—and if the whole truth were known—he was even guiltier than they claimed.

Ty Conn was never one to make excuses for his behaviour. Once while he was stealing a car, the lady who owned it tried to intervene and, in his haste and inexperience (he was sixteen at the time), he ran over her foot. In private conversations about his criminal record, he never ceased to lament this lapse in his otherwise successful undertaking to commit potentially violent crimes without physically injuring anybody.

He didn't hesitate before pleading guilty to the robbery charges when he appeared in court on May 18. The judge imposed a sentence of twenty-three months. It could have been worse. Because it was less than two years, he'd do his time in the provincial facility at Napanee, the Quinte

Regional Detention Centre. But nothing in the life of Tyrone Conn ever proceeded predictably.

His co-accused in the Belleville robbery, another seventeen-year-old named Richard DeHaan, did his time and, presumably, straightened himself out and got on with his life. But for Ty Conn, his time in the Quinte "bucket" would, like a bacterial culture, just grow and mutate until it consumed him and all of the life he had before him.

"He thought of himself as a quiet, polite and well-mannered individual who didn't swear or fight with other people until that point in time," the psychologist, Dr. Murray Brown of the Saskatchewan Penitentiary in Prince Albert, reported. He had a whole different view of himself when he left.

However, where institutions fail, life itself often intervenes with harsh lessons in reality. The Quinte bucket was the first in a series of such lessons.

About a year after his heart-to-heart with Dr. Brown in 1993, he admitted to a team of prison specialists that "my fantasy of life as an exciting criminal . . . all came crashing down" after that arrest in Belleville. And the big reason probably wasn't so much his anticipation of the jail time he was facing as the knowledge that, in the weeks before the Belleville robbery, there had been a string of holdups in the Ottawa area, and sooner or later somebody would pin them on him. He knew somehow that the system wasn't through with him just yet.

Sitting in a cell in Napanee, waiting for the other shoe to drop, he fell into a massive depression. If the criminal lifestyle he had planned . . . and hastily started . . . had been a mistake, what else was there to live for?

There was nothing to return to in his past. He had no biological kinfolk that he knew or cared about. All his previous substitute families, the Conns, Benches, Vreugdenhills, Coens, had been thrilled to see the back of him. With the termination of his Crown wardship on July 28, 1983, he had been expelled from the precincts of youth itself. He was, statistically, an adult, but he'd never really experienced a normal adolescence.

That kind of mental process eventually leads to despair, and it was sometime in the spring of 1984 when Ty Conn arrived at the outskirts of that bleak place. And he wasn't very far into it when he could hear the demons who lived there whispering to him about suicide.

It wouldn't be the last time. Frequently, in times of hopelessness, those soothing inner voices would begin to speak their tempting messages. There is no purpose. There is no hope. There is but one angry statement to be made: a principled refusal. And but one way to make it: in a purposeful and eternal silence.

He had more or less accepted suicide as a valid, if not particularly attractive, option when he realized that what he was really grappling with was an old fantasy in disguise. What he really wanted was to escape from confinement. Suicide was just one way of achieving that objective. Suicide was a form of running away, with one major difference: it was final.

So, before he tried to kill himself, he attempted to break out through a cell window but was unsuccessful. Then he tried to hang himself from the top bunk in his cell. That didn't work either. For all his efforts, jail just got worse. They tossed him into solitary confinement and left him there for the better part of a year in order to discourage any further escape plans. They also tacked another six months onto his sentence.

7.

JANUARY AND FEBRUARY 1985 were eventful, even though he had no control over his own life at this point.

He turned eighteen, and shortly afterwards a clergyman got in touch with him in solitary and asked if they could talk. Ty wasn't at all religious, but after many long months alone with his own grim thoughts, the prospect of speaking with someone who was intelligent and possibly sympathetic had a certain appeal for him.

The reverend turned out to be nice guy, and they spoke at some length during which Ty revealed a lot about his family background. The upshot of the conversation was a suggestion by the clergyman that perhaps he could arrange for Dr. Conn, for whom Ty seemed to retain some genuine affection, to pay a visit. And so he did.

From the brief accounts available, the meeting was a huge success. They talked for about an hour, and Dr. Conn seemed to be in an unusually friendly mood. Perhaps he was relieved that his troubled and troublesome son was finally settled and under control and unlikely to invade his privacy in the foreseeable future. Perhaps he was moved by Ty's difficult circumstances.

He reported that he was starting divorce proceedings against his unfortunate wife. He apologized for the way she had badgered Ty while he had been living with them. He divulged details of Ty's infancy and even told him the name of his birth mother and where she was from. At the end of the visit Ty hoped that they could stay in touch. Dr. Conn assured him that he would come and visit him again. Afterwards Ty felt as if a great weight had been lifted from his shoulders. Obviously he'd been correct in his opinion that Mrs. Conn had been the problem. Maybe, at long last, this was the beginning of a real relationship.

Dr. Conn's reference to his marital difficulties skipped past a lot of gruesome detail that his lawyer was in the process of including in an affidavit to support his petition for a divorce from his wife of more than twenty-seven years. Christmas 1984 in the Conn household in Ameliasburgh on Quinte's Isle had been a nightmare.

Mrs. Conn, after a couple of days' heavy drinking, was unable to prepare Christmas dinner. During the traditional gathering to open gifts, she announced that she was leaving the marriage once and for all. There had been prior separations, including a six-week stay at the Homewood Sanitarium in Guelph after a suicide attempt. But this time there would be no backtracking. Shortly after Christmas, she moved into the family cottage in nearby Consecon.

Dr. Conn didn't share any of these details with Ty during his visit, correctly assuming that, at this point, they weren't relevant to him since he was no longer a member of the family. On the other hand, they might have offered some comfort by letting him know that his problems in the Conn home weren't all of his making.

In any case, Dr. Conn's visit to the Quinte prison raised Ty's spirits enormously. The clergyman at the Quinte prison had accurately perceived that, in spite of all the fractious history between them, Ty retained a desire and a need for a relationship with the man who was legally his father. The sins of his father were only sins of omission, he figured: He wasn't home enough; he wasn't warm enough; he had responded to his wife's ailments by hiding from them and letting his children, and chiefly Ty, face the consequences of those problems. On the other side of the ledger, Dr. Conn had personal strength and the kind of intelligence that the boy admired. And he, of course, wanted to be admired back . . . for something. Now that Mrs. Conn was out of the picture . . . maybe.

Shortly after Dr. Conn's visit, Ty's criminal past caught up with him again. Ottawa authorities filed a slew of new charges against him: Five counts of robbery, including two holdups in Kingston; use of a firearm to commit robbery; and "disguise with intent." On February 14, 1985, an Ottawa judge added another fifteen months to his sentence, bringing his total to three years, eight months and twenty-seven days.

It could have been a lot worse. And as he sat there in an Ottawa courtroom on that overcast Valentine's Day, he couldn't have been unaware that there were a lot of far more prominent people who were in a lot worse trouble. The front page of the *Ottawa Citizen* that day was rampant with the scandalous travails of the defence minister, Bob Coates, who had just lost his job because of a dalliance in a West German strip club. The premier of New Brunswick, Richard Hatfield, was quoted in the same paper complaining that the RCMP were tormenting him by leaking details of how they'd found marijuana in his luggage. Cathy Evelyn Smith, formerly of Toronto, was being charged by Los Angeles police with murder in the death of John Belushi.

Yes, fifteen more months for a bunch of armed robberies wasn't the end of the world. But it added up to federal time. And on March 19 he was moved into Collins Bay Institution, a medium-security prison on the edge of Kingston. He was familiar with the place. He'd been in Kingston four years earlier at the age of fourteen, living in the St. Lawrence detention home, where they used to let him ride off on a bicycle to explore the city, and you didn't have to explore very far in Kingston before you ran into a penitentiary.

8.
———

COLLINS BAY INSTITUTION IS WHAT the system calls a "high medium" prison. It is informally known, among inmates and corrections personnel alike, as "gladiator school" because of the tough demeanor of the clientele, or "Disneyland" because of the architectural style of its main building.

The central administrative section actually looks more like the old railway hotels that were being built around the time they started building the prison, 1929. It's of Kingston granite and has a cheery red copper roof and the distinctive spiral tower that evokes the Disneyland reference.

It shares an eight-hundred-acre federal reserve with the minimum-security Frontenac Institution, which actually makes use of the surrounding land to raise a lot of the food required to feed the inmates in both establishments.

When Ty Conn first went to Collins Bay in 1985, there were more than 450 inmates living in four units, two of which were closed down in 1998 after rioting to protest outdated and Spartan living conditions. Collins Bay is regarded within the system as a "tough joint," because of the type of inmate selected to do time there. Most of them are doing sentences in excess of five years, and most want to do their time with minimum hassle from staff or other inmates.

In the careful wording of the prison bureaucracy, the cons there have also "demonstrated a tendency to resist co-existing with other inmates incarcerated for sexual offences." The absence of sex offenders contributes to a no-nonsense atmosphere in the place.

When eighteen-year-old Ty Conn moved into Collins Bay, he was entering a society of élite criminals, and the timing couldn't have been worse from the point of view of anyone concerned about his rehabilitation—if, in fact, anyone was concerned about it. The self-doubt and despair he felt in the Quinte Regional Detention Centre was soon replaced by an attitude that federal prison wasn't as bad as he'd been led to believe. Compared to most of the people in there, he, with a sentence of less than four years, was just passing through. And the hard men of Collins Bay were, for the most part, the kind of people a young fellow in search of self-worth could identify with.

One thing puzzled him. The male figure in his life whom he wanted to admire was once again proving hard to reach. Each time he tried to call his father's office to pick up where they'd left off in the January visit, he was told the doctor wasn't in. Usually the receptionist would explain that Dr. Conn was on vacation. But he continued to hope that some kind of a positive link had been established and would grow into a real bond.

What he couldn't have known, as he settled into the routine at Collins Bay in the spring of '85, was that Dr. Conn was preoccupied by a lot of unpleasantness in that divorce action he'd so casually mentioned during his visit. It's difficult to imagine how Ty would have reacted had he been able to read some of the allegations his adoptive father was now piling around the feet of his estranged and obviously disturbed wife.

His divorce affidavit was a shocking litany of Loris Conn's mental and emotional problems dating back almost to the time of their marriage, in 1957. She had plagued him with dramatic fantasies about illness and harassment by non-existent people. By the early seventies she was frequently drunk in and around the home. They had a meaningless sexual relationship. She was suicidal. Last, but from Ty's point of view, not least—she was abusive.

Throughout his life Ty was always reluctant to discuss abuse by his adoptive mother. Either he didn't trust his own memory or he seriously doubted that anybody would believe him. Perhaps he was simply unwilling to appear to be offering what he considered to be a bogus excuse for his later criminal behaviour.

But, in mid-1985, even he would have been shocked by what Dr. Conn was telling a judge of the Supreme Court of Ontario about his wife.

Loris Conn "frequently beat the children in cruel and sadistic ways. She railed against them with marathon lectures lasting from one to five hours during which she struck them on their heads, pulled their hair and kicked them."

She terrorized them in a game during which she would turn out all the lights in the house and pretend to be a witch, and she "continually humiliated and degraded the children with attacks against their personalities, looks and sexual abilities."

Perhaps the most shocking disclosures were in graphic descriptions of the sexual seduction of their eldest son, Jeffrey, by Mrs. Conn when he was a teenager. Lest the accusation be dismissed as the hyperbole of a divorce petitioner, Jeffrey provided a damning affidavit to support his father's accusation that his mother had molested him.

It is futile to speculate about the extent to which the Conn children would have been damaged by such a destructive domestic situation. Each of them, with the possible exception of the youngest, Loris Jeanette, seems to have come away from childhood with significant emotional and psychological scars. For Ty Conn, who had been adopted and whose disrupted infancy may well have caused additional problems, childhood became an agony that defined the rest of his tragic life.

Had he known it then or ever, the irony that in the summer of 1985 the Conn family was publicly declaring its own emotional bankruptcy would have hit him like a powerful electric shock.

It was an unhappy chapter of his life that was finally closing, but too late to be of any benefit to him. And yet, as that grim proceeding was playing out in the cold formality of a Belleville divorce court, another chapter of his life was reopening just a few city blocks away.

9 .

MARION CHAMBERLAIN HAD BEEN LED to believe that relocating a child who had been given up for adoption was extraordinarily difficult and often impossible. "I just thought what would happen is they'd think, 'You're the mother . . . aw get out of here.' They're going to pretend that they didn't even work in that office twenty years ago."

But she was pleasantly surprised at how helpful everybody seemed to be when she started looking for the boy she knew as Ernie. Perhaps it was easy because most of the people who had been involved in the life of Ty Conn up to that point were keen to let somebody else take over a lost cause.

But when she presented herself at the offices of the Picton Children's Aid Society in early 1985, they agreed that they could help her with "non-identifying information." This was a promising start. Shortly thereafter she had a phone call referring her to a CAS worker in Belleville. His name was David Harvey.

David Harvey remembers Ty Conn in terms that contradict the widespread view that he was a delinquent and destined for the criminal justice system from day one. As Harvey recalls it, a social worker spends 80 per cent of his time with 20 per cent of his caseload. Ty Conn wasn't part of the troublesome 20 per cent, and so he remembers him only in a general way: "a likeable lad" who "didn't pose a lot of difficulties."

He had his little scrapes with authority, but considering the problems in his infancy and the later rejection by the Conns, it was a miracle that he wasn't in a lot more trouble.

"I would think it would be a difficult bridge to get past, an adoption breakdown. The child would have to be asking why. How can you be more rejected than to have your adoptive parents relieve themselves of you, reject you and not want to see you again? A child would have to deal with that.

"I didn't see anything in him that would indicate he was having trouble making that adjustment. He was a fairly well-behaved teenager."

Marion Chamberlain remembers going to meet Mr. Harvey early in 1985. She was nervous and didn't expect much from the encounter. But she was pleasantly surprised when she found him to be warm and sympathetic.

They met and they talked at length, she remembers. He explained his constraints about disclosing information about her son's new life, but, she found out later, he actually dropped the name Tyrone twice during their conversation. She was too flustered to pick up on it.

Partway through the meeting David Harvey excused himself and left the office. Halfway across the desk there was a fat file, and she just knew that it contained all the information she wanted. But she was afraid to look at it. She was making progress and she didn't want to risk the success of her project by being sneaky. It never crossed her mind that there might have been a reason for Mr. Harvey's absence from the room.

At the end of the meeting, the social worker promised to make some contacts and to see if it would be possible to proceed toward some kind of contact with her son. She thanked him and she went away feeling like someone who was about to get a second chance at a life she'd failed miserably the first time.

"He obviously contacted the Conns. Then I don't know whether I got a phone call or a letter or whatever. It must have been a phone call saying that yes they had spoken and the adoptive parents thought that it would be very beneficial for him to know his birth mother."

Everything moved very quickly after that. With Dr. Conn's consent, the CAS wrote to Ty and notified him that his birth mother was anxious to meet him and that there would be no official objection if he was interested.

Then he wrote to her.

She remembers her son telling her, "I didn't want you to know that I was in prison because I thought that would turn you off."

"And I remember saying to him, 'I don't care where you are, I just want to see you.' I didn't care if he was there for twenty first-degree murders or whatever. I just wanted to see him."

CHAPTER SEVEN

The Road to Millhaven

The Primary Strategy Group for this offender was identified as Limit Setting. Clients in this group generally have a fair degree of comfort with a criminal lifestyle and often demonstrate a pattern of long term involvement with criminal activities. Members of this group often view 'being a successful criminal' as a major goal in their lives in preference to achieving success in a more conventional manner. This appears to be an accurate reflection of conn. conn indicated to this writer that he always knew he would be a criminal and that he strived [sic] on the excitement of such activities. In this writer's opinion conn has the intelligence and motivation to lead a successful prosocial life, however he has opted to focus and direct these attributions [sic] toward a criminal lifestyle. Good record keeping is often essential in dealing with these clients.

Case Management Strategies Interview
Millhaven Institution, October 1987

. . . when he walked through that door the first time, and when that door clicked and I knew he was going to be on

> *the other side, it was like everything I had ever hoped for*
> *and dreamed for had come true. It was like this is the end.*
> *You know, my God, I finally achieved what I wanted to.*

> Marion Chamberlain, October 1999

I .

IF TY CONN'S STORY WAS SENTIMENTAL fiction, this would be the beginning of the last chapter. And it would have a happy ending. But in reality unhappy beginnings seldom proceed to happy endings.

Marion Chamberlain is vague on details such as precise dates, but she has a vivid recollection of sitting in the visitors' lounge at Collins Bay Institution sometime in the late summer of 1985 listening to the clunk and clang of metal doors as her son approached from somewhere deep in the bowels of the prison.

The visiting area is usually aflutter with nervous wives and girlfriends and children and parents of inmates, but on that day it was empty, except for Marion and a couple of prison officers, who were also women. She hadn't asked for special treatment, but she sensed that the others realized that this was a very special occasion.

"It was a nice visiting room . . . and the girls who worked there knew why I was going. And I know damn well they listened to everything we said because it was like, oh shit, this is a real happening. But they were nice. They were encouraging and everything like that."

And then the last door opened and he walked in. She was quietly grateful that there were no other men around, because she knew she'd probably not be able to recognize him. To not know him would be too painful for both, too stark a manifestation of the abyss of time between them. It might have ruined everything.

Halfway across the room he stopped and they stared at each other, neither certain what it was appropriate to say or do in such circumstances.

Seconds froze and felt like minutes. Finally he uttered one word: Why.

She didn't have a clue how to respond. Not right away. The answer would take forever and she was prepared to spend that long working on it. But for the moment and for once in her life, she was speechless.

Then he said it again, more statement than question: Why.

She knew before she'd gone there that this would be a difficult moment. Of all the people responsible for his infancy, she was the only one left alive. Her parents both died in their mid-fifties. Jack Hayes had died in his forties. She knew it would be easy for her to blame everyone but herself. But she wanted to avoid that. She wanted to avoid any discussion of blame. Allocating blame at this point was futile.

She figured the situation cried out for a lot of information. But explanation could be difficult and very tricky from the point of view of honesty and fairness and truth. You start explaining things and you're soon sliding down the slippery slope of blame. Excuses. Expiation. She had so much to tell him but didn't know where to start.

Finally she went to him and hugged him. He didn't hug back. A long time would pass before he'd return a hug. She realized that it wasn't all about her. From what she was able to ascertain in future conversations, hugging had never been part of the protocols of intimacy in his life. In fact, there hadn't been very much intimacy at all. But it was the only way she could think of to break the ice. The stiffness in his non-response was like a rebuke.

Eventually they talked, and she was surprised how much he knew. She didn't realize that he had been briefed by his adoptive father earlier that year. Because they were both tireless talkers, their unhappy history didn't remain a barrier for long. In fact, it became the substance of a therapeutic conversation that went on for many years.

"And I'd stay right until the last minute, until they're hauling me out the door and then we'd make arrangements to go back down again. I'd be down on whatever day at whatever time. As soon as I get off work I'll be here, whatever. But it was good from the beginning. Once he found out—his first question was why, why. So it was heart wrenching to bring out those black boxes again."

The following months were an education for both of them. She spared him none of the embarrassing details of the early days. About her childish fling, at fifteen, with his father who was a dozen years older; of her unexpected pregnancy; of all the early difficulties and about the little boy named Ernie who got passed around like a hot potato and then handed over to the Crown when nobody had the means or the wits or the inclination to look after him.

It wasn't easy but it was penance, and penance shouldn't be easy. And according to the assurances of the religion she'd picked up from Big Max, penance is supposed to be rewarded by absolution, reconciliation and redemption. So she told him everything she could think of, painful as it was to both.

He reciprocated, and it was hard to listen.

"I can remember driving home and being real happy and some days being real, real sad. The fact was, after I found out what all he had gone through [I thought] that, oh shit, if only I had started to look earlier maybe I could have got him out of those homes. But it was like a written-in-stone thing. You don't interfere in these lives until they're of age and then can make their own decisions."

He told her about life in Collins Bay, and there were days it might have sounded kind of enviable to her if she'd been listening to somebody other than her own kid and if she hadn't felt so responsible for the predicament he was in. Most of the time she held multiple jobs, as many as five at a time, anything from driving a bus in the daytime to cleaning offices at night, to supplement the family income. It seems it's always been like that. Work days that never seem to end.

In Collins Bay, he told her, the day really started at 8 a.m. with "work up," inmates leaving their cells for schooling, rehabilitative programs or jobs. An inmate could refuse to take part in any of the activities, but that meant being locked in the cell all day just sleeping or watching television. She could think of worse ways to spend a day now and then.

At 11 a.m. it was back into the cells for a count, then a half-hour of open range, a free period for hanging out in the broad common space in front of the cells. Then lunch; back to work for a few more hours; another count at 4 p.m.; another free period on the range; dinner and yard.

The yard was an outdoor space with a baseball diamond and a running track where they could exercise or kill time until 8 p.m. in winter, 10 p.m. in summer. Ty spent a lot of time in the yard because he liked to jog. It kept his weight under control and it was good for his asthmatic lungs. He was startled to learn that Marion had a lot of bronchial troubles too, including asthma.

Prison might not sound so terrible to people who have never been there. The trouble with prison, he found, is that it puts your life on hold. Theoretically it's supposed to provide an opportunity to identify and maybe even correct the problems that caused criminal behaviour in the first place, prepare offenders for a second chance. But that's too big a job, given the resources available to the people who run prisons.

And what about exceptional cases? What if you were still young and you hadn't yet had a first chance? What if prison was your first exposure to the adult world? Instead of learning about the law and about life and how to cope with other people and society in the neighbourhood and school and university, you had to learn in a place designed for damaged people. The first rules you learned were rules for criminals, many of them established and enforced by criminals.

Prison, Ty would say, is the absence of life, and in that way it had something in common with the grave. Nothing good happens to people in prison. There is no growth in prison, just decay. Then people come out, usually more rotten than when they went in. That was how he'd react when he heard about people who wanted to make prisons worse.

Collins Bay is an old-style penitentiary, with ranges and its special segregated areas closed off behind barred gates. Ranges in the two older units, which are now closed and soon to be demolished, would be familiar to viewers of old movies: two long rows of small cells, one directly above the other, with barred entrances, all controlled by a central mechanism that was actually hand-cranked.

The two functioning units, Unit Three and Unit Four, are brighter, and the cells all have solid doors which, like the walls in the common area, are painted in pastels that might seem more appropriate to a daycare centre. The mix of colours and the daylight that penetrates the high barred windows give the place a more cheerful atmosphere than you'd expect in an old prison.

The cells, throughout, are little more than walk-in closets. There's a narrow bunk, a desk with drawers, a toilet, a sink. Long-term inmates fix them up fussily. Pictures and posters and personal mementos fight the confinement to personalize the space. If you live in it, you don't call it a cell. You call it home. But it still doesn't change reality. You could call it a castle. It's a cell no matter what you want to call it.

As in any community, people are the best part of prison and the worst part of it. Except that in prison, everything is extreme. The few good people are really, really good. They are the rare people who should never have gone there in the first place or who have defied the odds and outgrown whatever wildness steered them toward the prison system. The bad people are really, really bad. Most of the in-between are kind of unfathomable, either because their circumstances are so strange or because they just want it that way.

Inmates in Collins Bay are generally more comfortable with each other, because there is no danger of inadvertently encountering sex offenders or "rats" there. People who abuse women and children or betray other inmates are the lowest form of life in this harshly class-conscious society. Collins Bay doesn't accept people like that, only hard-ass cons who are too troublesome for other medium-security places, but who don't need the intensity of supervision they'd get in a maximum-security joint like Millhaven Institution, twenty minutes westward on the Bath Road.

Gradually, Ty even told his mother about the violence that is a constant factor in the daily life of the inmate. This is a society where self-esteem is hard won and rigorously protected. A challenge to the status or the image of an inmate by another inmate or by staff must never go unmet, because the consequent loss of face could mean the difference between life and death. A person who is considered weak or "a goof" is regarded as being unreliable and becomes a target of ridicule and abuse. Inmates must work for respect and be prepared to fight to keep it. In the simple equation of survival, strength equals respect, and respect equals strength.

The prison culture has changed a lot in recent years. Once upon a time moral strength was as highly valued as pectorals and biceps. Now many inmates rely on weapons, the weight pit and bravado to flaunt their strength. Prison styles favour sweat pants, tank tops and other kinds of muscle shirts. Frightening tattoos announce recalcitrance. And there is now a whole level of prison violence that has nothing at all to do with respect or personal honour. It has to do with drug deals and debts and the drug-related tendency of inmates to betray each other and steal from each other. And it has to do with the expanding number of inmates who are in the system because of serious mental and emotional problems which, in an earlier age, would have landed them in hospitals or asylums for the insane rather than penitentiaries.

There was one aspect of prison life that was taboo to talk about even though it must have been especially problematical for him: sex. People who know the system acknowledge that going into it as a good-looking boy he'd have been a constant target of the people he'd learn to call "chicken hawks." They are predators of no particular sexual orientation who are constantly on the prowl for younger people in the prison population to satisfy their sexual appetites either by seduction or coercion.

Rape and aggressive sexual harassment aren't as common or as overt in Canadian prisons as one might suspect from watching U.S.-made prison movies. Inmates tend to be homophobic and hostile to blatant sexuality in prison. But quiet pressures from sexual predators can make life almost unbearable for someone who is young or pretty or effeminate. Inmates and staff alike privately acknowledge that Ty Conn's early days in the prison system were at times hellish, because he was so young and so good-looking and so naïve.

Among all the people who knew him and agreed to talk about him, only one acknowledged having discussed this difficult aspect of prison life with him. He had no choice in the matter, according to his friend, a gay man who has never been in prison. Sentencing a feckless boy to incarceration in a world inhabited by damaged and sexually repressed criminals amounted to punishment by officially sanctioned sexual violence.

The friend, who cannot be identified, but whom we shall call Ian, became involved in Ty Conn's life at two crucial junctures, in 1989 and 1999, offering sanctuary at huge risk to himself.

"I saw a photograph of him at seventeen in prison sur-rounded by big tough cons and I just thought to myself, 'Oh, you poor kid,'" Ian said in an interview.

The big shots at the Brookside reform school hadn't talked much about these aspects of the criminal vocation, and it was a hard learning curve for an eighteen-year-old, with virtually no life experience, suddenly dropped into the middle of it. It was even tougher to explain to the mom you'd never known before you were stuck there, but who was quickly becoming your closest confidante and friend.

Marion Chamberlain, who in her varied life had not been unfamiliar with people from the world of ex-cons and petty criminals, found herself frequently depressed by the life her son described. And she quickly became determined to get him out of it somehow.

2.

OCTOBER 11, 1985, A PAROLE OFFICER from the Peter-borough district of Correctional Service Canada called on Marion and Max Chamberlain for a chat about Ty. The issue was whether or not he was ready for a visit or, in the jargon of the corrections system, a temporary absence from Collins Bay. The penal system really didn't think so, but they were clearly encouraged by the rediscovery of his birth mother. This was a positive development in the inmate's life.

Marion and Max were renting a little two-bedroom home in Belleville, but Max, who was self-employed, felt there was lots of room for Ty there if he was allowed out for a visit.

And if he was allowed a longer stay on the outside, Max was sure he could get him a job in construction.

They were forthright with Mike Kerr, the parole officer. Marion told him all about her unruly younger days and her failed marriage to Jack Hayes. Max admitted that he'd been through a few rough patches himself, but that he'd been a sober member of Alcoholics Anonymous for five years and that their twelve-year marriage was very strong.

The parole officer was impressed by them. "Although Tyrone is virtually unknown to Mrs. Chamberlain and her husband, they appear to be concerned and caring parents who are willing to give Tyrone a chance."

Marion really wanted to get Ty out of Collins Bay at least for a visit over Christmas in 1985, and if it had been solely up to them and Mike Kerr, it would probably have happened. But there were other people whose opinions had to be sought and considered.

According to Mike Kerr's report "a spokesman for the Belleville police department was contacted . . . and indicated that his department would be adamantly opposed to any form of early release for subject."

Kerr noted that while the Belleville police were usually "open and willing" to consider inmates for release into their community, they showed a particular animosity toward Ty Conn. Individual cops, such as the detectives Sam Morgan and John Ashley, liked him and figured he just needed some strong guidance. But there were others in the department who didn't share their view.

They considered Tyrone to be "a very dangerous individual," and the unnamed spokesman whom Mike Kerr consulted was of the opinion that the "subject, if confronted during the robberies by a police officer . . . would have used the loaded gun on them."

Mike Kerr also consulted a fellow parole officer, Warren Hendricks, who had prepared a pre-sentence report on Ty Conn two years earlier, when he'd been caught at age sixteen in possession of some stolen property. At that time Hendricks found Conn to be well on his way to a criminal career. Hendricks had noted that Conn seemed to be totally unprepared for life in the community. The judge in that case seemed to agree and prescribed five months in jail to straighten him out.

It clearly hadn't worked, and Mr. Hendricks's opinion of "subject" hadn't changed in the two years since he last saw him. He also drew Kerr's attention to the fact that the Conn family "had not been supportive of Tyrone nor offered their assistance in dealing with him for some time now."

Mike Kerr had actually made an effort to discuss the situation with Dr. Conn to form his own impression of the Conn family's attitude, but when he called up and asked for a meeting, Dr. Conn said he didn't think it was necessary. He said he was going through a divorce and "he considers it bad timing for Tyrone to visit him. He mentioned that maybe in the new year, once he is settled, he would consider it."

In fact, Dr. Conn had already divorced his wife, the decree nisi registered in Belleville on September 11. Loris, the ex-wife, was living alone at the summer cottage near Consecon on Quinte's Isle and, according to her friends, quietly drinking herself to death.

Dr. Conn had started a new relationship, with his secretary, and she seemed to share his first wife's aversion to the boy. In fact, she was the receptionist who had been deflecting telephone calls from Ty with the excuse that the doctor wasn't in or was on vacation. When she eventually became the second Mrs. Bert Conn, part of the understanding between her and her husband seemed to be that his adopted son, the jailbird, would be kept safely out of their lives, as the parole officer, Mike Kerr, discovered.

"I questioned Dr. Conn concerning the degree of support that he was offering Tyrone, however, it would appear that Dr. Conn has washed his hands of Tyrone," Mr. Kerr reported.

In his summary the parole officer noted that he personally had no particular objection to giving Ty Conn a pass to visit his birth mother. But "in view of the negative police opinion and that which was rendered by the probation and parole service," it would be too risky to let him out.

It was a big disappointment to Marion and Max who didn't yet know Ty as well as the people in the justice system. It didn't come as a surprise to Ty, though. He had a sense they wanted to keep him inside for as long as they could, at least for two-thirds of his sentence, at which time he'd be eligible for statutory release.

He was right on that score. He was going to cool his heels in Collins Bay for another year, absorbing the culture of the place along with instruction in criminal technique and twisted notions about how the world works before they would finally give him a shot at freedom.

3 ·

IN FEBRUARY 1986, THE CHAMBERLAINS had moved to a little house on Highway 2, just west of Belleville. It had been unoccupied for some time and was dilapidated, but Max had a lot of experience in construction and was fixing it up. He and Marion did that several times—bought an old place, fixed it up, sold it at a small profit, bought a better place. Late that month they were contacted by another parole officer, C. K. MacMillan, who used to know Ty "as the son of Dr. E. B. Conn, an eminent psychiatrist in the Belleville area." He was anxious to meet these new factors in Ty's life.

Once again, Marion and Max related the difficult circumstances of their past lives and assured Mr. MacMillan that they were solidly on track and that they were both anxious to do whatever they could to help Ty get his life in order. MacMillan spent a lot of time explaining how the parole system worked and how, in particular, it applied to Ty, who was guilty of crimes that the system took seriously because of the potential for violence in his actions.

All in all Marion made a quite an impression on him.

"I found Mrs. Chamberlain to be a very straight forward, honest individual who fully appreciates the severity of her son's offenses. While she is highly supportive of him, after having been just reunited after many years apart, she also realizes that Tyrone got himself into this mess and that he will have to decide that he will have to get himself out.

"The Chamberlain family will give him any and all assistance which they can, but are being quite realistic in their view of how an individual might change in time."

The Belleville cops had a less charitable view. The reaction of the local police was still "distinctly negative." The "criminal spree which Conn undertook," Mr. MacMillan said, "is one which is of major concern to police who state they do not wish to have him back in the area even under mandatory supervision although they fully appreciate that this will likely be the case."

And so it was. In October, yet another parole officer, J. C. Caryi, visited Marion and got the same impression as the others: "a very sincere individual . . . both she and her husband are prepared to lend as much emotional support as possible," though they were of the opinion that "subject is old enough to accept responsibility for his own actions."

The Belleville police remained adamantly opposed to having him around, though they "accept the subject's release on M.S. [mandatory supervision, or parole] as a necessary evil."

It was into this ambiguous environment of naïve goodwill and instinctive hostility that the corrections system released Ty Conn on December 1, 1986. Everybody was right about him, and everybody was wrong. He was, indeed, nineteen years old and legally responsible for his own actions. But he'd been in a state of personal turmoil from the age of eleven and in some form of prison almost continuously since he was fourteen. Emotionally he was a boy, his development paralyzed by a stroke of legal expediency December 27, 1978. That was the day he was tossed from his adoptive home and started bouncing through a series of foster homes and group homes and reform schools toward the oblivion of prison.

The problem for people who didn't know him—and by December 1, 1986, nobody really knew him, not parole officers nor police nor his rediscovered parents—was that he was a little boy masquerading as a healthy, rational nineteen-year-old man. He was a survivor, but he'd learned his rules of survival in the predatory world of misfits and outcasts.

4.

ON THE DAY HE WAS RELEASED HE planned to visit Dr.
Conn. He was going to need some advice and some help.
They had that productive visit nearly two years earlier, in
January 1985, at which time his father was friendly and talk-
ative and had promised to stay in touch. And while there
hadn't been any further encounters like that one, it seems
there was some correspondence.

At some point in mid-1986, anticipating his imminent
release, Ty had written a frustrated and carelessly worded
letter demanding a straight declaration on just where he
stood in Dr. Conn's life. And he said that if the doctor didn't
respond, he was going to go and see him face to face when
he got out. It seems he didn't know that Dr. Conn had
moved on with his life and that he was no longer included in
it.

He insisted later that it wasn't meant as a threat. It was
meant "like tell me what's going on," but the doctor seemed
to take it the wrong way and so did the institution, because
he later discovered that there was a note on his file alleging
that he'd made a threatening comment to his father.

But he figured it was all water under the bridge by the
time the big day came, December 1, 1986. It was a Monday,
clear and cold, and he was about to become a (relatively)
free individual for the first time in almost two years and nine
months, which is a long time in the life of a teenager.

In an interview he gave in July 1994, he recalled that he
got up early and "I was dressed and ready at 7 a.m." At
7.30 a.m. he got a letter from Dr. Conn saying "he didn't

think it would be productive to show up" and didn't think he could be of any help. "So I didn't [go to see him]." That was all he had to say about it, though it was clear that the cryptic account masked profound and bitter disappointment.

It almost spoiled the joy of release. But by then he was accustomed to rejection and he shrugged it off. In any event, he had this new relationship. His mom: a woman he didn't know from a stranger, working so hard to get closer while his legal dad, whom he did know, just couldn't seem to get enough distance between them.

The one time he did drop by the doctor's office, while he was on his release, "the receptionist yelled at me and threw me out." It isn't clear whether or not he was aware that "the receptionist" was the new Mrs. Conn.

5 ·

HE SHOWED UP THAT DAY AT THE little house where Marion and Max and their twelve-year-old son, Little Max, lived, at Bayside, on Highway 2 between Belleville and Trenton. It was a far cry from the massive country home he'd lived in with the Conns just outside Foxboro on the road to Stirling. It was half the size of the place they'd lived in on Leslie Street. It was a dumpy little one-storey bunga-low with three bedrooms. The central source of heat was a big old wood stove in the living room.

Big Max knew how important this was to his wife. She was a strong woman, but he'd learned she had a lot of regrets packed away in her black boxes. A couple of times a year she couldn't avoid delving into them. One day he could expect to be full of sadness was January 18. He'd found out that it was Ty's birthday, and it always dragged her back into the past, back before his time, and forced her to revisit a lot of the mistakes of her younger days. Who didn't make mistakes? But on that day there was no consoling her.

He seemed like a nice young kid, and for someone who'd been doing time at his age he seemed, at least on the outside, to be unscarred by it. He wasn't bulked up or marked up the way so many of them are these days, tattooed from asshole to eyeball. He didn't swagger they way they like to. He was actually well spoken and polite. Max knew his share of ex-cons from construction and working on boats. Ty was okay.

Right from the start they laid down some rules, and that was where things started to get sticky. Ty didn't really expect rules. Rules were part of the prison routine, for institutional controls or for punishment. This is supposed to be home. This is not an institution. What's with the rules?

His instincts were normal. At nineteen people are naturally inclined to rebel against overt rules, but for most people at that age the important regulation is already coming from within. Most people by then have incorporated a lot of rules into their consciousness without even knowing it. The same way they learned not to touch the hot burner on the stove, they learned not behave in a manner that would put them and others at risk. Through the healthy fear of punishment and the learning of "positive values," most kids reach nineteen with instincts that are more useful than external "rules." But Ty Conn wasn't like most people. And so the rules rankled.

The rules in the Chamberlain household weren't very onerous. Most were based on common sense. For instance: because the central source of heat was a stove in the living room, it was important that bedroom doors remain open to allow the heat to circulate. But Ty, from the time he was a toddler, had been sleeping behind locked doors. The Conns locked him in his room as punishment or to keep him from wandering and stealing food. Foster homes and group homes confined kids in their rooms as a form of household management. Prisons are all about locked doors.

One might have expected that Ty Conn would have had more than enough of closed doors in his lifetime, but the effect on him had been the opposite. He felt exposed and vulnerable when his door was open. He couldn't sleep unless the door was closed. He kept closing it. Marion kept opening it. They'd argue about it.

He wanted to go jogging at night, either to avoid his bedroom or just because he could. In prison, he only had one opportunity to jog: yard. He could only jog when the coppers let him. Free, he felt he should be allowed to go jogging any time he wanted to. What's wrong with jogging, even if it's dark outside?

Marion kept reminding him that they lived on a busy highway. Jogging at night was dangerous. Plus, he was new in the neighbourhood, and while the neighbours didn't have any reason to be suspicious of him, it looked weird for somebody to be out jogging at 11 p.m. or midnight. And if they ever found out where he'd just come from, there would be no stopping them from jumping to conclusions.

"It seems like everything he wanted to do," she recalls, "we were kind of against it."

Max gave him an old car and he was thrilled. But Max warned him that he couldn't drive it right away. There were some more rules. The car needed work to make it safe. He needed to get himself a driver's licence. The car needed licence plates. Things you shouldn't have to explain to somebody who is nearly twenty years old.

The big rule was about booze. Big Max used to have a big problem with booze. He worked hard to beat the problem and had been off it, with the help of Alcoholics Anonymous, for six years. Marion told Ty she didn't want any booze around the house and she'd be happier if he avoided it altogether. He had enough to deal with from the past without picking up new handicaps.

The ironic thing was that Ty really didn't care much about liquor. He'd tried it a few times and it didn't do much for him. It was the same with drugs. Hash and marijuana did not add up to a good time in his books. But booze and bars and drugs, because they were so adamantly prohibited in prison, were symbolic of the many freedoms that prison denied.

It was a freedom glamorized by media advertising and movies and television drama that tantalized inmates during their long hours of confinement. Fantasies of freedom usually included a woman or a bar or both.

Ty learned the symbolic significance of booze watching the pathetic efforts of older inmates trying to simulate the feelings of freedom by making and consuming noxious brews. He well knew that people risked their own security and that of family members by smuggling drugs into and around the institutions, swallowing them or sticking them up body cavities, anywhere they could hide them and carry them. They went to degrading lengths to experience what people take for granted on the outside. Now he's outside. What's all this about booze?

It was a house rule, they told him.

It was inevitable, rules or no rules, he was going to drink and he was going to party hard the way he'd heard inmates describe the fun they'd had before they lost their freedom.

Shortly after he got out, he met up with an ex-con named Joe Britton, whom he'd met casually once while he'd been under arrest. Joe was waiting for a court appearance. Ty came stumbling in with several other youngsters heading either to or from a courtroom in late '83. They were all handcuffed together, but the escorting officer had done it wrong. Instead of right hand to left hand, a couple of them were cuffed right to right so their arms were crossed and they were tangled up. Joe, who was about six years older, asked the officer to re-cuff them properly and was told to "shut the fuck up" for his trouble.

One of the kids, who turned out to be Ty Conn, just smiled and told him not to worry about it. The name stayed with Joe and he heard it again occasionally in the Quinte bucket and at Collins Bay. People talking about the young kid who came from a posh Belleville family and turned into a bank robber.

Joe got out about the same time Ty did and found out to his amazement that this Ty Conn was living with Marion and Max, both of whom he knew from the past. He'd worked with Max on some construction sites, and Marion had once been his supervisor in a plant where they made Cheesies.

Ty and Joe hit it off well the moment they met. Joe is big and easygoing and his crimes were clumsy efforts to get out of financial difficulties. Small robberies. There was nothing really bad about Joe, and Ty liked that. Also, Joe had his own apartment in Belleville and it became a place for Ty to escape to. There were no rules. There seemed to be a non-stop party in progress, music blaring, people drinking beer and smoking dope, girls dropping by looking for some fun.

When Ty wanted to try out a bar, Joe took him to the lounge at the Sherwood Forest Inn, even though he wasn't particularly happy about the way Ty looked, and he could tell by the way he acted that Ty really wasn't ready for the outside world. He wore a dopey hat and a long jacket that might have looked like a gun coat just for the effect. And he had that institutional attitude that meant you always had to be parsing people's sentences and watching their expressions for evidence of insult. He was always on edge, making sure never to miss a real or imagined insinuation or to allow one to pass. He was overly critical of people he considered to be losers or goofs.

This may have been necessary in Collins Bay, but in ordinary company in the bars of Belleville it could get you in a lot of trouble. Joe realized he had to keep an eye on Ty.

One night Ty got really plastered and Marion found him hanging onto the toilet bowl for dear life. He was sick as a dog, but she read the riot act to him and she grounded him. That settled him down for a while, but he was restless. He'd missed so much of what young people take for granted that he was continually edgy and resentful. Freedom is a powerful word, but it isn't worth much if you don't know what to do with it. Ty, as Joe could clearly see, was an accident looking for a place to happen.

It happened on New Year's Eve just before the start of 1987. It was a really stupid incident. Ty decided to get some use out of the car that Max had given him. He didn't think anybody would notice that he didn't have a driver's licence and you couldn't tell from just looking at it that the car was unsafe and uninsured. The one thing a cop would notice was that it didn't have licence plates, so he stole a couple off a truck in Belleville.

But the cops noticed that too and picked him up. He spent New Year's in jail and on January 6, 1987, they gave him two months for possession of the stolen plates. On January 23, they put him back in Collins Bay.

6.

THERE'S AN UNWRITTEN RULE IN PRISON that you don't ask people what they're in for. You find out because you have to know. But you don't ask directly because you don't want to be talking to the wrong kind of people. And, in Ty's case in January 1987, it was probably just as well. He could imagine it: You're back for what? Licence plates? To forestall further questions he'd simply volunteer the information that he was back for parole violation.

Marion and Max were disappointed and relieved at the same time. Ty had a lot to learn about living a normal life and they both knew well that people learn by their mistakes. It was inevitable that after the way he'd spent his teens there were going to be a lot of mistakes. They just hoped and prayed they wouldn't be big ones.

One thing Marion assured Ty was that they weren't passing judgment on him. They didn't think any less of him for his lapse. Yes, they were disappointed, but it was probably a good thing in the long run. Maybe now that he was getting another taste of the inside he'd realize that the things that bothered him outside weren't so bad after all.

The bottom line, of course, was that he'd be eligible for release again in a matter of weeks. But it couldn't have been lost on either one of them when January 18, 1987, rolled by that he was spending another birthday in jail, where, it seemed, he was destined to spend all his birthdays. It was a bad omen.

At some point Ty decided that things would be different the next time he got out. He'd make his own rules, and rule number one was going to be "Do what you have to do for survival," and after that, maybe, start trying to get your life together. Unfortunately, the only means he knew at that point for survival was taking stuff from other people. Certainly nobody was going to give him anything, except maybe Marion and Max, and the bottom line there was that they really didn't have much to spare.

On February 13, Collins Bay released him again. He dropped by his mother's place and there were some angry words about rules and especially about driving a car without a licence. Ty threw the car keys at her and stomped out. He checked into a run-down old hotel called the Belvedere and took up residence in Room 49.

He put the word out that he had his own place and that his friends were welcome. Welfare gave him some money, but it wasn't enough even to support a modest lifestyle, and so he started plotting robberies in order to make ends meet. Then he went off to Toronto for a weekend on a social visit. While he was gone some of his friends went overboard with the partying in his hotel room, and when he returned he discovered he'd been evicted.

It was time to move on, but he needed money. He knew from his past life in the foster homes that there was a Canadian Tire store in Madoc and that they sold guns there, so he made his way toward the little central-Ontario town. In broad daylight he walked into the store, sidled up to the gun rack, took a shotgun and walked out with the weapon under his coat. It was, he remarked later, disgracefully easy. *Anybody* could have swiped a gun from that place for any reason.

Then, armed with the shotgun, he headed off in the direction of Trenton, where he walked into a convenience store and ordered the clerk to hand over her money. It's unclear how he was travelling, but he headed toward Ottawa and en route stole another set of licence plates to disguise a car he was using when he got there.

If he gave it any thought at all, it's difficult to imagine that Ty Conn, with his acute intelligence, wouldn't have realized that he had just given the system about a dozen reasons to put him back in prison and throw away the key. And there was certainly nothing in his recent memory to give him any confidence that he was going to get away with this for long. Ty Conn, who had fantasized about being a famous criminal, was, even then, more famous for getting caught. There are a lot of old cops around who should be grateful to him for advancing their careers by making himself so easy to nab. It was so easy it's tempting to think he wanted to be caught.

He'd hardly arrived in Ottawa when the police there notified the Belleville police that they were following him. Because he was still under mandatory supervision, he had no business being there, and furthermore, he seemed to be using stolen licence plates. If Belleville had no serious objection, they were going to take him in.

On March 4 they pulled him over. He had a record and he had a shotgun and that added up to a conspiracy to commit robbery in their area, which he denied vehemently. But there was no contest about the stolen plates and about being outside his home area and about having the gun, all of which were prohibited either by law or by the terms of his release from prison. And he soon admitted to them that he'd used the shotgun to rob a convenience store in Trenton because he didn't have enough money to get by on and he didn't know any other way to get it.

He sat in jail for a couple of months until they got around to bringing him to court. When they did, on May 14 that year, he pleaded guilty to charges of conspiring to commit armed robbery, the armed robbery itself, use of a firearm and possession of a firearm while prohibited. He got six years for it. On May 20, he was escorted into Millhaven Institution, a place he would come to know intimately during the years to follow.

CHAPTER EIGHT

Gone Fishin'

The Correctional Service of Canada, as part of the criminal justice system and respecting the rule of law, contributes to the protection of society by actively encouraging and assisting offenders to become law abiding citizens, while exercising reasonable, safe, secure and humane control.

Mission Statement, Correctional Service Canada

"A prison guard at Millhaven Penitentiary was following procedure when he shot and killed a convict who was involved in the beating of another prisoner on Wednesday," a prison official said.

"This is one of those isolated things that, unfortunately, happen in a maximum security prison. That's not surprising. That's where the most dangerous people are kept."

The Globe and Mail, October 16, 1987

I.
___

A PRISON FIGHT IS NOT A PRETTY SIGHT. The objective is to inflict as much damage as possible as quickly as possible by whatever means available. Assume your life is at stake. There are no rules. If several people gang up on one, assume he deserved it. Do not get involved.

Ty Conn had only been in the general maximum-security population at Millhaven for a few weeks when a fight broke out not far from where he was standing in the exercise yard on the night of October 14, 1987.

The yard back then was about the size of a football field (it's smaller now as a result of renovations at the prison) and surrounded by a fence that's at least forty feet high. It's a place to exercise, if that's your thing, and there are always a few solitary joggers trotting around the perimeter while the majority huddle in groups or just stand alone. It's a place to chat and think and take fresh air. And as the days get shorter and darkness comes earlier, the yard becomes a little bit harder for the staff to manage.

At about 7:35 on the evening of October 14, 1987, the only light was coming from tall lampposts located at intervals throughout the yard. Ty was standing near one when the fight broke out not far from him. It looked like three guys on one, and it looked serious. Everybody was in close, pummelling and kicking. Somebody seemed to have a club of some kind. There were stabbing motions, indicating the use of a shank, a home-made weapon that serves as a dagger.

Ty Conn always hated violence. To the best of his recollection he'd never laid a hand on anyone in anger, with the possible exception of a few defensive skirmishes in the group homes when he was a kid. He was of average size, always looked fit and, most important of all, usually minded his own business. Even then he had a reputation for being a brain, and, while there's a fine line between being a brain and a nerd, he didn't look or act like one so people didn't pick on him. He never had to fight. But behind the calm exterior, a kind of nausea churned inside whenever he saw one.

This fight seemed to go on and on. Then he heard guards shouting and, following quickly, the unmistakable blast of a shotgun. What happened next would become the subject of a lot of speculation and misinformation and, eventually, a formal inquiry. By the end of the process the truth went missing or became irrelevant, since the guy who died was just a con.

The sound of the shotgun got everybody's attention, and as Ty Conn remembered it some time later, the three assailants moved back slightly from the beating victim.

Then there was the sharp crack of a rifle shot from a tower about sixty-five yards away. Ty looked quickly toward the sound, and when he looked back there was an inmate sprawled on the ground with a large red stain spreading rapidly over his back.

For a guy who was turned off by violence, he saw a lot of it in his lifetime. He saw three people killed in prison fights or because of them. One of the killings happened on that evening, October 14, 1987, in Millhaven pen.

2.
———

HOWEVER YOU LOOK AT IT, MILLHAVEN is a place of punishment. Institutions have roles. Medium- and minimum-security prisons are geared to the reality that some day the inmate will rejoin society. Whether it's Warkworth with its sex offenders or Collins Bay with its lifers, the management challenge is to somehow get difficult and troubled people on track for conventional lives, regardless of how unrealistic that might be. When they're sent to Millhaven, they're going in the wrong direction and they know it.

Millhaven, in the words of one manager there, is for medium-security inmates who screwed up. Nearly one prisoner in three is in for murder. There are no frills at Millhaven and the programs are designed to meet the most desperate needs: substance abuse, anger management, basic survival. The top priority at Millhaven is the minimum requirement spelled out in the mission statement, the exercise of "reasonable, safe, secure and humane control."

Most inmates will assert that three of those words are meaningless: reasonable, safe and humane. At Millhaven, the only word that matters is "secure." They are there not because they're any more of a threat to society than, say, the people at Collins Bay, but because they are a menace to institutional security and good order. They tend to fight systems or try to escape from them. At Millhaven, every aspect of the place is a loud, bold assertion: Trying to fight the system or escape from it is futile. Don't even think about it.

The hardcore population of Millhaven numbers about 140 men, of whom at least thirty are, at any given time, in segregation for security or disciplinary reasons. They occupy five ranges in a section of the prison called J Unit. It's a kind of limbo. When you're living in J Unit you're doing real time. The reality of the corrections system is that nobody goes from maximum security to parole. Nobody, by that rule of thumb, gets paroled from Millhaven.

Ty Conn was there for a year, until they moved him back to Collins Bay in June 1988. It was a year in which his mood alternated between resignation and despair. One day he seemed to be focused on the fact that he was only twenty and, all things considered, he could realistically look forward to getting past the Millhaven hurdle and back on track for parole in 1991. He'd only be twenty-four. Lots of time left to get a real life going. Other days he just wanted to die. According to a prison document dated November 18, 1987, a guard alerted his case-management officer that he'd found a last will and testament in Conn's cell. This was sometimes an indication that an inmate was planning something desperate.

On the bad days he couldn't get his mind off the dismal math: he'd been locked up since he was fourteen. Those crucial years of discovery and joy, the teens, had been spent bouncing off the unyielding walls of institutions, or in brief episodes of absurdity, running away from them. Adolescence was gone and he had nothing to show for it except a long criminal record. He didn't even have a high-school diploma, for God's sake.

Then he'd start speculating on freedom and how sweet it must be when nobody is chasing you. And all he missed and how little time he had left before it was all completely out of reach, and how much time he had to put in behind the bars and walls before he could freely experience any of it. Looked at in this light, it was almost hopeless. The only way he was going to experience even a small piece of his youth would be to escape while he still had it.

Escape fantasy became a kind of drug. He found that he could just shut his eyes and burrow out of reality through the tunnels of his imagination. He could almost feel the sunshine on his face and the pulse of the real world beating on his senses. And his despair would vanish for a while. Then he'd see something on television, or somebody new would come in, or somebody would go out, or he'd get a visit from his mom, and he'd be reminded that he was just deluding himself. And he'd sink into the darkness again.

He found Millhaven, generally, to be overwhelming. But on the plus side, after a year there he had a spotless disciplinary record. He hadn't done much to improve himself, but for a change, he wasn't getting any deeper in the hole. He asked for a transfer back to Collins Bay and medium security and, after a review of his file, the institutions agreed. On June 16, 1988, he moved back.

And, in retrospect, it seems he had made a serious commitment to settle down and get it over with. He'd met some hard cases in Millhaven, people who were lifers in the true sense of the word. They were the denizens of the justice system, as much a part of the landscape as the cops and lawyers, judges and guards. They were part of the community and there was something about them that was at once heroic and pathetic. He didn't want to be like them.

Life, as he imagined it, was too sweet to miss. He wanted to travel. He wanted to learn about the world and to help make positive changes in it. He wanted to meet women and fall in love with one of them. And the crowning achievement of his life would be to have a family. Something modest.

"It sounds crazy," he told a young woman who befriended him during that period, "but my idea of happiness is strangely austere. A small house, a workshop, a wife, a kid or two. A dog."

In a letter to Heather Atkins, a student at Queen's University in Kingston, he confessed that "I used to think I'd die a horny bachelor because I prefer being alone at times. But I now believe that I thrive on social contact with other people. I know that having friends can be a drag at times, but friendship and companionship are preferable to being alone."

Such simple concepts: a family, friendship, companionship. Most young people have the luxury of taking friendship for granted. Having a family is low on the list of things to do, below jobs and sex and wealth and fame. For Ty Conn it stood by itself, set apart from his other dreams, so idealized it often made listeners uncomfortable when he talked about it.

He was personable and handsome and bright and healthy, and yet this simple goal always seemed so distant. Like when a kid talks about becoming an astronaut.

Late in July 1988, Marion Chamberlain arrived for one of her frequent visits with some news. She'd been more nervous than usual driving down, not sure how to break it, or how to respond to his reaction. She had to tell him that his adoptive mother and his nemesis, Loris Conn, was dead. Mrs. Conn had been discovered by friends hovering between life and death in the cottage in Consecon where she'd been living since her divorce from Bert Conn just three years before.

Marion had read somewhere about the sad event. Needless to say the obituary notices spared readers the pathetic details of Mrs. Conn's isolation from family and friends in the cottage on Quinte's Isle and of her deterioration as she retreated farther into the darkness of alcoholism.

"He didn't react in a very strong way. He just said, 'Oh well. She's gone. Good for her.' That was about it."

She'd never met Mrs. Conn, and on the few occasions she visited the doctor at his office, once accompanied by Ty, "it was just like we were the Black Plague."

For Ty it was, in a way, a final break with the Conn family. He would continue an intermittent relationship with Cairine, but he had come to terms with the fact that Dr. Conn had purged him from his life forever. He would always feel bitter about that, but he was determined to put the bad memories behind him and to get on with building bridges to the members of his real family, people with whom he shared blood and genetic memory.

He wasn't back at Collins Bay long when he decided to do something about the lapse in his formal education. He'd actually worked off a few high-school credits at the Brookside youth facility while he was scheming to escape from there and, considering the amount of studying he did, the marks weren't bad. So he went back at it in mid-1988 and by the end of the year he had his high-school diploma.

Concentrating on his studies, the escape fantasies went away. A few years later, he would recall for a therapist that "for the most part I didn't seriously think about making any attempt to escape again because I wasn't serving an unbearable amount of time." But freedom remained a tantalizing subject of speculation.

The problem was that he lacked a realistic sense of what freedom meant, with all its constraints and countervailing responsibilities. For him it was a pure state of being, in which anything was possible. The notion that freedom is relative and qualified couldn't have meant anything to him, because he still hadn't experienced the real thing.

Freedom, idealized, becomes an obsession, and obsessions can become dangerous.

3 ·
———

SPRING IN CENTRAL AND SOUTHERN ONTARIO is a seduction. By late May and early June the days are long and loud with hints of summer. The countryside is vivid with green explosions and the public mood lifts from the earnest affairs of winter, lightened by the anticipation of approaching holidays. Even in a penitentiary there are stirrings of hope with the arrival of spring.

By the spring of '89, Ty Conn's mood had been improved by a couple of escorted passes which allowed him casual excursions into the community. His mother visited whenever she could, and he'd begun to look forward to their long chats. His personal history was finally beginning to make some sense to him.

He'd already met his kid brother, Max Jr., who was about to graduate from grade eight. He had high hopes he'd be allowed to attend as part of the family. He'd have an escort, of course, but that wasn't any big deal.

Rob Clarke was his case-management officer at Collins Bay, and he was looking forward to the graduation almost as much as Ty. He'd been the escort on three previous passes, and Ty had been on his best behaviour. He'd met Marion. He felt their new relationship was one of the best things that had happened to the young fellow in a long time.

"I thought he had intelligence beyond that of many of the other offenders I was working with. He seemed to enjoy the talks we had in my office," Clarke recalls.

The graduation was to be on June 29. Rob Clarke didn't go with him that day. The escort was a friendly and well-liked psychology testing clerk named John Green. Who knows how future events might have been affected had the hard-nosed Rob Clarke taken the assignment on himself. He didn't, and the consequences of that day would reverberate throughout the rest of Ty Conn's life.

Paradoxically, Ty seemed to have slipped into a state of despondency on June 29 just before they headed off to Foxboro, north of Belleville, to attend his brother's graduation. Perhaps the event reminded him too graphically of what he had missed out on. Perhaps, on that day, the prospect of parole, which most days seemed to be a mathematical certainty, wobbled under the influence of his natural pessimism.

Or maybe it was a lot simpler. Maybe driving toward Belleville through the lush spring countryside and witnessing the bustle of normal existence around him, he was overwhelmed by the need to be a part of it. Perhaps it occurred to him that he had not experienced a summer of freedom in nine years and even that last one, in 1980, was the qualified freedom of a group home, working at odd jobs for Gerald Suurdt in Frankford. In fact, he hadn't known a real summer since 1976, when he was nine and Dr. Conn had sent him to camp for nine weeks.

And now it was 1989. And he was twenty-two years old and staring at the dreary prospect of another summer of imprisonment. And then another. And so on.

Whatever triggered it, his mental technique for coping with feelings of depression by dreaming about escape, his "well-established method of lifting my spirits and ridding myself of persistent feelings of despair," seems to have kicked in hard that day.

The plan was to go straight to Max and Marion's place in Foxboro. They'd sold the little house in Bayside, where he'd lived briefly with them in December 1986. On the spur of the moment, he concocted a new plan. He told his escort that there had been a change in the arrangements and that his folks wanted to meet up at a Belleville restaurant. He always regretted the fact that the escort, who was a really decent guy, was so trusting, because it made what happened next seem kind of sleazy.

In the restaurant he said he had to go to the washroom and would be right back. But he didn't come right back. He went right out the washroom window, over a hill and away. And, just as in the summer of 1976, he was gone for nine weeks.

He had no plan. He did it on an impulse. He never really stopped to calculate the magnitude of the betrayal, and if he had, knowing what he knew about the culture of the corrections system, the inevitability of extreme consequences would have scared him to death. But he'd probably have gone anyway.

4.
———

MARION AND HER HUSBAND AND SON were worried and annoyed when the anticipated time of Ty's arrival came and passed with no sign of him. They became frightened when the police called and asked if they'd seen him. They didn't know about his long history of sudden disappearances. Then, apparently satisfied that they weren't hiding anything, the caller told them the news. Ty had run away from his escort.

Then Marion was angry. The day was important. It was to have been the first family celebration since she had rediscovered her first-born, and now he had committed this selfish act. And, down deep, she knew that it was a really bad move, bad for everybody, especially for him.

They gave some thought to skipping the ceremony, because they expected the place to be crawling with policemen. But it wouldn't have been fair to young Max to deprive him of this moment, so they went anyway. There wasn't a policeman in sight.

Marion had never been in a situation like this before. Ty was a fugitive. What do you do if he shows up? The police told her she had to get in touch with them. But he was her son and she felt she owed him a lot for all her past failures. She had worked hard over the years not to be overwhelmed by guilt, not because she wanted to be excused from responsibility for what had happened to her boy, but because she realized that guilt is a waste of energy. And she needed all the energy that she could muster to be a proper friend and mother to this troubled young man who was just as much her son as young Max.

Now the police were telling her that she owed it to her son to turn him in. That it was her duty to betray him again. No, she said to herself firmly. She wouldn't. She'd wait to see if he'd show up and she'd talk sense into him, but without a lot of cops looking over her shoulder. It would take a while before she'd get the chance.

Ty's first instinct was to head for Toronto. But he was broke and needed to make contact with somebody there very quickly. Six years earlier, during one of his rare episodes of freedom, an acquaintance in Trenton had given him the name of a middle-aged Toronto businessman who, to protect his identity, we have called Ian. Back then he was hoping that Ian would help him get a job.

Ian was well connected and well off. Ty, at sixteen, was a nobody, broke and fresh out of jail. Ian had taken one look at him and given him bus fare back to Belleville.

Now, in 1989, Ian was the only Toronto contact Ty had, and so he cooked up a fable about having spent the intervening years getting a university degree and working in the U.S. He'd run into trouble for working illegally there. He was in Toronto and broke. Could Ian help out?

Ian agreed to meet him in front of Fran's Restaurant near College and Yonge. The next day, Friday, June 30, they drove to Ottawa together, ostensibly for the July 1 festivities on Parliament Hill. The trip was really to enable Ty to pick up some money that some "business associates" there owed him.

That evening, he borrowed Ian's car for several hours and when he returned he was flush with cash. People who knew him then suggest he had loot from previous holdups hidden somewhere nearby.

On Saturday they watched the activities on the Hill and the evening fireworks. Ty appeared to be bored by it all now that his primary mission in Ottawa was accomplished. On Sunday they returned to Toronto. On the Monday they went to a birthday party where, Ian reports, Ty charmed a large group of upscale guests that included lawyers, the headmaster of Upper Canada College, one of Canada's most exclusive schools, and at least one police officer.

By then, Ian knew the truth about his young guest. A brief item in *The Toronto Star* had blown Ty's elaborate cover story, which Ian had found to be highly improbable from the start. Now Ian knew he was harbouring a hunted fugitive from Collins Bay Institution and that he was potentially in a lot of legal trouble himself. But by then Ian, who is gay, was besotted by his dangerous young guest.

Ty was instinctively heterosexual, but he would have been accustomed to sexual advances by other men in prison. It's impossible to know how he'd have been affected by the coercive sexual attention of dangerous people, or how he might have responded.

Sexuality is the darkest and, to outsiders, least understood part of the prison culture. Ty Conn would not have been the first youngster to be confronted by the need for compromises that could have confused and damaged him.

To be faced, outside prison, with the offer of a relationship that wasn't coercive with a man who was cultured and generous and on whom he now depended for survival would have left him in a complicated situation. But it couldn't stay complicated for long. They were together for a few weeks, by the end of which Ian gave up on any fantasies he had about a relationship of any real value with the young fugitive. Ty liked girls. And that was that. Plus, he was a wanted criminal.

They spent most of the time they were together in the Muskoka region. Ian had a friend there with a yacht. It was a safe and enjoyable place for Ty to hide out temporarily. He committed a couple of robberies in the area, though he was never caught for them and never specifically admitted where they were. Once, years later, when he was considering negotiating with the authorities to close outstanding files from past activities, he confessed privately to being responsible for unsolved robberies in Oshawa, Barrie, Gloucester and Nepean, as well as Ottawa and Belleville. It's likely that the robbery in Barrie was during this period.

He was getting large amounts of money somewhere because he gave a lot away. He gave one thousand dollars to the Irish National Association just because he felt there had been "a lot of injustices committed against the Irish people over the last eight hundred years."

He also gave a substantial sum to an old friend and former inmate he described as "a relic from the sixties" who was living in the Oshawa area. His friend was investing in a sailing vessel that he hoped to take down the inland network of rivers and canals that leads from the St. Lawrence to the Gulf of Mexico.

Late in July he robbed a bank in Ottawa, but just as he and an accomplice were leaving the scene, the police showed up. It was probably a coincidence, but it was a bad omen, and it was only as a result of some skilled driving (by the friend) that they escaped. He was badly shaken by the experience. He realized how desperately he wanted not to go back to prison, especially considering the amount of new time he'd get for escaping and reoffending. And the prospect of a violent confrontation with the police left him shaking in his boots. His view of death as just another kind of escape may have been, considered in retrospect, just a little hasty and glib.

His driver had some connections in the Halifax area, so they agreed that it would be a good idea to hide out there for a while. So they picked up his family, gathered up a pile of money and a few belongings and headed for the Ottawa airport.

Ty's life hadn't provided him with a lot of travel experience. He'd never been on an airplane and wasn't familiar with airport security. Approaching a metal detector, he realized that, along with his pocket change, he was carrying a handcuff key. Just in case somebody might recognize what it was, he popped it into his mouth.

At that moment he overheard a male passenger behind him notify the security guard that he "had a hot ticket" in a briefcase. The guard asked to see what it was. Ty couldn't resist turning to look, and when they opened the briefcase he saw, to his horror, that it contained some documents, a badge and a gun.

He turned away quickly, realizing that with the key in his mouth he couldn't warn his friend, who was in front of him and who at that moment was in the process of empty- ing his pockets into a little plastic container. Helplessly Ty watched as his friend dumped a handful of change and detritus out of his pocket into the little tray, and in the middle of it all, now sailing on the conveyor belt toward the X-ray machine, there was a massive chunk of hashish. He almost swallowed the key.

Miraculously, the security people were so interested in the cop's gun that they didn't notice the dope or that the young sweaty guy in front of the cop had a piece of metal in his mouth.

And, then, just to complete the total discomfort of his first airplane ride, the policeman sat in the aisle seat right across from him all the way to Halifax.

They stayed in Halifax for three weeks and Ty claimed that he fell in love with the place. Knowing that he had a genetic connection with Newfoundland (through his biolog- ical father) made the ocean particularly mystical and mean- ingful to him. He went out to Peggy's Cove and stood on the barren rocks below the famous lighthouse, hypnotized by the slow swell and roll of the sea, the deep resonance of its hollow voice. He went for a cruise on *Bluenose II*. He took a moonlight sail on the *Mar II,* a charter sailboat out of the Historic Properties complex on the Halifax waterfront.

He rented a little house overlooking Bedford Basin and every night he had dinner at an Italian restaurant called Lino's. Every morning at 3 a.m. he'd be one of the last to leave the Misty Moon Show Bar downtown, his ears still ringing as the heavy-metal music decayed to silence. This was a vacation. He'd never had one like it before, and down deep he knew there was a strong possibility that he never would have another.

The entire trip was marred by only one criminal act. He later confessed in a private conversation that he stole a thick wad of large-denomination bills out of the hands of a bank teller as she innocently walked past him. He was in the bank to exchange some U.S. money, part of an earlier heist in Ontario, when the young woman came walking toward him carrying the money in front of her, clasped between her palms as casually as if she were delivering a sandwich. He said later he just couldn't help it. The bank was guilty of a terrible security lapse. He couldn't resist teaching them a lesson. He was sure such an incident would never happen again.

"I just said: 'Excuse me, I'll take that.'"

The young woman looked at him as though he were making a joke, but he politely plucked the money from her grasp and walked out. He proceeded quickly in the direction of Historic Properties, where he knew he could disappear in the crowd of summer tourists. Fortuitously, the *Mar II* was just preparing to set sail on one of her regular two-hour trips around the harbour and into the Northwest Arm.

He couldn't have planned anything more perfectly. He was the last person to walk on board.

He never enjoyed anything as much as he enjoyed Halifax, with its music and its bars and its vast population of young people from the universities and the armed forces and the government offices that gave the city a permanent air of prosperity and fun. His only regret was that he never got around to eating lobster. He'd probably have stayed, except that near closing time at the Misty Moon one morning there was a ruckus and he was marginally involved. He figured it was time to move on.

Halifax, besides its other charms, had felt lucky for him. Going back to Ontario wasn't. Within two weeks, he was back in jail.

On August 21 he walked into the Frankford and District Credit Union, ten miles up the Trent River Valley from Trenton, with a shotgun. When he walked out again, he had a substantial amount of their cash in a bag. It was not a clean getaway. Every way he turned there seemed to be a roadblock. The net was closing fast. He realized that he really had only one place to hide: his mother's house in Foxboro.

When he finally showed up, Marion realized just how complicated her situation really was. He had a pistol and he didn't try to hide it from her. It was clear that he was bent on committing crimes and that there wasn't much that she could do to stop him. To give herself a little comfort, she stole his bullets and hid them in a flower vase. It was, she remembers, all very difficult and confusing.

He stayed for a couple of days, sleeping on the living-room chesterfield. He told her a little bit about his trip to Halifax. He even gave her some photos. He was especially proud of one that showed him with his Ottawa friends on board the *Mar II*. After Ty had been there a couple of days, Big Max put into words what Marion already knew: "He's your son, but we have to start thinking of our son, Max."

Ty also knew he had to leave, since it was only a matter of time before the police tracked him to his mother's place, and the scene wouldn't be a pretty one. They'd all be in trouble then. He said goodbye, and as he left, Marion knew in her heart what she had to do. It was horrible to contemplate, but once the thought crystallized, she bit her lip and did it. She went into town, found a pay phone and called the police.

"I was selfish," she says sadly. "I didn't want him to be hurt. I knew he hated prison. But I also knew that he'd be safe there. And if he was there, I'd be able to go to see him. And I would. For as long as I had to."

She called an officer she trusted, Glen West of the OPP, who had known Ty since his first scrapes with the law when he was living in the group homes and who seemed to understand what made him the way he was. West arrived with another police officer, John Ashley, the Belleville city detective who, in his own words, had once been Ty's "babysitter" when he was still a child and living with the Conns. They chatted for a while, then she handed over the bullets she had stolen from him. While there, one of the officers spotted the photograph from Halifax and told her he was confiscating it.

The photograph led them to Ottawa, and the focus of the search shifted to that area. And on September 6 they found him there. He surrendered quietly, his excellent summer vacation behind him.

Mixed in with the relief, Marion felt a profound sadness. After all the time it had taken to find him and to restore the bond between them, it was probably over between them. She couldn't imagine that he'd ever forgive her for her treachery, well-meant though it was. She knew how he felt about prison and that, for him, going back was just a different kind of death. But she was determined to confess to him the story and let the chips fall where they may.

Ty already suspected that Marion had something to do with his capture, and when she showed up at the jail in Ottawa, she fully expected him to tell her to shove off. He certainly looked hostile when he arrived in the visiting room. There was a thick security glass between them, and she felt a wave of relief when he picked up the telephone on the other side.

His first question was: "What are you doing here?"

"I came to see you," she said.

Then the question she had been waiting for, the generic question that seemed to apply to every aspect of their lives: "Why did you do it?"

"To save your life," she said.

And they both just stared through the glass for a while, because they knew that it was the generic answer that was and would continue to be appropriate to all the questions that defined their relationship. And that it was true.

The excellent vacation cost him plenty. He'd stolen, spent and given away a small fortune, acquiring a resource of rich memories out of which to weave fantasies for years. He would pay it all back on the instalment plan, in time. The courts added another eleven years to his sentence, and when the arithmetic of justice was complete, he was looking ahead to nearly eighteen years of imprisonment.

But it hadn't cost him everything. He still had the unqualified support of this complex little woman who was staring steadily at him through the glass with a look of stubborn adoration on her face.

<hr>

5.

<hr>

AFTER A BRIEF SPELL IN THE MILLHAVEN transfer unit, he was back in Collins Bay on November 24 that year. He had become a bit of a celebrity among the other inmates. But celebrity carried a serious downside. From the institutional point of view he'd committed a major no-no, an offence far worse than any of the holdups for which he was now notorious. The celebrity of being an escaper carried with it an equal and opposite measure of distrust and, in some cases, outright hostility from staff and administration. He'd burned one of them. They'd never forget it.

It wasn't long before that old companion, despair, was back and asking him a troubling question. Why had he let them take him down so easily? He'd been armed, but when it became certain that they were going to catch him, he threw the gun away. Why didn't he keep it? Why couldn't he have finished it then and there? All it would have taken would be to point his weapon at them, maybe fire off one round, even if it was straight into the air. Then it would have been over. Of course, when the moment is at hand, the option is never that simple.

It is this reckless line of thinking that police officers fear most. Sam Morgan, a veteran of the Belleville City police department, always considered Ty Conn to be non-violent by nature. But non-violent people can also be dangerous. Ty would never deliberately try to physically harm anybody, Morgan felt. But despair and desperation were wild cards that could make anyone behave unpredictably, even out of character.

"You never know what the person will do in the stressful situation," he said. "It doesn't matter who, no matter how decent or well trained . . . I felt that if he was trapped, he would have done anything."

Long years of police work had taught him that in unusual circumstances people will do "the most unimaginable things." Ty Conn was just lucky that it never came to that a lot sooner, he believes.

An Ottawa policeman, Detective Derek Love, says he once asked Ty whether he'd actually have used his gun if confronted by an officer, and the answer was immediately affirmative. There was no hesitation. Ty told the policeman that, all things being equal, he'd probably have blown them away if they'd suddenly come face to face in an uncontrolled situation. That, in the opinion of Detective Love, made Conn a dangerous man, no matter what anybody else said.

Of course, when Ty made that sinister comment he was under arrest and sitting in a jail cell, and one has to wonder how much of this was bravado, the angry defiance of the impotent. And there's the more sinister possibility that he was consciously cultivating a dangerous reputation as a way of increasing the likelihood that some policeman would, one day, do the job that he, in several attempts, had failed to do through lack of courage.

On several occasions he had been on the brink of doing serious harm to people. Given a moment to think about it and to make a choice, he chose not to. The Ottawa grocer, for all his mad bravery, would have been a dead man when he showed his knife to a desperado with a gun if there was the slightest disposition in the gunman to shoot people. Ty Conn ran away.

He once recounted the story of a bank teller who, during one robbery, locked him inside the bank with her and the customers when he tried to leave. First she'd broken the rules by insisting on speaking to a manager when Ty announced that he was robbing the place. Then, instructed by her boss to just give him the money, she activated an automatic device that locked all the doors.

"If I was ever going to shoot anybody," Ty once remarked, "that was the day it would have happened. And if anybody ever deserved shooting . . . !!!"

Instead he managed to open the door himself with a hard kick, and he fled. But he never forgot the woman who was prepared to risk her life and the lives of the other people in the bank for the sake of a bag of money. It frightened him and made him more cautious. But it didn't make him stop.

It is probably true that all people have the capacity to kill other people in certain circumstances. People who live in the underworld of crime with its attendant violence are most likely to find themselves in such circumstances. But how dangerous is someone like Ty Conn, who ends up in the underworld by default, and who is instinctively repelled by acts of violence?

In an unusual letter written November 24, 1990, to student Heather Atkins, he seemed genuinely remorseful as he confessed that "I've had tellers faint, piss themselves and freeze, yet I never really realized how much I frighten them.

"I guess the question is, what gives me the right to do that to people?"

In the same letter he also admitted that on his last escape he had been "frozen with fear . . . I didn't want to do any banks, yet I had to . . . living on the run costs a lot of money.

"I thank God that I've never hurt anyone," he wrote. "I know when I go into a bank that I'm not going to shoot or harm anyone unless someone tries to jump me. Even if someone jumped me I'm not sure what I'd do. I hope deep down I'd prevail and not shoot or hurt anyone. But you can't know what'll happen until it happens."

There is a consensus among people who knew him— criminals, policemen, prison guards and acquaintances well outside the world of cops and robbers—that he didn't belong in the underworld and he never belonged in prison, no matter what he did to get there. His lawbreaking was part of a perverse attempt to break out of an existence that was shaped for him by a lot of people who never really cared much about what he needed, wanted or deserved. Breaking the law was a way of breaking into the real world.

6.

EIGHTEEN YEARS IS A LONG TIME. CONSIDERED at the age of twenty-two, it is a lifetime. Even in the calculus of corrections, eighteen equals twelve years of imprisonment if the inmate has to wait for his statutory release date. Even in the best of circumstances, he's going to be close to thirty when he gets parole. When you're twenty-two, you tend to view thirty as the beginning of old age.

The first months of the new sentence were uneventful. He settled in and busied himself with prison activities. But he was never allowed to forget that, as far as the institution was concerned, he was a different person after the summer of '89. He was under intense scrutiny, always under suspicion. He sensed that guards were always waiting for a chance to pounce.

There seemed to be no end to the charges against him for disciplinary infractions that he considered to be nothing short of harassment, so he started fighting them. They found a "pen toker," used for smoking hash, in some other cell but said it was his. He contested the charge and won. They accused him of gambling and he beat that too. Some cigarette ash on a mirror led to a charge that he was using cocaine. He fought that accusation and beat it too. The list grew.

It became clear to him that he was being doubly punished. The man he'd betrayed during his escorted release for the graduation was a popular member of staff. They seemed to be looking for ways to make his time longer and his life more miserable than it already was. And they were succeeding. He already felt a lot of guilt for the way he'd escaped. It was low and sneaky. He felt badly for the guard. But he was doing an additional eleven years to pay for his crimes. What else did they want?

Early in '91, the management at Collins Bay threw him in the hole, a segregated punishment cell, for another infraction that he considered to be bogus. They left him there for thirty days, and in that dark and silent time he slipped into another deep depression. And, once again, to escape it he fled into the dangerous world of fantasy.

He described it in an interview three years later: "I was getting really depressed and when I get depressed I get suicidal sometimes. And then I thought, why should I feel like this? Let them shoot me in the head as I'm going over the wall. It's more productive . . . at least I'd die for something, instead of hanging myself in my cell."

It wasn't all that simple. For one thing, the notion of escaping again presented him with a challenge and a project and a whole series of problems to solve. People frequently escape from prison, but rarely over the wall. That only happens in the movies. The wall is just part of a complex system of constraints and, in some ways, the easy part. It's backed up by systems to make sure nobody gets to it in the first place. There are dogs and electronic detection devices and cameras and factors the inmates don't even know about. And there are towers where bored men with loaded guns have nothing to do but wait for somebody to try.

Then again, he thought, the presumed infallibility of all systems tends to sometimes make the people who depend on them complacent. People get too dependent on the systems. They take naps and coffee breaks and play cards and read in a state of relaxation because they assume those systems present such a daunting psychological barrier that nobody is even going to try to surmount them. At Collins Bay, guards even had exercise bikes at some of the control points in order to fight boredom and fatigue and fat at the same time. That, he realized, is the inherent strength of the system: its psychological effect. But that could also be its inherent weakness.

With that realization, his strategy became simple. Attack the wall under the cover of institutional complacency.

The strategy couldn't have been more astute even if he'd been privy to the internal files of the Collins Bay pen. A lot of staff considered the perimeter detection system there to be next thing to a joke and had been lobbying for improvements. In January 1991, there was a review by security experts and they agreed with staff. They recommended additional razor wire and spur fences on the walls, a new high-tech motion detector and an extra patrol. Eleven months later, the improvements still hadn't been implemented.

Ty was living at the time on the second-storey B Range of 3 Block, one of the better neighbourhoods in the place. Occasionally he'd make phone calls to his family and friends from a little common room on the north side of the range. Ever curious, he discovered that there was a relatively unused toilet there. Inside, there was a barred window overlooking the interior of the prison courtyard. He could see the backside of the administration building, the chapel and the northwest corner of the wall which was more than twenty feet high. He could also see that many of the windows facing the yard were covered with heavy security screens. This one wasn't. The first elements of an escape plan clicked into place.

It isn't clear when he actually started the project, but it appears that he was determined to move slowly. His last escape suffered from impulsiveness. This one would be planned down to the final detail. Its elements were basic and traditional: a hacksaw blade, a ladder and a rope. The blade and the rope would become available sooner or later. The ladder had to be invented.

Thinking the project through, he realized that there were three possible outcomes, and he had to deal with them in his own mind before he could seriously focus on the task. His greatest concern was that he would chicken out at the last minute, when stress and fear hit their peak. Then there was the likelihood that he'd be caught in the act. And there was the related and very real possibility that somebody would shoot him in the back as he fled.

He realized that a key part of his plan would have to be to drop hints with the right people in his immediate circle. They'd have to be absolutely trustworthy, but indiscreet enough to create a vague buzz that alerted the other inmates that Conn was up to something. That would lock him on his course, for to back out after people knew would be to suffer a loss of face, which could be very dangerous in the prison world.

On further reflection it became obvious that his second and third concerns were closely related. Getting caught and getting shot could easily be one and the same consequence, and the more he thought about it the closer he moved to accepting the fact that escape, in the end, could well be through an even darker passageway than the one he was in. That, he finally decided, was okay.

Somehow he acquired a hacksaw blade and slowly began the tedious process of cutting through the washroom bars. A long electrical extension cord, stolen and stashed, would serve as a rope. Routine security precautions included regular cell searches and bar inspections, but Collins Bay didn't have the people to carry out these functions as often as they would have liked. Ty was able to work on his project in relative peace.

The centrepiece in the plan was a ladder, and he knew from the start he'd have to build one. Hiding a twenty-foot ladder in the cell might have been risky. Even in the strained security circumstances of Collins Bay in '89 somebody might have noticed. Hiding it anywhere in the joint would have been difficult, so he designed one that could be assembled quickly from prefabricated components.

One of his intellectual gifts was an impulse to examine things in detail. In his mind, he was constantly dismantling computers and machinery, figuring out how specific components related to the whole. He did the same thing with ideas and theories. Because he spent a lot of time in the library, he couldn't help noticing that bookcases were usually of modular construction, and on closer examination he discovered that bookshelves in Collins Bay were supported by metal uprights.

On reflection he realized that those solid strips of metal, engineered to carry the weight of hundreds of pounds of books, could be bolted together to infinity. He was only 160 pounds and he only needed twenty feet. The wall was higher than that, but he figured if he got that far the rest of the distance would be no problem. Somehow he gathered up pieces of bookshelves and short lengths of oak, for rungs, and a lot of two-and-a-half-inch bolts to put the device together.

Corrections officials won't disclose where he stored the materials, even if they know. What they do know is that some time between 9:30 and 10:30 on the night of November 5, when the focus of the institution was on the exercise yard, Ty Conn was busy in the prison chapel putting his ladder together. At 10:42 somebody briefly spotted him on top of the north wall just as the perimeter defences went into a state of panic. By the time the emergency response people got outside to look for him, guns loaded and shotguns cocked, he was gone.

One of Ty Conn's favourite secrets had to do with how close he came that night to being caught before he got more than a few feet away from the outside of the wall. His feet had no sooner hit the ground than he heard the second most terrifying sound imaginable: a truck engine roaring to life no more than a few yards away. The only worse sound would be that of a shotgun being cocked.

Then he was drenched in light, clearly outlined against the prison wall as the truck began to move. For an eternal moment he stood frozen, blinking in the sudden light. The vehicle moved in his direction, then to his everlasting astonishment veered away and left him with his stomach churning as the tail lights grew more distant and finally vanished into the smear of light on the Bath road.

He was still in a state of shock as he ran across the highway, but was brought to high alert by a horn blaring and the screech of rubber as an oncoming car braked and swerved . . . and almost missed him. He heard the bump before he felt it, and he swerved and stumbled, and he almost fell. But he stayed on his feet and he kept running until he reached little Collins Creek, just west of the institution. He plunged down the embankment and into the frigid water and started limping north toward Highway 401.

Afterwards, when they searched his cell, they found a cryptic entry on his calendar at that date, Tuesday, November 5, 1991. "Gone fishin'," it said.

CHAPTER NINE

Forty-seven Years

A bank robbery and shooting Friday led to the arrest of an escaped convict, police said.

Ottawa Citizen, December 22, 1991

I.

THE SMALL RED DOT OF LIGHT WAS motionless on the refrigerator door when he first spotted it. Just sitting there among the bits of trivia from the domestic life that normally unfolded in the apartment. Perhaps it was just a fridge magnet. Because he was near-sighted he had to squint to try to see it better. He really wanted to know what it was. Something about that little red dot made him nervous. Then he told himself it was probably just a reflection from the Christmas lights that splashed the exterior of the apartment building with festive colours. It was, after all, December 20, and normal people were getting ready for the biggest celebration of the year.

Normal people. It was at Christmastime, thirteen years earlier, that the family who had provided him with the only "normal" home he'd ever known dumped him. He felt the familiar surge of anger and sorrow he always experienced whenever he was reminded of his exclusion from "normal" people's lives. But he quickly caught it and squeezed it back down to where he tried to keep such unwelcome feelings, back in the deepest and darkest recesses of his memory. Anger and self-pity were enemies at any time. On this critical night they could prove deadly, and not just for him.

Slouched on a chesterfield, a Ruger Blackhawk .357 Magnum in his hand, he allowed the fleeting moment of despair to be replaced by weariness. It had been a long and eventful day. It had, in fact, been a long and eventful forty-four days since the night he'd scaled the twenty-foot wall of the Collins Bay penitentiary. Forty-four days. More like one day, the various parts all welded together by fear and the ache of unfamiliarity in the strange and qualified freedom he'd been experiencing.

Now it was all about to come to an end in a stranger's apartment in Ottawa. The question nagging at the back of his mind was: What kind of an end? How much of an "end" was he really ready to deal with now? The ultimate end? Eternity? It was the one part of the situation that he could control. How it all would end. The thought felt good. Control. What a rare, intoxicating feeling.

The room was cold. He'd had to shoot out the patio door in order to get inside, and now the chill Ottawa December night was wrapping around him. He wasn't happy about having to do that. He knew and admired guns and he liked the empowered feeling they gave him. In addition to the pistol, he'd picked up a couple of other impressive weapons since his escape: a Winchester Defender 12-gauge shotgun and an

Marion (Wood) and Jack Hayes, with infant Ernest Bruce Hayes, in 1967.

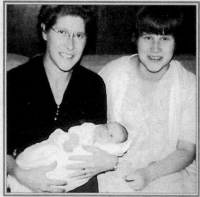

Marion Wood Hayes, right, and her mother with infant Ernie Hayes.

Ernie Hayes, near his first birthday, 1968.

*Ernie Hayes with family neighbour
in Picton, NHL star Bobby Hull.*

*Ernie Hayes, undated,
during his parents'
breakup.*

*Photo taken while a ward of
the Crown, and prior to
his adoption.*

*Ty Conn, 1978, a few weeks before he was
returned to the custody of the Children's Aid
Society as a Crown ward.*

*Ty Conn, reunited with his mother, Marion (Hayes) Chamberlain, in 1985,
while he was an inmate at Collins Bay Institition.*

Collins Bay Institution's administrative centre with architectural features that have earned it the nickname "Disneyland" in the corrections culture. In November 1991, Ty Conn escaped over a section of wall to the right of the main building.

Photo taken during the summer of 1989. Unlawfully at large, after escaping from Collins Bay Institution, he visited his half-brother, Max Chamberlain Jr. (right), in Foxboro, not far from Belleville, Ontario.

July 1989, while at large from Collins Bay Institution.

Collins Bay, about 1990, with Heather Atkins (centre), a university student who visited inmates, and exchanged letters with Ty until his escape in 1991.

Ty and half-brother Max Chamberlain (left), in 1991.

Ty Conn, while an inmate in the Special Handling Unit, at Saskatchewan Penitentiary in Prince Albert. By this time, in 1993, he had two sucessful escapes from Collins Bay and one unsuccessful attempt to flee from Millhaven Institution.

Returned to Millhaven, he enjoys a weekend "trailer" (personal family visit) with his mother and half-brother, Max (left).

Millhaven Institution.

At Kingston Penitentiary, in 1998. Ty Conn is on the left, with
Mike Larrabie, Jeremy Conway, Clint Suzack and Wally Pitt.

August 8, 1998, ten
weeks after transfer to
Kingston Penitentiary,
with the authors,
Linden MacIntyre
(centre) and Theresa
Burke (right).

The stress of life in Kingston Penitentiary is apparent in this photo, just before his escape in May of 1999. On the right, his friend Clint Suzack. On the left, an inmate-friend identified only as "Bear."

Main public entrance to Canada's oldest prison, Kingston Penitentiary.

old M 1 Carbine, altered to fire its entire thirty-bullet magazine with one press of the trigger.

He just didn't like shooting things. He didn't entirely trust firearms. You never know whom they'll hurt. Especially the M 1. Whoever had altered it didn't do a very good job. It had a nasty habit of continuing to fire, even when you took your finger off the trigger. Even a handgun has a powerful effect on ordinary people. The poor fellow who'd been sitting here watching his television set had looked like he was going to have a heart attack when the real guns went off and the wild man came charging through the broken glass where his patio door had been. He must have broken some kind of a speed record getting out of here.

The risk of harming innocent people is high when you pull a trigger of any gun. It's one of the reasons he always avoided doing it when there were people around. It was a source of pride with him. A couple of dozen armed robberies in seven years and he never fired a shot.

Sure, he'd scared the shit out of a lot of people, and their faces often came back to haunt him. Especially the loathing in those faces. He recalled the cashier at Nate's Deli on Rideau Street. Those were his early days, and he couldn't forget that expression which said something like: You are a lesser creature and a loser, a predator, and my only desire now is to live to see you brought down. Or, more recently, that young woman in Colborne. At the Bank of Commerce. She had that spacey look of the newly married. You could almost see into her brain and the images there of her mom and dad. Her husband. Maybe a baby. She was pretty, the type he'd like to have dated, if he'd ever had the chance. Her expression was pure terror. He'd have been happier with hate.

His memory was a virtual gallery of frightened, hateful, hostile faces.

It was getting colder by the minute. It was a shame about the patio door. He'd hoped it would be unlocked. It wasn't, and he didn't have time to pop it off its track, which would have been quieter and less destructive. And there was a guy in here. And then some cop fired a shot and his ears were still buzzing with the noise of it and the shattering of brick in the wall a foot above his head. Why did they have to do that? If he'd wanted to hurt them he could easily have picked off one of them from his vantage point on the balcony before they saw him. And there was the cop who'd managed to get up on another balcony just a few feet away. He'd have been a dead man. But instead of gunning down a cop, he'd shot the glass out of a patio door. Knowing them, they'd probably use that as an excuse to kill him. Maybe even claim that he'd fired first, at them. It wouldn't have surprised him. One species he knew well was cops. Cops and robbers.

His eye returned to the refrigerator door. The little red dot was gone. Outside he could hear the mutter and crackle of police communication. They were still there. Seemed like there were a hundred of them. Probably more like a dozen, with their rifles and shotguns and drawn revolvers. Waiting like duck hunters in a blind. Maybe if he just didn't move they'd think he'd got away and they'd go away too. He strained to hear sounds inside the building. It was silent. Not even the flattened murmur of television sound. It was much too quiet. Nobody was moving. Then he saw the little red dot again. This time it was travelling, silently and randomly, across the wall of the dining area. And that was when he remembered a movie scene.

It was a war movie, or a cop movie. And there was some kind of armed standoff. And they brought in sharpshooters with laser sights on their rifles. He remembered then, the meandering red dot silently seeking out its target.

He looked quickly for the red dot again, but couldn't find it. Now, with panic setting in, he searched desperately, up and down the walls. When he finally caught up to it, the dot was just crossing his shoulder. Then it settled on his chest. Horrified, he rolled to the floor and lay there, heart pounding. The laser beam was just above him. He could see it clearly, a thin shaft of blood-red light, its focal point motionless on the cushion he'd been leaning back on moments earlier.

He was helpless, but at least he knew the answer to the question he'd asked earlier. How much of an end? He knew then that he didn't want to die. Not then. Not in some stranger's fourth-floor apartment at 1375 Prince of Wales Drive in Ottawa. Not at ten o'clock on a Friday night just before Christmas 1991. Not when he was only twenty-four years old. Not yet.

2.

THE BIG ESCAPE OF '91 CAUGHT everybody by surprise, it seems, including himself. Yes, he had planned everything meticulously and pulled it off with aplomb. Yes, he had an accomplice (never identified) waiting for him somewhere up near the big highway. After that, however, events show no evidence of any overarching plan. This was typical.

Perhaps it was his innate pessimism or his low self-esteem or both working to convince him that he'd never get away with it.

Somebody met him and delivered him to the Belleville area where he stole a car. He made a brief phone call to his mother, but remembering what happened in 1989, he didn't tell her much. He told her not to worry, that everything was going to be okay, and rang off quickly.

Joe Britton, whom he knew from various past scrapes, was staying on a farm near Foxboro at the time with his then-girlfriend, Janice MacDonald, who raised pedigreed dogs. Joe raised a little pot in the cornfield and occasionally worked at construction with Ty's stepfather, Max Chamberlain. And he helped Janice with the dogs. Joe had a criminal record and had done time for robbery and some minor offences but was trying to stay straight. Having an escapee from Collins Bay for a house guest was perilous, but Ty was a friend. Joe was old-fashioned.

Notwithstanding the intensity of the convicts' code, true loyalty is rare nowadays, and as the inmate culture changes and loses its integrity, it has become extremely risky to trust anybody. But Ty trusted Joe and Joe assured him that he could stay there for as long as he wanted. Janice laid down the condition that he had to refrain from criminal activity while there.

He consented, but he wasn't there long before Joe realized he was up to his old tricks. He was carrying a lot of cash. A couple of days later while Ty was out, Joe heard a news flash on a local radio station that there had been a holdup in a nearby community.

He just knew in his gut who did it, and his instinct was verified later when he saw Ty's car racing up the lane with a plume of dust behind it. Ty was dressed in black and in a sweat and he was as high as he could be on pure adrenaline. He had a bag of money. By the look of it, there seemed to be in the neighbourhood of fifteen thousand dollars.

His car was clearly hot and their first priority was to get rid of it. They took it out back of the barn and spray-painted it black and stripped off a telltale luggage rack. On the roof, Joe sprayed the word "copsucker" and they both got a big laugh out of that. Then Ty drove it down a nearby country road, with Joe following, and ran it deep into a farmer's field and left it there.

They were both unnerved a little bit, driving back into Joe's yard, to see a strange car parked in front of the house. It was almost exactly like the one they'd just abandoned. It was a little Chevy Malibu, and they wondered whose it could be. Ty nearly fainted when he walked into the kitchen and saw his adoptive sister, Cairine Conn, sitting there. He hadn't realized that she and Janice were friends or that Janice, unaware of his agenda, had called her and suggested that she drop by and surprise her brother.

He was surprised, but he wasn't entirely happy to see her. He liked Cairine, and though she was six years older than he was, they had always got along well. But this was complicated. He was on the run. He was committing crimes. He didn't want her involved. But Joe was thinking realistically. It was only a matter of time before the cops were on his doorstep, having figured out the history he shared with Ty. They had to hit the road. Cairine had a car that wouldn't attract suspicion. She thought the idea was pretty cool.

They partied a bit, then Joe, Ty and Cairine struck off for Ottawa. It was a hilarious trip, the three of them high on drugs and booze and tension, but they arrived without incident and checked into a centretown motel. The party continued. Joe was loaded and Cairine was stoned most of the time, while Ty, who wasn't much of a doper and tended to get sick on liquor, came and went mysteriously.

Then they headed off to Montreal to launder some money and to pick up another car, and it was at about that point they started getting worried about Cairine. For her it was all a lark. For them it was business. They sent her home to Belleville so she wouldn't be there when the situation turned nasty.

Joe and Ty headed for Toronto then and holed up in the west end on a section of Lakeshore Boulevard that's notorious for strip bars and hookers and seedy motels with employees who are blind to the comings and goings of the clientele. It's easy to imagine a Hollywood scene: a couple of serious hoods cavorting on the spoils of a crime spree. But there's an actual photograph from that trip, and in it a slightly stupefied Ty Conn is posing with a nearly naked stripper in one of the Lakeshore bars. He looks more like a bedazzled schoolboy than a heavy criminal. The photo captured the comical pathos of the moment and the empty futility of his project.

3.

BACK IN OTTAWA, AFTER TOO MUCH hearty partying in Toronto, Joe became seriously ill, probably from alcohol poisoning. He told Ty he had to go home.

Joe was tall, about six feet four, and weighed more than two hundred pounds, and he considered himself Ty's big brother and bodyguard. But he had a blood condition called porphyria and the boozing was getting to him. He had no choice. In addition, Janice had all those dogs to look after back in Foxboro. He was concerned about leaving, but Ty assured him that he had a lot of friends in Ottawa and that everything would be just fine.

But everything wasn't just fine, and he had no way of explaining his conundrum to Joe or anybody else. Sure, Joe had done time, but nobody could be expected to relate to or understand what he was really going through. His life had been mostly time spent in some kind of custody. Freedom, it suddenly seemed, was just an empty space. It was his challenge to fill it with a life. But where do you start?

Faced with the reality of making choices and organizing a variety of circumstances to give some kind of shape and meaning to his new existence, he felt a growing paralysis.

"I felt," he later explained to a psychologist, "like a lost soul. Instead of solving all my problems, my freedom and . . . being wanted by the law created a multitude of additional concerns. For two weeks I hibernated in an apartment, not out of concern that I'd be seen in the street, but rather in a state of confusion and doubts about what was going to happen to me. I once again rationalized any robberies I had to commit as being necessary for my continued survival. I experienced brief moments of happiness, but for the most part, I was overwhelmed by a constant fear of capture, and [frustrated] over not knowing what to do next, I inevitably became depressed in the very environment that I had believed held solutions for the discomfort I had felt in prison."

When he was in prison it all seemed so simple. The movies and the storybooks all ended with the escapers vanishing into exotic distances, or dying. When he was in Collins Bay, either outcome seemed preferable to the status quo. But the distances and the means of getting to them were a lot more daunting when he actually sat down and tried to make a plan. Death, the closer you get to it, becomes uglier and uglier. Could it be that he was a loser? Too stunned even to die?

Making a life with any kind of value requires roots and reliable links with other people. You have to know things, not just from literature and movies, but from actual experience and from structured learning and the formation of instincts. Life is a continuum, and getting to where he really wanted to be would have required starting out very young. But from the time he was very young, life had largely been an exercise in avoiding punishment. Punishment for being bad. Punishment for being worse. All he knew, when he got right down to it, was how to be bad and how to avoid or cope with punishment.

He gradually began to realize that he was boxed in, not by the law, but by his own limitations. He had no real options other than to be who he was and to play out the hand he'd been dealt. He was a bank robber. He belonged in prison. Those were the two defining realities of his existence after twenty-four years and nine months on the planet. Looking at the situation in such simple terms didn't make him feel much better, but it simplified things considerably.

· 4 ·

CINDY HICKMAN DIDN'T EVEN KNOW she was pregnant at the time which, thinking about it later, was really merciful.

The experience would have been a great deal worse if she'd realized that it wasn't just her life that was at risk, but also that of her unborn baby. Remembering the day the robber walked into her branch of the Canadian Imperial Bank of Commerce was bad enough without that. It was November 20, 1991.

The bank was in Colborne, just south of Cobourg. And it was about noon when the young guy walked in, kind of stiffly wearing a pair of overalls. Something about the determination in the way he moved caught her eye and then she saw the shotgun. It had been concealed down his pants leg and he hardly slowed down as he drew it out. And when she heard the loud click that told her he was cocking it, she just went numb.

She couldn't remember what, specifically, he said but it was something like "No one move or I'll blow your fuckin' head off." He knew exactly what he was doing. He strode straight through the passageway in the tellers' counter and started emptying out all the right drawers as if he knew all along where the money was.

Cindy knew from her training that her job now was to keep very quiet and to memorize as many of the details as she could. His face, she remembered later, was smeared with some kind of colouring. He had something weird on his head. Mostly she remembered the overalls and the click of the hammer on the gun. And she remembered that he was very nervous and very quick.

"He's in a rush and that obviously stresses you too . . . they're just in a real hurry. I also wondered about an accident happening because he was moving so fast. And if you don't know the person, you don't know if they intend to do anything. Nowadays you don't know if they're on drugs or anything like that."

Then he's gone as quickly as he appeared, but the uncertainty and the fear doesn't end. You can't help wondering if he noticed that you were concentrating on memorizing what he looked like so you'll be able to identify him later and help put him away. What if he comes back looking for you? What if he finds out where you live?

"They didn't catch him right away. I'm sure there were a couple of banks after that . . . so there's always the fear that you don't know where they are afterwards, and I don't know, you have all these things going through your head that he is coming to get me. It's not rational, but these are the things that go through your head afterwards."

5 .

AT THE END OF NOVEMBER, COMPELLED either by boredom or some deep-rooted resentment going back to his days with the Vreugdenhills and the Suurdts, he headed back to Frankford. He had to have known he was pushing his luck. He'd already knocked off the credit union there in August 1989, and he'd broken into Consumer's Carpet and stolen cars so many times it was a pretty safe bet that he'd be the prime suspect in any crime that happened there forevermore.

But that was the last thing on his mind as he slowed down in front of the little credit union building in Frankford at the end of November 1991. He noted that they'd changed the name of the place. It was now the Bayshore Credit Union. Maybe that was a good sign. Like a fresh start.

But once again he could feel the creeping fear that worked its way through him every time he focused on the critical details of the one activity that had become, regrettably, the primary purpose of his life. Robbery, like escaping from prison, had, in his dreams, been the means toward an end. In reality it had become an end in itself and it didn't make any sense. It was fundamentally wrong and it was dangerous. It wasn't supposed to be like this. So you grit your teeth. You take the money. Then hopefully you use the money to gain access to a better way of life.

But one robbery just seemed to lead to another. And sooner or later he'd fail and the consequences would be huge. That, it was becoming increasingly clear, had been the main flaw in his entire plan of escape. He had no longer-term game plan.

Heading southward on Highway 33 later, he knew from experience where the police would put the roadblocks. In his mind's eye he could already see the intersection points and all the stealthy cop cars slinking into position. They'd know exactly where to go looking for him, because they'd know exactly who they were looking for.

So just a few miles south of Frankford and just before the factory village of Batawa, he turned up a sideroad and then tucked into a wooded field where he planned to lay low overnight. Rest up for the task ahead. He had detailed maps of the area and he planned to plot an escape route that would avoid any of the roads that were likely to be under police surveillance. Then he allowed himself to relax and he dozed.

It was getting near midnight and he was only semi-conscious when the probe of headlights brought him to a state of full alert. There was a car moving slowly along the far side of the field. It could have been some local kids looking for a place to make out or drink beer or both. But he immediately recognized the squared-off double headlights and the careful movement of the approaching vehicle, like a stalking animal. Then the moonlight revealed the outline of a light bar on the roof of the approaching vehicle and he knew he was in trouble.

There was a shotgun on the car seat. He grabbed it, slipped out the passenger's door and started running blindly toward the trees. And then he was flat on his back, struggling to breathe. He felt as if his windpipe had been broken. The stars in the sky were fuzzy. Had they shot him? Is this what it felt like? No. Nothing so dramatic. He'd run into a tree. Christ. The money from his recent robberies was still back in the car. And a lot of personal stuff, including personal photographs. Him and Joe. That stripper in Toronto. He had to go back.

But by then there were three more cars moving into the field and they weren't stalking. Their headlights bounced wildly as they tore across the field toward where he'd been moments before. Or was it hours? How long had he been lying on the ground? Injured or not, it was time for him to get out of there, and there was only one means of escape available. He started running.

He made it to Trenton, about seven miles away, and with the help of some acquaintances, he hid out there for a few days. But he needed money, and so on December 6 he went to Toronto and robbed the credit union at Morningside and Lawrence avenues in Scarborough.

He was finally able to return to the sanctuary of Ottawa's underworld. But by then the sense of futility was weighing so heavily on him that he could hardly breathe. He was finally immobilized by the emotional paralysis that had been creeping through him for weeks. The near-miss at Batawa signalled to him that the police were closing in on him.

For two weeks he rarely moved out of the Ottawa apartment he shared with a group of people he hardly knew and barely trusted.

On December 20, possibly to break free of a growing despair, or perhaps even to precipitate a crisis, he stuck a gun in one pocket and a ski mask in another and headed for the Central Guaranty Trust branch at 888 Meadowland Drive. It was just a couple of blocks from where he'd been living.

A few days earlier he'd bought a Christmas card for the warden at Collins Bay, Al Stevenson. He stuck a five-dollar bill inside and wrote a little note: "Have a Merry Christmas and have a beer on me." It was with his stuff back in the apartment. He'd mail it tomorrow. Maybe it was cheekiness. Maybe black humour struggling out of inherent fatalism. It must have occurred to him on his way to his last robbery, or shortly afterwards, that the warden was going to have the last laugh.

6.
———

MARION CHAMBERLAIN WAS JUST SETTLING down for an evening of television when the phone rang. The sound of the voice made her nervous because she didn't know where he was. Next door? In jail? Timbuktu? His name had been popping up unexpectedly on newscasts during the past seven weeks and it frightened her. It seemed that he was behind every crime in the region since he'd escaped from Collins Bay. They were making him sound like a one-man crime wave.

He hadn't come to stay with her this time, and she was grateful for that. His surprise appearances in the past frightened her. Perhaps it was the menacing characters that sometimes came with him. Maybe it was the awareness that he was probably armed. Maybe it was the storm of memory that the voice revived. Memories stored carefully away in what she considered to be her "black boxes." But here he was on the phone.

"Hi, Ma."

"Hi, son. How are you anyway?"

"Not good, Ma. They've got me in the crosshairs."

She turned to her husband, Max, and asked: "What are 'crosshairs'?"

Max told her.

"What should I do, Ma?"

"There's only one thing to do, Ty."

"I know."

"You've got to give up."

After he put the phone down he knew she was right. But still he wondered. Is it really that cut and dried? Just give up? Are those the only choices, give up or die? There had to be other options. But what were they?

Trying to figure out options had always been a problem. Life, from his very first moments of self-awareness, had been some kind of custody. Social workers. Parents for whom he was always inconvenient. A responsibility that had to be delegated or deferred or forgotten. Then there were cops. Wardens. Guards. Lawyers. Judges. People who were always trying to figure him out and straighten him out and always, ultimately, making choices for him. Where he'd live and how. Foster homes, reformatories and prisons don't offer much to develop the faculties for recognizing and exercising options.

Lying on the floor with that menacing beam of light probing above him, he felt the return of the suffocating frustration that experience told him could lead so easily to self-pity. In prison, he learned early on, self-pity is an early stage of death. The death of the spirit. Maybe even death in the most final sense. Solid cons fought self-pity. Or at least denied it. Or concealed it. People who surrendered their souls to pity couldn't be trusted, and in prison everything starts with trust or ends with the loss of it. Distrust is the beginning of breakdown, usually ending in destruction.

Calling Ma was probably a mistake. She already had enough on her plate.

7.

BY 10:30 THAT EVENING THE CHILL was starting to get into the bone marrow of the dozen or so members of the Ottawa Regional Police tactical squad who'd been positioned outside 1375 Prince of Wales Drive for about an hour and a half. An armed standoff is always unpredictable, even when there are no hostages and when the immediate area has been secured. But they had the place under control. They had the upper hand. Young Mr. Conn wasn't going anywhere, except back to jail. There were just two wild cards in the deck, impatience and despair.

The officer in charge scanned the dark outlines of his men, crouched and watchful beside their vehicles. They were trained to deal with the impatience, which is just another form of fear. It comes from wanting to get the job over quickly, to end the peril. But of course any policeman knows that impatient haste leads to carelessness, and that just increases danger.

The other factor, despair, was of course most likely to affect what was going on inside, where the young hoodlum was probably doing a lot of soul-searching at that very moment. And if the soul-searching led him to anger, it wouldn't be long before they'd all be in danger. Despair was the enemy. The police were betting instead that their quarry would first encounter fear. That's when the person in control should offer him some hope and a way out.

Inside, waiting for just that opportunity, Detective Derek Love of the Ottawa police major crimes unit was stationed in the building stairwell at the fourth-floor landing. His partner was cautiously making his way to the apartment adjacent to the one Conn was holed up in. The plan was to initiate some kind of contact, offer hope, end the affair peacefully.

The situation started out unsteadily. They'd been hoping for a quiet takedown, but as often happens they encountered the wrong people first, a couple of guys and a woman who had been in the apartment with him. While officers were taking charge of them, Conn dashed for the balcony and disappeared. He couldn't have gone far, but he'd become the proverbial loose cannon. And they knew he had a gun.

Since then there had been two gunshots. One of the SWAT officers took a shot. A bad idea. But the officer claimed that Conn had waved the big silver Ruger in his direction and that was all he needed. He'd been carefully climbing around the balconies and, unwittingly, almost stepped on Conn.

He fired the shot to distract the fugitive and Conn fired back . . . or somewhere. Then kicked the broken glass out of the patio entrance to unit 403 and vanished inside. The police promptly cleared the entire fourth floor of all the remaining residents. Otherwise there might have been hostages by now. You never know how these people will respond when they're cornered. Conn was already doing eighteen years when he lit out from Collins Bay. Faced with the prospect of what . . . another dozen, maybe more . . . there was no telling what he might do. A hostage-taking would have escalated the situation into a crisis.

8.

THEN HE HEARD THE SOUND OF someone shouting his name through the wall from 402.

"Tyrone," the voice called out.

The tone was that of a concerned parent attempting to get the attention of a sulking child.

"Tyrone. It's Eric Hanson. Ottawa police. Are you near a phone in there?"

"Yes," he replied.

"I want to talk to you," Sergeant Hanson said.

I bet you do, Ty said to himself. And of course he already knew how the talk would go and where it would end. It was always the same. It was actually kind of amusing the way the coppers seemed to think they were being original in their friendliness. It was always as if to say, Hey, I'm a cop, but I'm different. You and I probably have more in common than you can imagine. I know what you're going through. Etc., etc.

Of course, the result was always the same. Face jammed into the carpet while a couple of the assholes try to break your arms putting the cuffs on so tight that within five minutes you think your hands are going to fall off.

Ah well. It's Christmas. Maybe they'll have a bit of the seasonal spirit in them.

"What's the phone number? Get me the phone number and I'll call in," the policeman said. "We can talk, okay?"

"I'm going to go to the phone," Ty shouted. "I don't want somebody taking a shot at me."

"Go ahead," the voice replied patiently.

He crawled slowly to the telephone, conscious of that lethal red spear of light, now apparently gone from the room. But there was no number to be found on the telephone.

"There isn't any number on it," he shouted.

There was a long silence. Then: "There must be."

"No," he said, impatient. "There isn't."

Another pause, then: "Okay, Tyrone. Here's what you do. I want you to dial this number. I'll call it out. You dial. Okay?"

As the officer called the number, digit by digit, he poked carefully at the buttons on the front of the telephone, remembering how much he disliked it when people called him Tyrone. It sounded so officious. The cop wanted to sound friendly, but calling him Tyrone ruined it. So full of authority. The authority of strangers. And of course it wasn't his own name anyway. Just a name a bunch of strangers decided to stick on him when he was three. A bunch of strangers who promised to be his family, but never were.

9.
———

ACCORDING TO THE SYNOPTIC POLICE report, "after a period of negotiation the suspect agreed to surrender and he was arrested at 23:42 hrs.

"Found in the apt was a .357 caliber Ruger revolver ser. #35756250. Also found was $11,105,00 dollers [*sic*] in bills in a plastic bag. Also shells for the gun."

There's an intriguing hint of betrayal in the police report of Ty Conn's capture. "On Dec. 20, 1991, information had been received and the suspect Tyrone Conn was arrested at 1375 Prince of Wales Drive in Apt. #402."

In plain English, somebody ratted him out. The enigmatic passive voice conceals anything that might disclose who did it. The former OPP officer, Glen West, who had known Ty Conn since he was a boy, has confirmed that it was he who indicated to the Ottawa police where they could find Ty that night. But how did he know? He was based in the Belleville area and that isn't anywhere near Ottawa.

Back in '89, Marion Chamberlain, his mother, helped the police take him down, assuming correctly that they were already closing in on him and that the longer he continued to duck and dodge them, the greater the likelihood that some-body was going to get hurt. She made no bones about it at the time. And the policeman she contacted then was Glen West. But it wasn't Marion this time.

Joe Britton believes it was somebody involved in the early part of Ty's escape from Collins Bay. And he continues to suffer from a recurring depression that it might have indirectly been his fault.

After he returned, ill, from Ottawa where he'd been running with Ty, he discovered that the police had ransacked the farm where he and Janice lived, looking for evidence that Ty had been there. Joe wasn't sure about what specifically went down in his absence, but they found drugs there and they'd been putting some serious heat on Janice to help them with their inquiries.

Then one evening, after he'd been back in Belleville for a while, Joe was driving along a city street with a few scotches under his belt when a policeman pulled him over for some minor driving infraction.

The cop asked Joe for a breath sample and Joe blew orange, enough for a brief suspension. But Joe, figuring he was near the end of his rope anyway, suggested to the cop that he should check his communications system and that he'd probably find something about Joe Britton there. That made it a matter of record that Joe turned himself in.

The cop obliged. Joe called his lawyer, Eddie Kafka, and before long he was out on bail. He discovered that he and Janice and Cairine were in some potentially deep trouble and it wasn't just about drugs. They could go down for aiding and abetting an escapee and bank robber.

Janice was all for cutting a deal, but Joe refused. Then he went on a bender and everything dissolved into a kind of nothingness for the next while. By the time he pulled out of

it, Janice had a deal with the cops and the Crown and it
included him. They avoided prosecution for serious drug and
felony charges. In return, the police got some crucial information. And the information undoubtedly helped them get
Ty Conn.

The ex-policeman, Glen West, is coy about the wheeling
and dealing that went on. But he has disclosed one significant
element: that there was a separate deal with the accused, Ty
Conn. For his part he'd plead guilty to most, if not all, of
the twenty or so outstanding charges against him if they'd
withdraw any charges pending against Cairine Conn. He was
adamant that she be allowed to avoid the taint of a criminal
record. The family name was sufficiently besmirched already.
The cops agreed and Cairine walked.

On Thursday, February 20, 1992, Ottawa Judge Dianne
Nicholas confessed that she was emotionally overwhelmed at
having to punish Ty with the stiffest sentence she'd ever
handed out. She gave him sixteen years for the Guaranty
Trust robbery on December 20 and for the Toronto credit
union holdup on December 6. The crown had asked for
twenty years, but she said, "the thought that kept coming
through my mind was . . . there are people who kill people
who get less than twenty years."

Someone might have pointed out that there are also
people who kill people who get less than sixteen years. Ty's
sixteen years would, in the end, really be more than thirty-
three years when tacked onto the sentence he'd already been
serving when he broke out of Collins Bay on November 5.

She was at a loss, she said, to understand how Ty Conn
had become a bank robber, with his background and his tal-
ents. But she offered this encouragement: "Your life is not

over. You are still young. You have lots of time to think about it. I hope you change your life."

On February 26, 1992, he was back in the Millhaven reception unit where he was "penitentiary placed" on April 6 in the notorious J Unit, which is reserved for some of Canada's hardest criminal men. On June 29, he returned to court in Belleville to face more charges: possession of housebreaking instruments, theft over, theft under, possession of stolen property, break enter (of a business) and commit (theft). This added another eighteen months. On July 6, he was convicted of robbing the bank in Havelock, east of Peterborough, on November 27, 1991, and got another three years.

On July 23, he got another thirteen months for breaking out of Collins Bay. The judge acknowledged that it wasn't much of a rap for such a serious offence, but considering what he was already dealing with, it would be sufficient.

Then, on October 7, back in Cobourg he got another six years for having "terrorized Colborne Canadian Imperial Bank of Commerce staff," including Cindy Hickman, as he stole $8,050 the previous November 20.

The lead story in the Cobourg *Daily Star* on October 8, 1992, by reporter Valerie MacDonald, presented some contrasting images.

Ty pleaded guilty to the offence while "wearing hand and feet shackles and guarded by two OPP officers."

Crown Prosecutor David Thompson told Judge Jenkins that Conn had entered the bank wearing earflaps and makeup "changing the colour of his skin." He was armed and told everyone not to move or he would "blow their f . . . ing heads off." He then went behind the counter and took cash from two of the tellers' drawers.

After the sentencing, one of the OPP guards remarked to the reporter that "he seems like such a nice guy."

Heading back to Millhaven after his October 7 court appearance, it was all a bit too much to comprehend. Even the corrections system would need months to get an accurate tally of the total sentence they were dealing with.

Ty Conn was only twenty-five years old. All he knew was that the sentence ahead of him was for a period of time well beyond the length of the life behind him. It was really quite overwhelming.

In May 1993, Tyrone Conn, FPS 690154B, received a memorandum from Corrections Canada's chief of sentence management informing him that, after consultation with the attorney general's department in Ottawa, "your sentence calculation has been amended to . . . a revised term of 44 years, 3 months, 22 days."

That was the bad news. The good news was that they were counting from June 2, 1987. Six years down, he thought. Thirty-eight to go. Then they recalculated it again. This time it came to forty-seven years, four months and six days.

CHAPTER TEN

Three Wishes

His three wishes are to be free, to have no compulsion to commit crimes when he needs money, and to have a family.

Dr. Murray Brown
Saskatchewan Penitentiary
March 26, 1993

He wrote me saying "I really want to hear something good. Tell me about school. Tell me about your life." And it made me so sad when I got the letter because it was so unlike him to do that. I never got letters from him that sounded hopeless.

He asked me once to take some pictures of a river . . . and send them to him. I took pictures of ducks and sent him the pictures. He was so happy with them. After that he always wanted me to send him pictures. Just anything outside.

"P," a friend, 1999

I .

FOR SOMEONE WHOSE LIFE WAS SWIRLING rapidly out of control and about to disappear down the toilet of justice, he seemed to have been in remarkably good cheer. According to the *Ottawa Citizen* of February 21, 1992, he was "smiling and relaxed looking" as he absorbed a sixteen-year prison sentence for a flurry of charges relating to his December robberies in Ottawa and Toronto.

A contemporary newspaper photograph presents a more appropriate image. He is handcuffed and closely escorted by a large and angry-looking policeman. His expression is one of solemn hopelessness. He doesn't seem to be afraid, just lost. He looks like somebody with forty years of imprisonment ahead of him.

That, or a similar photograph, had a deep impact on at least one person who saw it. Most people who met him found him easily and instantly likeable. And one young Ottawa woman who saw his picture in the paper obviously fell in love with it.

Ty Conn was a study in contrasts. Handsome and bad, materialistic and generous, a thief with a conscience, dangerous but unsullied by violence. His appearance and his story were the stuff of tragic romance. He was obviously available and, for the foreseeable future, settled down.

Such contradictions are sometimes irresistible to people who are sentimental or burdened by loneliness and idealism or the need to fix things. And sometimes people who act on such sentiment risk causing great harm to themselves and even to the object of their affections.

In February 1992, Ty Conn was an emotional mess. The capacity for self-loathing carried out of a loveless childhood was now fully realized by the awareness that he had failed miserably at the one vocation that he thought would fulfil his need to make a living and to rebel at the same time. Crime is, by definition, deviant. Deviance, no matter how we analyze it, is a product of some kind of failure, social or personal. Ty Conn finally had to admit to himself that he was a failure even at failure.

He had a staggering prison sentence and it gave him a certain cachet in the prison subculture. It made a hell of a starting point for conversations. But, considered in the privacy of a locked cell, it made him want to throw up. There was a real chance that he wouldn't get out before he was fifty years old. There was a pretty good chance that he'd be on parole and under scrutiny until he was sixty-five. Among the fourteen thousand prisoners in the federal system, the typical inmate was thirty-three years old, a robber, serving forty-six months. Ty was twenty-five, a robber, doing more than forty-seven years. One of his pals at Millhaven was in for killing somebody. He was doing eight years. There was something wrong with that picture.

Who in her right mind would want to get involved with somebody carrying that kind of baggage? It was a long way from the first thing on his mind when he got a letter from the young woman who had seen his photo in the paper. He was starved for affection. He needed some kind of a stake in the future to make the present tolerable. He wasn't about to question the motives or the mental health of someone who was offering it.

He never disclosed her name, just the effect she had. She surfaced at a time when he was coming to terms with the realization that fate had never, in his entire life, shown a single kindness. Fate was perversity personified. Fate owed him a favour. And then the letter came. He responded.

It was, at first, the cautious and superficial chit-chat of pen pals. A feeling-out for mutuality, common interests, probing for a place to set the footings on which to build a friendship or maybe more. Maybe if he'd been more mature and healthier emotionally it wouldn't have meant so much. Coming as it did when his self-esteem was in a deficit position, the new friendship became a lifeline.

For the first time in a long time the old escape fantasies disappeared. He started to make optimistic calculations: with perfect behaviour and some luck he could hope for a chance to make his case before a parole board in ten or eleven years. The subject of marriage came up and he thought it was a serious possibility. He had, for the first time, a trustworthy accomplice in the perfect escape plan.

It's futile to speculate where the relationship might have led. It might well have had infinitely more potential than the young Ottawa woman realized. Ty Conn, for all his unhappiness and for all his crimes, was a relatively healthy young man. Internal prison reports consistently describe him as a highly motivated individual who got along well with everyone, inmate and officer alike. The former case-management officer at Collins Bay, Rob Clarke, used words like "sensitive," "intelligent" and "articulate."

"Tyrone was always what was considered a model inmate. Very polite, very respectful and well mannered. He would help other inmates. He was a tutor at the school in Collins Bay . . . and I think helping out in the institutional library. Things like that."

Another female acquaintance, whom we shall call "P,"

knew him then and was intrigued and, in a way, infatuated by him. But for reasons of her own she was determined to keep the friendship platonic, which in retrospect was wise, at least for her.

"All you had to do was have a conversation with him to know that he wasn't the typical con in jail. I did and even back when I first met him I thought, 'Wow, what are you doing here? You just don't belong here. You can do so much more than this.'

"He always impressed me as a person who got lost. He tried to find the right way and I would always say to him, about escaping and stuff . . . 'Why are you doing this? Because you're just making it worse for yourself.'

"And he'd say these really good things like 'I know it's wrong and I know I shouldn't do it.' And I'd tell him, if you break out, people will never see you in a good light. And getting out and robbing a bank is even worse, because you're just saying to people, look, I'm exactly what you think I am.

"And it really bothered him that people saw him in that way. It really bothered him that people saw him as just another convict, just another low-life. He never wanted people to see him that way, but he didn't know how to get them to see him another way."

His conversations and correspondence with "P" seemed to reinforce a flickering resolve to come up with a new plan for salvaging what was left of his life. However, much of it was doomed to be undone by another young woman who, in retrospect, seems to have had no sense of the volatility of the emotional compound with which she was experimenting.

She visited him at Millhaven several times and they were beginning to think ahead toward the possibility of conjugal visits. Prisons like Millhaven have secure living units where families and couples who are either married or in a stable (at least one-year-old) relationship can spend time together in privacy. The units are called "trailers." Trailer visits are precious to inmates, and because they're discretionary privileges, they encourage civility and stability in the population.

It was shortly after they started discussing trailer visits that she got cold feet and decided to break off the relationship. Sometime during the summer of '92, he got the Dear John letter.

The effect was devastating. He slipped into a profound depression during which he bungled an attempt to hang himself in his cell. Then he withdrew to that safe place from which he regarded everybody with distrust, especially people from the street who seem incapable of relating to others without groping toward superficial insights which inevitably turn into judgments.

But he knew he couldn't stay there for long. It was too dark and it was too painful. And so it wasn't very long before he was once again studying the perimeters of his nasty little world, wondering what, if anything, awaited on the other side.

2.
———

MILLHAVEN DOESN'T HAVE WALLS. IT has a pair of high chain-link fences with barbed-wire spurs and coils of razor wire on top running in parallel around the perimeter of the institution. Something about these fences makes them more daunting than a wall. It is more difficult to get over a fence because there are two barriers instead of one. Fences are transparent, both sides visible at the same time. You can't run along the top of a fence and it is extremely difficult to go over a high one. But it is easier to go through one than it is to go through a thick stone wall.

Some time in early autumn of 1992, Ty once again began translating fantasies of escape into what would later look incriminatingly like an active plan. He was working as a clerk in the Millhaven social development office and had access to a computer. Authorities would later find, encrypted in the hard drive, the elements of either a novel about a prison break or a real plan in progress.

There were lists of tools, clothing and disguises necessary for a successful escape attempt. There were names, addresses and phone numbers of people to remember in the event of a flight to the outside. There was also information on how to acquire a passport and, suspiciously, a list of recent deaths of people who were twenty-five years old.

It is difficult to imagine a serious escape artist entrusting the details of a flight plan to an institutional computer. Which raises the possibility that it wasn't a real plan at all, but just an exercise in literary doodling. He was constantly sketching plot lines for novels and screenplays and collecting raw information that would lend authenticity to the thrillers he hoped one day to write.

He would, during his long incarceration, be called upon frequently to explain worrying files discovered in his own computer: particulars on design and function of firearms and explosive devices, hydroponic production of marijuana, hostage taking.

On the other hand, in the fall of '92 he was not feeling particularly constructive or creative, and it is entirely possible that he had also lost some of his innate capacity for common sense. Subsequent events seemed to confirm both possibilities.

Saturday, November 21, 1992, was damp, and the chill in the air made your bones ache. It wasn't particularly surprising when guards on the northeast edge of the Millhaven complex saw a fire flickering in a distant corner of the exercise yard that night. Guys just trying to stay warm. Let them have it for a little while.

What they couldn't see was that at a particularly dark section of the fence far away from the fire, a small group of inmates were huddling on the ground and one of them was snipping through the wire. As the exit hole neared completion somebody on the far side of the yard prodded the bonfire causing the flames to leap. The guards, focused on the now blazing fire, didn't notice that about a dozen of the seventy-five inmates who had been taking the air in the yard were now scrambling through the hole in the fence and sprinting through a loading zone called the Sally Port.

Many found places to hide among the empty packing cases and debris that was stored there, while four of their number headed for the Sally Port gate and furiously began cutting at the thick wire that was the final barrier between them and the outside world. Once through, it would be every man for himself, and there were parked vehicles just outside the gate and the woods beyond, offering the faint hope of freedom.

But everything was happening too fast. An alarm began to blare. There were security vehicles and armed men closing in on the area, people shouting. Some of the would-be escapers were already heading back toward the yard where a new situation was developing. The last to give up were the four at the gate and they hustled toward the yard only to discover another group of inmates had hacked another hole in the fence near the health-care centre. There was the sound of smashing glass as they assaulted the medical facility, presumably to get access to the pharmacy and all the goodies one would expect to find there.

The escapade quickly fizzled, however, as increasing numbers of guards arrived and began herding the prisoners back to their cells. Ty Conn was later identified by "sources" as being one of the four main instigators.

It would not go down as one of the great escape efforts of Canadian penal history, and it was quite out of character for an escaper who, on previous escapes, always preferred to work alone. He always maintained that he did not initiate the Sally Port uprising but that he found it irresistible once it got underway. It had a quality of recklessness that resonated in his miserable soul.

The authorities at Millhaven were not inclined to entertain any doubts about his role. He was a known escape risk. Prison escapes are an administrative nightmare. The public gets riled up. When escapers reoffend, sometimes violently, politicians get on their high horses and suddenly become experts on corrections, though rarely with any useful results. They start agitating for more repression, more punishment. And that doesn't work. It makes good people bad and bad people worse. It feeds the anger and worsens the neuroses and personality disorders that offenders bring with them to the institutions.

People who are always dreaming about escape are a big pain in the ass for everybody, including themselves. Even if he was only marginally involved, Ty had given the institution an excuse to get rid of him. And if they needed any more cause to seal his future, he handed it to them on February 25, 1993, while they were still sorting out the administrative aftermath of the November 21 incident.

As a favour to another bank robber, Ty had agreed to take the fall for a robbery he hadn't done. They had calculated that the courts really couldn't punish him any more, so he readily agreed to show up in Ottawa to claim that his pal was innocent and that he was the culprit. However, while he was cooling his heels in the Ottawa detention centre awaiting his moment in court, guards conducting a routine search discovered a handcuff key.

A handcuff key? Sure, he had a handcuff key. Lots of inmates had them. They were easy to make. He vehemently denied that he'd been planning to use it to get away. It was more like a good-luck charm. A status symbol, etc., etc. But nobody was listening any more.

On March 8, 1993, under heavy escort, he was bundled off to the old penitentiary in Prince Albert, Saskatchewan, where Corrections Canada maintained one of two Special Handling Units for the most difficult inmates in the country. The other one was in the Archambault Institution in Quebec, a place with a frightening history. The SHU in Prince Albert (which has since reverted to regular security status) was a thousand miles away from the only personal support he had (his mother and half-brother). It was Canada's most secure prison, and if his goal in life had been to become an élite criminal, time spent in a super-maximum security SHU would help him earn that status.

But the SHU was supposed to be a dead end. It might make him seem like a élite criminal, but "élite prisoner" was probably a more accurate description of what he was becoming.

The SHU was designed for Canada's most dangerous and incorrigible offenders. The message conveyed to an offender at the SHU is that, as matters now stand, you are never going to be fit to live among free citizens. Ty Conn was neither dangerous nor incorrigible. But he was an institutional problem, an escape risk, so he belonged at the SHU with the lifers and the psychos and the hopeless.

It was, probably, the darkest moment of his life since that day almost fifteen years earlier—December 27, 1978—when he had been legally banished from the Conns' home and made a ward of the Crown. He was still living as a ward of the Crown and it was beginning to look like a certainty that he would die one.

Paradoxically, the SHU, considered in retrospect, may well have been exactly what he needed at that moment in his life.

3.

AN OUTSIDER'S FIRST IMPRESSION of the SHU is one of calm and order. The Prince Albert facility had eighty beds for the fifty-eight inmates. They were monitored at every moment and every movement by seventy-one guards, most of them armed. A visitor to the SHU couldn't help but be struck by the quiet. It almost seemed empty. The sense of efficient order and control all but banished any awareness of the real purpose of the place: to segregate a lot of extremely bad people from society and from other prison inmates. To the visitor, it might have been a very strict school or a very secure monastery.

Living there was another matter. In his 1996 survey of the corrections system, *The Slammer,* Kevin Marron observed that "prisoners in the SHU are . . . guarded more closely than most caged animals.

"SHU inmates are buried so deeply in the prison system, so cut off from everyday life, that they have little left to lose. Many of them have little self control and the SHU provides them with an environment where they do not have to take any responsibility for their actions."

He observed that some inmates actually "thrive" in the flattened existence of the SHU. In the absence of any personal responsibility, they are presented with an opportunity for deep introspection. For some, it is precisely what life has never before proffered. Ty Conn was one of those special cases with both the need and the capacity to benefit from a stretch of quiet time.

On the day that Ty moved into the SHU in Prince Albert, he had to be aware that he was taking up residence with Canada's most loathed sex offender and murderer, Clifford Olson, and the notorious Charles Ng, a serial killer from California.

Six days after he got there, the neo-Nazi Carney Nerland moved in. He'd been serving a four-year sentence for manslaughter for the unprovoked killing of a native trapper named Leo Lachance two years earlier. He'd been doing his time in Stony Mountain Institution in Manitoba, but was back in Prince Albert, where the killing occurred, for a public inquiry.

They had to put him in the SHU because native inmates in the general population seemed inclined to react violently to his racist views. And, even if the natives didn't get him, there were a lot of white cons who were anxious to have an intimate discussion with Carney about how he got his reputation as an RCMP snitch.

Ty Conn was probably appalled by his first impressions of the place: the crushing regimen, blank-faced inmates shuffling around in shackles, the coldness of the guards, the guns. Even the colours were flat beige and brown. Prisoners wore drab-green prison outfits, and in spite of their subdued demeanor always seemed in a state of high alert, ready to spring at the slightest provocation, which could be as inadvertent as a sighting of Olson or a slur from a guard.

He had never seen so many doors. You could hardly move more than a few feet without having to be buzzed through another barrier. He was conscious of being under constant scrutiny, usually at gunpoint. The unseen faces behind darkened glass or behind the gunports could get to you if you gave them a lot of thought. Most movements within the institution were with hands cuffed and ankles shackled.

For the first ninety days there he would have no close contact with other inmates, except, after thirty days, he was allowed to participate in group exercise.

Judging from sparse institutional sources available, he settled in without any serious problem. There was "a minor institutional charge" for which he was punished by five days' loss of access to the common room and the gym. He was seeing a drug and alcohol counsellor, though he didn't have problems with either substance. Eventually he'd enrol in two programs that would have seemed tailor-made for him: a twelve-step program for adult children of dysfunctional families, and a two-week program called "the gift of self-esteem." There isn't any evidence that he got much out of them, except approval from institutional managers who always regard participation in their programs as a good sign.

Ty's self-esteem would probably have received its greatest boost if he'd been able to read over the shoulder of the penitentiary psychologist, Dr. Murray Brown, who took an interest in him shortly after he got there. Dr. Brown's observations weren't exactly flattering, but his insights revealed a high level of personal concern for "the inmate," and that was unusual in Ty's previous experience within the system.

According to institutional records, he opened up readily for the psychologist, speaking candidly about "his past crimes and why he is always thinking of escaping."

Dr. Brown noted that "the inmate was polite and co-operative . . . and eager to tell his story." He was "frank and direct in expressing himself and stream of thought and emotion was appropriate and fitting."

Dr. Brown's report is eerily resonant of the observations, twenty-three years earlier, by another psychologist named Ingrid Bateman, in Belleville, Ontario, when she assessed a little boy of startling charm and intelligence for the Picton Children's Aid Society. Ernie Hayes, a.k.a. Stephen Wannamaker, a.k.a. Ty Conn, hadn't lost much of his charm or his wit for all the misadventures of the intervening years.

"On the Raven's Standard Progressive Matrices . . . he obtained a score placing him in the very superior range of mental ability. His raw score surpassed that of 98 per cent of his age peers. This non verbal measure is often thought of as measuring inductive reasoning ability and intellectual flexibility. His display of verbal comprehension ability, conceptualization and expression during the subsequent clinical interview was judged by this interviewer to be decidedly above average."

Personality testing, not surprisingly, revealed some old scar tissue, "a certain amount of significant psychological and emotional stress," which can make people who score as he did, "moody, changeable, dissatisfied, opinionated, restless, unstable and self-critical."

"At the same time," Dr. Brown added, "these individuals also have good ego strength, independence, self-reliance and a wide variety of coping skills to deal with ordinary problems in daily life."

His report, which was dated March 26, 1993 (six weeks after Ty Conn arrived in Prince Albert), continued: "Individuals who obtain similar profiles often exhibit situational depression and agitation in response to some external problem or difficulty. Problems and complaints often include social acting and societal or family problems and substance abuse problems. These individuals are often hostile and resentful and perceive rules and regulations as unduly restrictive. Such people tend to be impulsive, unreliable, egocentric and irresponsible.

"The findings also indicate an individual who feels depressed, unhappy, sad, and pessimistic about the future. Such a person often feels inadequate, helpless, and lacking in self confidence. There were further observations to suggest feelings of alienation, depression and despair and the conclusion that life is not worth while. Such an individual is likely to brood and cry easily."

It must have been a startling experience for Ty Conn. In an environment which, in his own later estimation, was "the worst place in Canada," a stranger who worked for the joint was actually leading him through a thicket of emotional and psychological underbrush that had been baffling and confusing and tearing at his psyche for years. It would become, in retrospect, a crucial turning point.

It *was* the worst place in Canada. But Ty Conn became one of those prisoners who actually grew in the SHU, not because of the repression or the elimination of personal identity, but because of something much more basic. It should have happened a lot earlier in his life, and without such a horrendous prologue: the personal interest of a few concerned individuals, people with the time and training to explore deep questions and issues about who he was and how he got there.

Miraculously, it would be at the SHU, in the arid badlands of corrections, that new growth began.

4.

A DEFINING CHARACTERISTIC OF PRISON goofs and other undesirables is that they whine a lot. Conversation seldom goes far before they're talking about their bad luck and experiences with all kinds of systemic injustice. Ty found, after he finished his initial ninety days of isolation, that you even ran into goofs at the SHU.

There was a guy there twenty-two years into a life-to-twenty-five sentence, and he was in the SHU because he'd killed two inmates and wounded "countless others." He was wanted in the U.S. for murder. Yet he couldn't resist telling anybody who would listen that he was an innocent and misunderstood man. He was even bothering Ruben Carter's organization, AIDWYC (Association in Defence of the Wrongfully Convicted). He was, in Ty's opinion, "guilty as hell," but kept boring people with claims of innocence.

He was a whiner and a bore, and nobody wants either label in prison. A bad encounter with the wrong person can get you killed.

One of Ty's closest friends at the SHU was Robert Ford, a thirty-six-year-old lifer, a one-time cocaine king in the Comox Valley of B.C. who had been convicted of murder. Ty wasn't ordinarily impressed by drug dealing or killing, but there was one entry on Ford's résumé that he just loved: an escape from the maximum-security Kent Institution near Matsqui in June of 1990 . . . by helicopter.

It was one of those unbelievable scenes, right out of the movies: the chopper swept in and hovered over the industrial yard for forty seconds while the inmate and a buddy scampered from the soccer field, past a sweat lodge, over a fence and aboard, and off into the wild blue.

For all his trouble, he was only out for two days when they caught him on a little island in the middle of Harrison Lake. But it was a display that would earn him the respect of convicts wherever his name was mentioned aloud forevermore. He and Ty were natural buddies. Ambitious escapers who got caught.

Ford was "solid." Cons who do their time stolidly and with appropriate contempt for the judgment of "the system" stand out as solid people. To be solid is to merit respect. To be respected is to be safe. That was how Ty Conn wanted to be regarded, and so he made sure to avoid any kind of self-reference that could be interpreted as complaining. Most of the people in a prison, including the people who worked there, had enough problems of their own without having to listen to some whiner feeling sorry for himself. "Own up to the crime and put up with the time" became his personal motto.

It was a commendable display of integrity and it guaranteed him a lot of respect from other cons who were also aware of his record of escaping and robbing banks. Most of them would have been less impressed had they been able to read his mind—or witness his inner struggle to turn his self-image and his life around.

From the early stages of his self-consciousness, Ty Conn regarded himself as a reject and a thief. He was aware of his own intelligence but felt it had no purpose other than to help him avoid punishment for his inevitable transgressions long enough to enjoy some of the fruits of his wickedness. He was, somehow, predestined for deviance. His life was, therefore, programmed to become a series of unhappy consequences probably ending in violent death. The only joy he would ever know would be in the brief and unpredictable intervals between episodes of punishment.

His life had become, not surprisingly, a self-fulfilled prophecy of doom. The project, as defined by Dr. Brown at the Saskatchewan Pen, was to somehow get behind that wall of twisted certainties and find out who he really was and what he was really worth, beyond his innate value as a human creature.

Ty spoke readily and objectively about his early life. He related that he'd been adopted. That "from an early age" he stole food and sweets. That he graduated to stealing money to buy things and quickly discovered that when he shared his ill-gotten goodies, others rewarded him with their approval and that made him feel worthwhile. Eventually he was breaking into places and stealing food and clothing. At fourteen he was sent to a training school for stealing a car. That started him on the road to the SHU.

Dr. Brown must have heard a thousand such stories in his time. But he hadn't heard many that were so well and compellingly told. He wasn't used to hearing them in the absence of self-serving excuses or attempts at manipulating him. And he wasn't accustomed to hearing them in such circumstances from the son of a psychiatrist.

"He described his adoptive mother as 'insane,' who once slashed her wrists and who was an alcoholic . . .

"Mr. Conn described himself as coming home terrified and on most days would stay in after school to avoid the environment at home."

As bank robbers go, he was an odd specimen: "Mr. Conn now claims he realizes he scared 'the shit' out of people. He relayed he was in a store once when a robbery occurred and he was scared. However, he said, he can suppress his feelings of empathy if he himself is doing the robbing. [But] he is not thrilled the way he once was if he can get away with the robbery. In contrast, he is worried about being caught . . . there is no partying afterward.

"His three wishes are to be free, to have no compulsion to commit crimes when he needs money, and to have a family."

This, for a therapist in a penitentiary, is a hopeful sign. Of course, such sentiments are unoriginal and easy to utter. They are only significant if the inmate means them and if they represent a new development in self-consciousness and

a genuine commitment to change. Dr. Brown and the rest of
the team at the s н u would have two and a half years to find
out whether or not Tyrone Conn really meant what he said.

5 ·

TY CONN TOOK HIS TELEVISION SERIOUSLY. His interests
favoured information programming. He rarely missed newscasts in the evenings and tried to watch the magazine and
documentary shows—*60 Minutes, Witness, Venture* and *W5*—
whenever he could. One of his regulars and favourites was
the cbc's flagship, *the fifth estate.*

He tuned in late on the night of April 12, 1994, and was
immediately startled by the sound of a man shouting
obscenities and abuse. And when he turned to watch, he was
chilled to see that the target of the verbal fusillade was a
skinny boy who seemed to be caught in a posture of cringing
defiance that Ty remembered all too well.

As the onslaught by a large man in a jacket and ball cap
continued, he could feel deep emotional tremors. The brutal
sounds and the image of the unfortunate boy tore at soft tissue in the dark recesses of his own memory. He couldn't take
his eyes from the screen. And when the program broadened
its sweep to include a group of teenage delinquents in a
group home called Portage, near Elora, Ontario—sad boys
incarcerated for thievery and vandalism and violence—he had
the raw feeling that he was watching his own life unfolding.

He was one of more than a million Canadians that night
who tuned in to watch a documentary called "The Trouble

with Evan," a two-hour special on the effects of verbal abuse. He would become one of more than four thousand people to respond to the show with letters, faxes and phone calls.

"The Trouble with Evan" was the brainchild of a gifted Scottish-born television producer named Neil Docherty. When his wife, Nina, died of breast cancer in 1993, Docherty became the single parent of two small boys. He had always been a thoughtful and participatory father, but he quickly realized that raising a couple of bright and active children alone presented challenges that he'd never thought much about before.

Parenting is stressful, but stress management in the home is generally random and improvised on the spot by people who are already stressed out. Stress is a recognized problem in most occupations, but it's usually up to individual parents to become aware of the potential for conflict in the emotionally intense relationships with their kids. And it invariably falls to individual parents to do something about it before the stress translates into abusive behaviour.

Social norms and the laws of the land mandate severe sanctions for physical abuse. But what about the more common varieties? What of the psychological and verbal bullying that people too frequently indulge in, not necessarily from any particular malice or cruel intent, but just out of ordinary frustration?

There wasn't much likelihood that the good-natured Docherty was going to become an abusive parent, verbal or otherwise. But as a journalist, he was soon asking a lot of questions. The big one had to do with the quality of the social resources available to assist those parents who, for lack of luck or wisdom, find themselves overwhelmed by the task of properly raising their children. "The Trouble with Evan" was the final product of these inquiries.

He'd met a couple named Karen and Mike who were at their wits' end because of the incorrigible behaviour of their eleven-year-old son, Evan. They were in a parenting course learning how to cope with him. Docherty persuaded them to let him monitor the effectiveness of the course by installing motion-sensitive video cameras in their home. The cameras would record routine encounters between Evan and his parents and perhaps reveal improvements in technique and results as they progressed through their parenting program.

Docherty was unprepared for what the implacable cameras would reveal. Soon the videotapes were piling up on his desk. The material extended to many hours of raw footage. But random checks were exposing an unexpected and disturbing situation, something so intensely private that Docherty wasn't sure he should continue watching, never mind recording it.

Evan's problems, it was beginning to appear, were about more than Evan. A significant factor seemed to be the troubled relationship between Mike (who was Evan's stepfather) and Karen, and the violence of Mike's mouth.

Eventually Docherty and an associate producer on the project, Sheila Pin, went to see Karen and Mike to explain that the tapes were beginning to show a situation they'd been unprepared for, and that maybe they should reconsider their decision to take part in the documentary. The focus was unavoidably shifting beyond Evan's behaviour. As the situation was unfolding, Karen and Mike could find themselves as much in the spotlight as Evan was.

To the surprise of Docherty and Pin, the parents were keen to continue the project, hopeful that it might lead to improvements in their family life.

A crew from *the fifth estate,* also under Neil Docherty's direction, had simultaneously been taping at the Portage group home for young offenders. Portage had a program for young people who had abusive family backgrounds and who felt there might be a connection between family failures and abuse and their subsequent criminal behaviour. The stories of their early lives at home soon began to echo the situation that was unfolding in front of a couple of video cameras in Evan's home.

Inevitably, the two projects converged. CBC executives agreed to clear the network of commercials for two hours on the night of April 12 and move the national news (then seen at 9 p.m.) to 10 so they could run, uninterrupted, what they realized would be one of the most disturbing and controversial documentaries in a long time.

The reaction was swift. Telephone lines were blocked as the callers rushed to their phones and fax machines with tales from their own experience. There was an avalanche of mail. Docherty and the program managers soon decided that the responses should all be screened carefully. Thousands of people had been touched by the show. The issue of verbal abuse seemed to be sufficiently serious to warrant a followup program.

For three days after the program, Ty Conn couldn't get the sounds and the images out of his mind. It was frightening. The kid, Evan, reminded him of himself when he was eleven and near the end of his rope in the Conn household. Evan stole, and he sought the approval of his friends by various deviant means because he needed it to offset the effects of the verbal battering that he was getting at home. Mrs. Conn rarely if ever used language the way Mike did, but the tone and the effect were the same. And look where it got him.

He'd never considered himself to be unique, but he hadn't given much thought before this to the possibility that there was such a direct link between verbal violence and criminal behaviour. He conducted an informal survey among thirty of his fellow inmates in the SHU, and it revealed that of the fourteen who had been incarcerated as juveniles twelve had experienced turbulent home lives and had gone on to foster care and group homes.

Finally, on April 15, 1994, he sat down and wrote a letter to the program.

"My mother," he wrote, "was the one that was aggressive as opposed to Evan's father, Mike. She used to yell and scream to no end, constantly berating me. I used to join soccer teams, cross country teams, anything to avoid coming home after school.

"The scene where Mike and Karen tell Evan he's no longer a member of the family was reminiscent of my having to stay in my room except for chores, not allowed to play outside, go to movies, snowmobiling, etc., for lengthy periods of time.

"I was once stripped naked at about age 10 and told to leave, go my own way if I wanted to. My father told me I was going to be kicked out at age 16. I eventually came to a point where I tuned them out, wouldn't do what they said, talk to them or . . . care what happened. My adoptive mother was just like Mike except she didn't use vulgar expressions as often. I hated her implicitly!"

Theresa Burke joined *the fifth estate* during the production of the Evan documentary and got the task of sifting through the responses for material that might be relevant for another program. The letter from Ty Conn stood out because it was on the topic of verbal abuse and because of its disclosure that the writer, who was twenty-seven years old, was serving a prison sentence of forty-seven years. She was also impressed by the uninhibited honesty of its tone.

"The over riding emotion I feel in response to your program is sorrow," he wrote. "Sorrow for Evan. I feel that he is being abused in that setting and sadly I see him possibly ending up where I am. The similarities between him and I are eerie. I hope that things work out for him, however."

Theresa Burke referred the letter to Docherty and they agreed that, should there be a follow-up, Conn would be a prime candidate to be approached for an interview.

6.
___

WINTERS IN NORTHERN SASKATCHEWAN can be brutal, but for Ty Conn the summers were worse. It was in the summertime that the air grew humid and the smoke from forest fires infiltrated Prince Albert and the penitentiary, and with his chronic asthma he often felt that he was smothering. Any distraction from the suffocating environment of the SHU would have been welcomed.

In July 1994, he was surprised when a corrections officer informed him that somebody from a television program had been phoning for him. Wanted him to call her back. Collect.

It was entirely up to him. The woman's name was Burke. She worked for the program *the fifth estate*. It was then that he realized it was probably about the letter he wrote back in April.

He'd never talked much about his childhood, except to the occasional social worker and psychologist and, with the exception of Dr. Brown at the Sask Pen, nobody seemed very interested. Theresa Burke, however, seemed extremely interested, and there was a quality of warmth and friendliness in her tone that put him at ease. When she mentioned that she, too, had been adopted as a child, he couldn't resist talking to her.

On July 18 they had a long chat on the telephone about life at the Conns, about the circumstances of his birth and about his criminal behaviour. He was frank and articulate and surprisingly objective. By the end of the conversation he agreed to sign consent forms that would grant Burke access to personal information on file at the Belleville Children's Aid Society and at Corrections Canada. There were more phone calls, and eventually he agreed to be interviewed on television.

The interview took place on September 1, and it should have been a classic. In person his appearance was impressive, and he spoke well and had a story that was unique. *The fifth estate* researchers had already sifted through his criminal records and were surprised to have found no hint of violence, other than the potential for it in his tendency to carry weapons. The fact that he'd always had access to weapons made the knowledge that he'd never used one during all the scrapes he'd been in seem significant. Who was this guy?

Unfortunately, he wasn't prepared to reveal the answer to that difficult question in an hour sitting in front of a video camera. He imposed conditions. His birth mother was not to be approached or mentioned by name. He was to be identified by his first name only. The Conn family was to be left out of it.

Theresa Burke had actually telephoned Dr. Bert Conn to seek verification for some of what she'd been hearing from Ty and reading in his files. He hung up on her without saying a word.

Ty Conn was hesitant speaking on camera about his upbringing, and he seemed unwilling to say anything that would blame other people for his predicament. Yes, his adoptive mother had been abusive. Yes, he seemed to have been the family scapegoat whenever anything went wrong. Yes, it was unfair that when he became hard to handle they dumped him. But he wasn't going to link those facts directly with the consequences of his subsequent choices and actions.

This, he was told, was okay. He didn't have to explicitly blame anybody. Just tell your story. Let people draw their own conclusions. Eventually he divulged enough to flesh out at least part of his file. And a truncated version of his life appeared on a segment of *the fifth estate,* among those of many others who talked of the impact of verbal abuse, on November 1, 1994.

Journalists meet scores of compelling individuals in the course of their work. Journalism is usually about people who are caught up in dramatic events or circumstances. Such relationships, while sometimes intense, are situational and change when situations change, then end. Ty Conn seemed, from the start, to be one of the exceptions.

Perhaps, as happened with the infatuated young woman from Ottawa, some jaded journalists were smitten by the fascinating contradictions between his character and his personal history. He was thoughtful, and his efforts to recall his own troubled history revealed a surprising empathy with people who might, in a less objective telling, have become villains in the tale. He was struggling to be accurate and striving to be fair—or he was pulling the wool over the eyes of some professional skeptics.

On close examination the contrast between what his record said he was and who, up close, he seemed to be was less contradictory than it seemed at first glance. His criminal record had accumulated in a few brief bursts of ill-considered behaviour during the very few days of his life when he was responsible for his own actions.

In thirteen years—since June 1981, when he was fourteen years old—he had been legally at large for a total of 69 days. He had stolen another 131 days of liberty in various absences from youth detention and two futile escapes from Collins Bay Institution. All the other days of that long and vital period in his young life had been spent in a prison of one kind or another. His chances of experiencing another day of freedom, legally or otherwise, in the second millennium were, at best, remote.

He had needs, but they were so complex and their roots so deeply embedded that any kind of friendship could have become perilous for him (because of expectations) and for his friends (because of cumbersome new responsibilities). But it soon became apparent that for him friendship was, in and of itself, a priceless gift. Friendship, in Ty Conn's value system, was not a vehicle for personal improvement. This, in one whose life was so damaged, was the mark of a rare integrity. And so he became a friend to those who met him in the cathartic backwash from "The Trouble with Evan," and the friendship would change everyone involved in it.

7.
___

HE SEEMED TO EXPERIENCE A KIND of epiphany at about that time. Dr. Brown of the Sask Pen had triggered an exercise in profound introspection shortly after his arrival at the SHU. Theresa Burke seemed like a kindred spirit with whom he might explore remote regions in his past. Her own experience, growing up as an adopted child, was a common factor in their lives, not unlike blood or a hometown. Now his self-examination would take on a new intensity.

On September 6 and 7 he produced a torrent of disclosure in the form of two letters to Theresa Burke and a personal mission statement that ran to a length of nearly eight thousand words for his case-management team at the SHU. The longer document set out, more explicitly than ever before, a critical personal assessment of his past and specific goals for the future.

The first letter to Burke was a reflection on the experience of having been interviewed for a television program and why he did it. He couldn't help analyzing his own motives to reassure her, and possibly himself, that his decision to appear hadn't been based on narcissism.

"No doubt I saw it as a novelty," he wrote. "But I don't really think I had some need to see myself or be seen on TV.

I also can't say I did it for the classic reason of helping others. I don't put much faith in testimonials having any effect in changing one's opinion or attitude. I think that sometimes it serves to make people pause and think, but usually people are set in their ways and it takes a lot more than a TV show to change them.

"I certainly hope that maybe something I said could help, but I don't think so. Who knows though? I'm sort of feeling concern for Evan now. After finding out he's in the process of being transferred to Crown wardship. I really hope that he's fortunate to find a place that he fits in. Knowing the CAS that's not likely but I hope he can avoid the feelings of alienation that I felt."

He noted that "if something doesn't happen [for Evan] soon, he'll no doubt end up in contact with the justice system and it seems that once someone gets involved with the justice system there's no looking back."

The second letter, on September 7, was in response to a package of CAS files that Burke had passed on to him. The files contained many revelations, some painful. His letter was ten pages long.

He hadn't known that he'd been adopted in order to give the Conn family a bright and attractive slightly older brother for the baby, Loris Jeanette. And he hadn't known that CAS workers were aware that his placement was less than perfect.

"I find it extremely insightful that it says I was 'miscast' in my role and was 'a scapegoat in a shaky and unsatisfying marriage,'" he wrote in a letter to Burke.

"Of course that affords me the position of being of no blame which isn't entirely true. But for once someone saw another reason for my problems than my behaviour."

He was mortified to read in the CAS documents that he'd been reported for urinating around the Conns' house and that he used to soil and hide his underwear. These disclosures were, apparently, evidence of his deviance and justification for his banishment.

Incontinence, he blustered in his own defence, was a natural consequence of being locked in his bedroom for long periods of time. The accidents only happened in that bedroom and it was only "embarrassment and shame," not some pathological twist, that drove him to hide the evidence.

Overall, the files saddened him, he said. He was surprised that they explicitly validated many of his own observations about his troubled adoptive mother. He, obviously, hadn't been the source for the CAS references to Mrs. Conn's alcohol and emotional problems. He hadn't told anybody because he was certain nobody would believe him. Of course, he couldn't have known that his bitter memories and the CAS workers' careful references to Mrs. Conn were insipid compared to the explicit damnation of the unfortunate woman by her husband during their divorce.

"Seems strange," he said, referring to the CAS comments on Mrs. Conn's troubles and his own return to Crown wardship in 1978, "she's the one with mental problems yet I was the one booted out."

Near the end of this long and confessional letter to Theresa Burke, he assured her that while he had "minor grievances" about his treatment over the years, "I willingly traveled down the path that led me here.

"I don't know what I feel. I'm angered, sorrowful, regretful and depressed. If anything, it reminds me of all I've ruined or missed. I could have had a fuckin' life. But essentially I've thrown most of it away."

In the longer document, written for the corrections managers, he was frank about the futility of virtually all that had gone before in his experience.

He described his criminal activities as "a rather dismal attempt to live my life the way I chose to by thwarting any legal constraints imposed by society."

From the time he went to the training school in Cobourg at age fourteen, his youth had been infected by "romantic notions of a criminal lifestyle" and those notions soon evolved into a conscious decision to rob banks for a living. It was a choice he said he made freely, but one he never felt comfortable with.

"It may sound unlikely but it was very difficult to push myself to do robberies. It became more and more difficult as time went on as opposed to the common belief that it would get easier. The fear of getting caught not only persists during the day I actually commit the act but even days and weeks afterwards."

He'd concluded that it wasn't worth the aggravation. As for escaping, he'd always known it to be futile, but he kept trying because, at best, freedom gave him a taste of the world he'd missed out on. At worst, an escape always carried with it the possibility of a fatal mishap . . . euthanasia for someone who just didn't seem to have the gumption for suicide.

He'd arrived at a point, he wrote, "where I now realize that a parole is my only remaining option and, far off as that may be, it is more concrete and realistic than any of the plans that I have tried in the past.

"Instead of dwelling in a fantasy land where I could envision escape rather than deal with the discomfort I was feeling in a productive way I should have been thinking about being released into the community the easiest way and the most sure way, by getting a parole.

"When I think of all the time I wasted on thinking about the many aspects of escaping and living life on the run I'm filled with a great amount of anger at myself and then embarrassment that I could've been so stupid."

At some point in the summer of '94, having finally rejected the belief that crime offered viable career possibilities, he decided that he'd better explore some more realistic options.

He found computers fascinating and was saving up to buy one. He knew he could excel at computer work, perhaps even as a systems analyst. But he also knew that his criminal background would close off jobs that required high-security clearance.

He felt that his personal background had given him experience and insights that might be useful for work with young offenders. But he knew he wasn't ready for that kind of a commitment just yet. He had a lot more work to do on himself before he could presume to be of any assistance to others who needed and wanted rehabilitation.

Building design and home renovation interested him. He was keen to learn the fundamentals of architecture as well as practical skills in carpentry, masonry and plumbing. He launched a campaign of inquiries to find out how to improve his formal education in order to work in that direction.

He wrote to an open learning institute in British Columbia. He wrote to the Association of Universities and Colleges of Canada for some guidance. He mailed letters to thirty-nine universities across the country, asking for details about their programs. He wrote to the assistant commissioner of Correctional Service Canada (csc) for corrections programs and to the deputy commissioners for the Atlantic, Ontario and Pacific regions about possible vocational programs in their areas. He even wrote to a shop boss at Millhaven about programs there.

As was the case so often in the past, his timing was bad. The csc was cutting back educational and vocational training programs. The system had stopped funding university courses for inmates, and the csc was turning vocational shops into maintenance departments for the institutions.

Most of the people he wrote to looking for help in planning a more productive future didn't even answer his letters.

8.

EVENTUALLY HE FOUND A COURSE that he could study by correspondence. It was a civil engineering technician's certificate program at Fanshawe College in London, Ontario. He'd have to pass fifteen courses in all, thirteen of which he could take through the mail. It would, if he succeeded, get him close to a legitimate occupation if and when the system ever decided to let him out. The csc agreed to pay for the program for as long as he could make passing grades.

In October 1994, obviously impressed by his new attitude, his case managers offered him a deal: continue psychological counselling and the program for adult children of dysfunctional families, and they'd recommend that he be transferred back to a "normal" maximum-security joint in about a year. All things considered, it was a hopeful development.

In December he made an appearance before the National Parole Board. It was a formality. There was no hope, given his recent past, that the board would even remotely consider parole. He knew it would take years to get to that point, but the appearance was worth the time he spent, and in the end he made a good impression on the august group. Conn, they noted afterwards, was an inmate "in the very early stages of expressing motivation to address his major factors of emotional/behavioural instability, long term institutionalization and entrenched criminal attitudes and values."

It wasn't exactly a commendation for the Order of Canada, but given what he was accustomed to, the faintness of the disapproval amounted to high praise.

The daily experience of the Special Handling Unit was perilous for an inmate who was attempting to get a fresh start. He found out late in February 1995 just how easy it was to get in trouble.

While he was eating supper in his common room, two other inmates went after each other with fists and shanks. They struggled and sprawled and eventually landed on his table, scattering the contents of his food tray. As soon as the struggle rolled on past, he tried to retrieve what was left of his meal. He was in the process of wiping spilled food from the place where he'd been sitting when the guards descended and broke up the fight. Then they busted Ty for having picked up what was left of his dumped food, accusing him of destroying evidence.

The natural response of someone on the outside might be "They must have been kidding!" But they weren't. Inmate Conn had to appear in an institutional court to fight the charge. He won. It seemed trivial, but if he'd lost, his hopes for a transfer later in the year would have gone up in smoke.

He was no stranger to prison violence. But the ferocity of violence at the SHU was a response to the intense repression there and the consequent frustration of inmates with deep-seated emotional and psychological problems.

In July 1995, he watched in horror as two inmates set upon a third with knives. Guards stood by watching indifferently as the attackers inflicted at least fifty stab wounds on the victim. Then, assuming that their work was done, the attackers stopped and, as Ty described it later, the guards "just opened the door to allow the victim to crawl out.

"Miraculously the victim survived. He was stabbed in the eye, the heart, one of his lungs, a kidney. One leg was savaged by 20 wounds, and he was wounded in an area that men fear most.

"Amazingly I watched him walk by 9 days later. His eye is OK. Nothing is wrong with his heart etc. The theory is he survived because of the extraordinary physical condition he was in. He was the guy in the best condition in this place.

"I've been a witness to three killings and I've never been so shocked as I was this time. Usually very few strikes are made. But this time it just kept going on, and going on . . ."

9.
―――

ON AUGUST 24, 1995, PSYCHOLOGIST Murray Brown reported that Ty was making commendable progress: his escape fantasies had lessened and he was working out plans for improving himself as he dealt with his formidable sentence.

He was twenty-eight years old. He was obviously approaching a crucial turning point in his life. It is a passage that corrections officers recognize as the beginning of genuine rehabilitation. And it is not uncommon among bank robbers, who are frequently more "normal" than many offenders whose crimes are the result of psychological and emotional ailments and extreme personality disorders.

Robbers seem to outgrow the impulses that shaped choices and behaviour during adolescence and their early twenties and, approaching their thirties, experience a genuine desire to do something constructive with their lives. Ty Conn arrived at that important junction in Prince Albert. With it came a flood of constructive optimism that would survive for almost exactly three years.

On September 20, 1995, he was formally advised that the management of the SHU was recommending that he return to Millhaven as soon as a formal review of his progress could be finished.

LETTER, SEPTEMBER 27, 1995.

I'm starting to think that I'll most likely end up spending another Christmas here. I'm not too concerned about that though . . . Short of killing somebody there's not much that can prevent my transfer [now].

LETTER, OCTOBER 29, 1995.

Hello. I'm now located in Millhaven Inst. I got transferred just a week after my approval. I hadn't expected it to be that quick. I got here on Oct. 11/95 and I am currently being held in segregation because there is a shortage of bed space in the normal population unit of Millhaven. I've heard that it might be six to eight weeks before I get into population. I've been here almost three now. It can't be too much longer.

10.
———

PEOPLE WHO SPEND TOO MUCH time around inmates and criminals seem to develop a prophylactic cynicism. They are quick to spot the insincerity and the deception in jailhouse conversions. They are quick to point out that psychopathy is a common feature of the criminal personality.

Ty Conn was not a psychopath. People with that personality disorder find it difficult, if not impossible, to even fake self-criticism. Ty Conn was self-critical to the point of being tiresome. Psychopaths are consummate liars. Ty Conn, at least as an adult, was passionate about the truth. During a five-year relationship with the authors his disclosures, where they could be cross-checked, were remarkable for their accuracy and their consistency.

It is therefore safe to accept at face value the honesty of his commitment, late in 1995, to reform his outlook and his life. It did not come out of any need to impress the corrections establishment. He'd been in prison long enough to know the futility of that. It came instead from a sudden realization that he wanted to live and to enjoy life, and that the lifestyle he had contrived up until that point was not viable, let alone enjoyable.

He would spend three years working hard to rise above circumstances that were consequences of the failures and the pathologies of many people, including himself. That his efforts were doomed to fail would reveal more about the system in which he was attempting to reform himself than about any failing or duplicity on his part.

CHAPTER ELEVEN

"I Must Have Faith . . ."

I must take it for granted that if I work hard and am sincere about my intentions some will notice and I will inevitably end up with some support along the way. I cannot simply conclude that it is hopeless. Instead I must have faith that there is a possibility . . .

Ty Conn, September 7, 1994

Millhaven Institution has long been one of the most difficult federal penitentiaries to manage. It has had a tumultuous history of rioting and violence and houses the most disruptive and volatile group of maximum security inmates in the Correctional Service.

csc news release, January 13, 1998

I.
___

FOR A YOUNG MAN KEEN ON SELF-IMPROVEMENT it's difficult to imagine a worse place to be than Millhaven

Institution at the end of 1995. The joint was seething with repressed frustrations when he arrived, and it wasn't long before he saw the first of what would be many disturbances during the next two years.

On New Year's Eve forty inmates refused to return from the exercise yard when they were supposed to, at 8 p.m. They had decided to see the arrival of 1996 in the clear air with the stars for a backdrop. It was a harmless, almost poetic gesture. And it was a Sunday night and bone-chilling outside. The guards shrugged it off. If they wanted to freeze their asses out there, let them.

They came in at midnight, their point made. Of course there had to be a counterpoint. Management locked the whole institution down for a few days, allowing only one hour of yard per day, and they punished the fresh-air forty by revoking weight-pit privileges for a week. But in the tit-for-tat culture of Millhaven, it couldn't stop there. All 130 inmates in the general population then decided to lock-down voluntarily for a week. They would stay in their cells, boycotting all prison activities, including the ones they enjoyed—yard, weight pit, visits, etc.

For Ty Conn, just back from the SHU, it made no sense at all. It was, he opined, "childish." But it was just a foretaste of what was to come.

He knew he'd be happier just about anywhere else on the planet, but his options were limited. He was a maximum-security inmate, and except for Kingston Pen, Millhaven was the only place available to him in Ontario. Nobody in his right mind wanted to go to Kingston.

He could have tried for another region. A lot of people were opting for Kent in British Columbia. There was a new joint in Renous, New Brunswick. He had, however, just gone through nearly four years without a family visit and he found he'd missed his mother terribly. Kent was too far away. Renous was closer but was in the middle of nowhere. There was always the new institution in Donnacona, in Quebec, but everything he heard about the prisons in Quebec sent shivers through him. For one thing, they were allegedly dominated by biker gangs, and if you hoped to survive there, you had to pledge loyalty to one of them. He'd have been hard pressed.

There were medium-security institutions like Warkworth and Joyceville and, of course, his alma mater, Collins Bay. But he knew that it would be a long while before any of the people who ran those places would consider him for occupancy, because of his notoriety as an escaper.

As 1996 began, he was resigned to the fact that "the 'Haven" was going to be home for the foreseeable future. And he knew it wasn't going to be easy.

By the end of January 1996, they were locked down again. The inmates discovered that the warden had imposed a collective punishment because one or a few of them were smashing up their food trays. He confiscated $1,200 from the inmate welfare fund to pay for replacements.

Food was always an issue. Food is the only legitimate source of pleasure in the joint. People living on the margins of sensory experience react badly when the food is bad. And there was a consensus at Millhaven that the food had gone seriously downhill ever since the Bath Institution next door, where meals for both places had been prepared when it was minimum security, went up to medium.

Millhaven inmates, since that development, had been getting meals from several serveries located throughout the institution, and nobody was happy about the arrangement. It was general knowledge that the daily budget for feeding an inmate at Millhaven was only $3.40. Probably that was another reason people were smashing the trays early in 1996. In time the protests would escalate.

For the moment, the warden, Jim Blackler, decided that everybody should pay for the foolishness. Inmates decided that the punishment wasn't fair. The protests began slowly. First the prisoners became sullen and cranky. Then they became balky about rules, especially about returning to the ranges and cells from the yard and the gym. Then, one range just above where Ty lived decided to smash up.

They destroyed everything they could get their hands on. They even trashed their microwave, telephone, toaster, washer and dryer. Then, using a heavy, stainless-steel cart for a battering ram, they broke through the locked barrier at the end of the range. Once past it, they turned on a fire hose, and the situation soon became serious for people in the range below.

The first thing Ty thought about when he saw water flooding down a stairwell and pouring into nearby cells was his new computer. He'd been saving pennies and loonies for ages, and he'd finally reached the magic figure of $1,900 and bought a computer and printer.

He managed to put a plastic garbage bag over the computer itself, but as he scrambled to protect the rest of his stuff, he dropped five hundred sheets of computer paper and the computer's mouse in the water. They were ruined. The cell was a mess. Water came through the wall and ruined his new calendar and its lush landscapes from Ireland. A stinking black fluid poured through the ceiling and drenched his bed.

By then guards in riot gear and armed with shotguns were clattering up toward the riotous range, and soon he heard four loud bangs as they launched tear-gas canisters toward the melee. But there was a downdraft and the noxious fumes spread throughout the lower range. He couldn't go to bed because of the mess. His eyes were so runny from the gas he couldn't read. He could hardly breathe. It was going to be a long night.

Near dawn, sitting on the toilet, which was the only dry place left in the cell, and leaning back against the concrete wall with his feet propped on the clean end of his bunk, he fell asleep.

2.

———

LETTER, FEBRUARY 1, 1996.

Dear Linden

Sorry that it's been a while . . .

I'm assuming that we'll be locked up for quite a while which is OK with me. I'm quite sick of seeing most of the faces I see every day and I could use the break for doing schoolwork and to get some reading done. At least as soon as my eyes stop bothering me so much.

Now for the good news. I got approved for a trailer visit with my Ma and I'm assuming it will be sometime in the next two months. That will be a welcome relief for a couple of days. I haven't had one in five years. I'll get to relax, eat some good food, and rap with my Ma. Despite our age difference and the mother/son relationship, I have a good time talking to her. Sort of like a really good friend. I hadn't noticed this previously in our relationship. I've only known her a little over 10 years. Since she found me when I was 18 it's been kind of weird relating to her. Now I guess I'm beginning to feel really comfortable with her, and appreciate her as a part of my life.

3 .
___

LIFE GRADUALLY SETTLED DOWN at Millhaven, at least for a couple of months. Ty was busy with his correspondence courses, upgrading his math. He took on the demanding job of allied co-ordinator, looking after the basic needs of inmates and their grievances involving various departments in the institution. It gave him new insights into the inmate personality. There were more whiners than he'd realized. He couldn't believe how much trivial issues bothered hard-assed cons.

Of course the institution didn't make his job any easier. A lot of the work was with the social development department, which at the time was particularly inefficient and further handicapped by the fact that one of the women who worked there was so frightened of the inmates she could hardly function.

There is no good time to do time, but from 1996 to 1997 in Millhaven was about as bad as anybody could recall.

For about ten years the system had been feeling the impact of a growing public perception that society was becoming more dangerous because of an exponential increase in criminal activity.

There was no solid statistical basis for the neuroses. But that didn't stop budget-conscious police organizations, right-wing ideologues and button-pushing journalists from inflating it and encouraging the notion that the only way to control the criminal hordes was to nab them early and hit them hard. Lock 'em up in places like Millhaven, deny all human comforts, add as much pain and humiliation as the law allowed, and throw away the key.

Incarceration was the answer, and the population of the prison system grew 26 per cent between 1986 and 1987 and 1995 and 1996. There was a major impact on the provincial system (for people serving under two years), but it was compounded in the federal institutions by a simultaneous trend in the parole system. Fewer people were getting out when they were eligible. In the winter months of 1996, there were nearly one thousand non-violent federal inmates occupying penitentiary cells after their parole eligibility dates had passed. Medium-security institutions in Ontario were overcrowded, so there were people stuck in Millhaven who really didn't have to be there.

Rehabilitation programs were overworked and, if you listened to the inmates, they were laughably naïve and ineffectual anyway. Health was a serious concern. Diseases like AIDS and tuberculosis were becoming frightening realities in the prison environment. In tests on 468 prisoners at Kingston Pen in February 1995, 100 inmates showed positive traces of TB. Racial friction and tensions from drug dealing were making daily life perilous. The front-line workers, guards and unit managers, were feeling the lash of inmate anger and frustration—and some of them found it hard to resist lashing back.

Early in April 1996, the entire system was buzzing about a report by Madam Justice Louise Arbour, who had investigated an incident at the Prison For Women (P4W) in Kingston. Guards had used excessive force in extracting women from their cells during a disturbance. There was a national uproar when *the fifth estate* broadcast an institutional video that showed guards manhandling and forcibly stripping the women. Justice Arbour had broadened the inquiry report to offer a damning critique of the whole corrections system.

She charged that the system was crippled by inefficiency, duplicity and contradictions, and there was hardly a con in it who didn't agree with her. The notorious strip search at the P4W was merely symptomatic of a larger unacceptable situation. A system mandated for correction and rehabilitation was dehumanizing people who were already frighteningly flawed.

Ty Conn, with twelve years in the federal system under his belt, had seen the so-called P4W segment on *the fifth estate,* and while he was appalled by the casual brutality, he wasn't surprised or shocked. He knew the scene well. Probably any man in Millhaven could have recounted a similar experience.

"To tell you the truth," Ty Conn wrote, "that tape is pretty tame . . .

"I have been held down by men while female guards looked on. I was naked and forced to do the familiar dance routine that accompanies a strip search. 'Lift your arms . . . shake your hair . . . head up . . . mouth open . . . lift tongue

. . . turn around . . . lift up one foot . . . the other . . . bend over.' All with women looking."

Inmate Dave Biggins at Millhaven would give a similar account to Kirk Makin of *The Globe and Mail*.

"Five or six female staff stand there, seeing you totally naked," Biggins said. "You either let it happen or you go off to seg for three or four months."

One might have argued that female officers passively watching a strip search isn't quite the same thing as a gang of men, dressed in Star Wars' outfits wrestling women to the floor and using scissors to cut their clothes off. The overall point, however, is valid: humiliation is gender blind, and it can leave a harmful imprint on anybody, man or woman, child or adult.

Prisons have changed a lot in the modern era of corrections. In the words of the French writer, Michel Foucault *(Discipline and Punish, The Birth of the Prison)* "[t]he expiation that once rained down upon the body must be replaced by a punishment that acts in depth on the heart, the thoughts, the will, the inclinations."

This might be an improvement over the maiming and mutilation that characterized earlier forms of punishment, but it is still punishment and it doesn't seem to have been any more effective in correcting human behaviour than the rack and the gallows. In fact, punishment that "acts in depth on the heart" can have social consequences as frightening as those arising from the inflicting of physical pain and even death. In the absence of programs and attitudes that will rehabilitate "the heart, the thoughts, the will, the inclinations," people will usually come out of prison worse than when they went in.

As spring approached in 1996, Ty Conn tried to get out of Millhaven by a more conventional method than his past hook-and-ladder technique. He submitted a formal request for a transfer to another region—Quebec or the Atlantic. He'd have a better chance of improving his security status in a completely new setting, he thought. And he was right. People in other regions wouldn't have felt personally burned by his past escapes. But they turned him down anyway.

A transfer at that time would unquestionably have improved the quality of his life. And though nobody could have known it at the time, a transfer might have made all the difference in the world to the length of it.

4.

LETTER, APRIL 27, 1996.

Dear Theresa

We are currently locked down due to a guy getting stabbed in the gym yesterday. Apparently he is still alive but I tell you he must have friends upstairs because the wounds he received should have guaranteed death several times over.

I just had a private visit with my Ma . . . I enjoyed it but I hadn't had one in five years and I really noticed something. I'm quite used to being alone and having someone else around you is strange to say the least. I guess it was slightly uncomfortable to share your privacy with someone else. It kind of spooked me cause I wonder if this is a sign of things to come. Will I always feel strange when I'm not alone?

5 .

THE JOB OF ALLIED CO-ORDINATOR WAS getting to him. Half in jest he remarked that he was beginning to understand the real reason most of the convicts were in the custody of the Crown: "They could never take care of anything themselves."

But he was soon to move on to another assignment. The federal government was funding a pilot project in Millhaven, a furniture shop in which inmates would be employed making desks, chairs and beds under contract. There would be special wage incentives to induce inmates to work in the new shop. Level 1 pay in prison, basically for doing nothing, was $1.60 a day. Depending on the nature of their chores, inmates could earn $20 to $30 a week working. In the new shop, it would be possible to earn as much as $125 per week.

This was crucial for Ty. He'd been advised that the government would no longer pay for his correspondence courses and he was going to have to find the means to pay the shot himself. The new shop was a godsend.

And by May he was in it, at least on a probationary basis. Probation was just fine since he'd been afraid that his reputation as a security risk would have disqualified him right away. He loved the work. It was "hard monotonous and dirty" but it made the time fly, and he looked forward to the paycheques.

After a two-week trial, they approved him for regular employment in the new shop. Institutional reports on his attitude and behaviour were glowing. A shop instructor gushed that "he's almost too good" at the work. They were having trouble keeping up with him. The reports indicate that he was also working hard on his studies and was "excellent with staff."

In early June he discovered that he was actually making less money in the furniture shop than he'd been making in his old job. But he resolved to hang in.

6.

LETTER, JUNE 11, 1996.

Dear Linden

I just heard a news conference from Justice Minister Rock and he's put forward a bill to change section 745 of the Criminal Code which outlines sentencing for first degree murder. He wants the 15 year review that is present in the current law to be put in the hands of a judge who will first decide whether a guy gets the chance to get the review.

Then the 11 members of the jury will have to be unanimous in their decision rather than the current two-thirds majority. Multiple murderers will be ineligible for any type of review and will have to complete the 25 years before ever seeing a parole board. The best part is that, aside from the multiple murder ineligibility, he wants this law if passed to be retroactive, essentially denying most guys the chance to ever see a judicial review.

I figure that will go over real good with the 2,000 guys sentenced to life with eligibility at 25 years.

On the news shows that I watched tonight it said that of those 2,000 only 31 have been granted a parole as a result of their review and only one has

subsequently been charged with a criminal offe...
namely armed robbery!

These are pretty impressive statistics yet I still hear
people screaming about criminals getting out early and
killing their loved ones. Every year or so some high
profile case hits the news and, wham! Canada is
besieged by rampaging criminals.

Statistics consistently show both the crime rate and
the murder rate declining yet no one will believe
them. They'll believe politicians who consistently lie,
but they won't believe the people who have absolutely
nothing to gain from lying about the statistics.

Well, enough of my preaching for today, I guess . . .

I'm doing as well as can be expected. Things in
here are either bad or good, but neither lasts for very
long and, in between, you find yourself constantly
awaiting a change in either direction just to liven
things up a bit.

7.

HE WAS STILL SUBJECT TO MOOD SLUMPS, but even when
he'd slip close to depression, he seemed to avoid the old
coping mechanism of dreaming up escape plans. Rare disciplinary infractions, however, were enough to keep alive the
suspicion among penitentiary staff that he remained a serious
escape risk.

In August 1996, they found a dismantled fan in his cell.
The motor from a small fan, in the resourceful world of

prison, can easily become a grinding tool. A grinding tool can be used for making other tools or weapons. He denied the allegation that he was planning a break-out, insisting that he was simply repairing the appliance. It was, after all, August, and it was hot and humid and he had asthma. And the thing wasn't working! They cleared him.

Events that bring significant change seldom occur fully developed. Like wedges, they start thin-edge first. Anyone studying Millhaven Institution in the summer of 1996 would have noticed that the primary functions—incarceration of maximum-security offenders and the classification of new admissions to federal corrections—were at cross purposes, and you could see the consequences in the new furniture shop.

The need to keep the two populations apart to prevent violence made the place cumbersome to manage at the best of times. Prisoners from one unit or the other had to be moved in small groups for yard or social functions or meals. Simple transactions took a lot of time.

Because prisoners picked up their food and ate in their cells, mealtime became a particular challenge. Getting them to and from the serveries required a plan that prevented them from bumping into each other. One consequence was that people like Ty who were working in the shops were losing a lot of their work time just getting to and from the workplace.

The basic problem was that they lived in J Unit, with the solid cons, but the shop was closer to A Unit, where the untouchables lived. You could lose a couple of hours of your work day just manoeuvring the short distances between home and meals and work.

Then somebody got a bright idea: move the shop workers to a new range in A Unit. They needed extra space anyway, since new admissions to the Millhaven population were being kept in segregation for months at a time just waiting for space in J Unit. The idea was not popular.

The shop workers were assured that the new range, 2D, would really be a part of J Unit and sealed off from reception, and there was no real danger that they'd be tainted with the stigma of A Unit. And, of course, in the final analysis, they really had no choice in the matter. Take it or leave it. If you want to work in the shop, go live on 2D.

The paycheques had improved substantially. He was earning about $110 a week after taxes. He decided to hold his nose and accept the move.

He was, in general, making a highly positive impression on the management of Millhaven. Everything about him, except his criminal record, seemed so normal.

Millhaven case managers knew that to get a meaningful parole hearing Conn would have to show evidence of rehabilitation. But they couldn't see much to rehabilitate—except the story of his life. And it was too late for that.

A staff psychologist finally suggested, theoretically Ty thought, that there might be something useful for his rehabilitation available at the Regional Treatment Centre (RTC), a psych unit located inside Kingston Penitentiary. He didn't realize that she was discussing a plan and not a theory. Or that it would happen so fast.

Late one day in mid-August she advised him that he was leaving for the RTC the next morning. What happened next was like a scene from *One Flew Over the Cuckoo's Nest.*

8.

LETTER, SEPTEMBER 4, 1996.
Dear Linden

I'm not exactly certain if I've described the particular nature of Kingston Penitentiary to you. It is a Protective Custody Institution where those individuals that cannot survive are housed. Either they've 'checked in', which means they've requested such protection for whatever reasons, debts, fear etc. Or they are people who simply couldn't survive in general population, such as sex offenders and informants.

RTC is a building/institution housed within the walls of KP but is strictly segregated from the population of KP. I arrived to find myself housed in an ancient brick and stone cell which ironically was huge. Open bar cells are the norm at KP since it dates back to 1830.

I was housed on a range with about 12 guys . . . I didn't know anyone and it was prudent to be more than a little wary of them.

I was never interviewed for the six days I was there but garnered what little facts I could from various nurses. There was going to be a personality disorder program beginning sometime in the fall and I was there to be assessed to see if I was eligible. A note about the nurses though. After years of looking at rather unattractive female guards it was very pleasant to look at the many pretty nurses.

After three days there I was in my cell for the 11:30 a.m. count and was suddenly informed that I had to 'stand to' for count. That means stand up during the count period so that you can be seen clearly. These stand up counts were initiated after several guys were killed and propped up to look alive. Believe it or not, one corpse was allowed to stiffen up and actually stood up against the toilet . . . they didn't discover he was dead until the smell became a little overpowering.

There have been several battles over this standing up for count but . . . most have been lost. In the SHU they tried to get us to do it, but after hiding under our beds for several days they just gave up. Millhaven's maximum security unit, of which I am a part, does not stand up for counts, but the guys in the assessment units do.

Well, I felt that I couldn't give in to this type of thing and refused to stand up. The guard threatened to charge me and have me sent back to Millhaven. That made up my mind right there, that I was going to go back anyway and not complete the assessment.

The next day I stood on my head for the count, laughing the whole time. The third count, I sat on the toilet. On the fourth day I mentioned to the range that we should all sit on the toilet and surprisingly they did!

About two hours later I was told to pack up and as punishment they locked me in what we commonly refer to as the refrigerator truck. It's made of high grade stainless steel and resembles an old milk truck. Well, for that week we'd experienced a spell of absolutely horrendous humid weather and I must say it wasn't that pleasant to sit in that damned thing all afternoon.

I was back in Millhaven by 4:30 p.m.

9.

ON SEPTEMBER 12 THERE WAS ANOTHER stabbing in the exercise yard. Management locked the institution down for two weeks. At the end of that time the inmates refused to work or take part in programs or activities and the lock-down resumed, lasting for another four weeks.

Inmates then blocked the windows in their cell doors so guards couldn't see inside. This meant that normal supervision, including counts, had to be achieved by teams of tactical-response personnel dressed in bullet-proof vests, helmets and visors, carrying shields and forty-inch batons, forcing each cell door open to inspect the interior. And each time the guards removed the paper blocking the cell windows, the inmates replaced it.

After meetings with the inmates' committee, on which Ty Conn represented the new 2D range in A Unit, there were some concessions on yard time and food, and the place set-tled down. But not for long.

Ty Conn was being severely tested by the unrest. He was firmly in support of activism to deal with what he perceived to be real grievances. And, living on 2D, he had to make a special effort to maintain his recognized status as one of the "solid" cons. At the same time, it was costing him money.

The shop had a backlog of contracts and the lockdowns were getting in the way of his long-term plans, which included education. Education cost money, and he wasn't earning very much twiddling his thumbs in a locked cell.

By then there was a new warden and a new management style. The previous Blackler regime had been notably hard-nosed. Al Stevenson, formerly the warden at Collins Bay, had a reputation for being a more conciliatory manager. Perhaps to signal a new management style, the inmates got turkey for their Christmas dinner that year. The previous year they'd had chicken.

But a new management approach wasn't enough to over-come the virus of anger that was running through Millhaven in those troubled days. There was a relatively benign uprising New Year's Eve when the inmates of 2D decided to stay out of their cells until after midnight. Anticipating that guards would attempt to prevent such action by an early lockdown, they blocked their cell doors in mid-afternoon and, as a result, an attempt to lock them in at 4 p.m. failed.

It was a harmless gesture. They played cards, cooked with improvised utensils, gabbed and hung out in the common area until after midnight, then quietly returned to the cells and went to sleep. It cost each a twenty-five-dollar fine, but nobody seemed to be terribly upset. They considered it the price of a cheap ticket for a New Year's celebration.

The unrest was taking a toll on Ty, however, and it wasn't only in his paycheque. His studies were suffering. Ominously, he'd failed an important exam for one of his math courses.

On the night of January 21, the Millhaven situation began to go downhill rapidly. One of the J Unit ranges blocked cell doors and refused to be locked up after supper. Then they covered the barred entrance to the range so guards could no longer see what was going on inside.

They had about thirty demands and they included ending a policy of fines for bad language, more recreation and yard time, better jobs and programs, recognition of special social and religious needs among members of minorities, and the always thorny issue of food. Millhaven was the only maximum-security joint in the country, they said, not to have its own kitchen. They were demanding one, and they wanted the max inmates to get jobs in it.

The demands, later printed up and distributed, seemed reasonable and, according to the people speaking for the population, were only meant to bring Millhaven in line with every other prison in the country.

Ty Conn drafted the summary paragraph in their formal statement: "We aren't asking for anything more than what other cons in other regions and institutions are entitled to. It appears that past as well as current administrations are only interested in controlling and warehousing the population of the MSU [maximum-security unit] rather than treat them humanely and provide them with opportunities for vocational, recreational and social development."

It was clear from the start that the hard men living in J Unit were prepared to take desperate measures to demonstrate their frustrations. There was a rumour on Ty's range that unless the administration reacted quickly with dramatic reforms, "they were going to get a body."

Late in the afternoon of January 21 guards reported that one prisoner on 2K range had been singled out, tied up and assaulted. Just before 6 p.m. a guard advised Warden Al

Stevenson that the victim, a forty-nine-year old Italian named Giuseppe Sereno, had been swaddled in toilet paper and that inmates were threatening to set him on fire. By early evening they were destroying anything that wasn't bolted down, and the riot squad was soon clattering up the stairs. They shot tear gas into the rebellious range and forced their way in, taking control in about ten minutes.

In one of the cells they found Sereno's body. He'd been doing four years in a Quebec institution for drug dealing before transferring to Millhaven. He was facing deportation to his native Italy after Millhaven. He'd been on the unit for just over a month and was regarded by staff and inmates alike as troublesome.

For reasons nobody in authority could ever discover, he'd been selected for death, either for some breach of the inmates' code or to get the attention of the brass or both. It was, according to unofficial informants, a slow and vicious execution. Two inmates armed with a knife returned to him repeatedly as he continued to show signs of life even after multiple stab wounds. Prison and police officials were never able to accumulate enough evidence to lay a charge after the grisly murder of Guiseppe Sereno.

The following day the inmates were braced for the usual repercussions: lockdown, no meals until perhaps late in the day when "bag lunches" would arrive, and a serious escalation in tension. To their surprise they got breakfast and were being politely asked if they were planning to work that day. The answer was no. Improvements promised in September hadn't materialized. By midday another of the six J Unit ranges had started smashing up and the riot squad had to go to work again.

Four days later, the trouble spread to Ty's range, 2D. Half the people on the range went on a rampage. Management then ordered all power and water to be turned off. After almost two days locked in their tiny cells without light or water, some inmates smashed the windows in their solid cell doors and threw burning rolls of toilet paper and debris into the common area in front.

Guards rushed the range with fire extinguishers but couldn't control the outbreaks. Finally they hooked up the main fire hose and flooded the place. Inmates then started burning bedding and their clothing, and the range soon filled with acrid and, Ty suspected, toxic smoke. Guards set up large fans at one end of the range to blow the smoke away, but they just blew it all down to the other end . . . where Ty Conn lived in cell 29.

Afraid that the smoke would poison him, Ty broke his cell windows to let fresh air in. Locked up and feeling impotent, he wrote a letter.

"Here I sit, my windows wide open to allow the smoke to escape, freezing half to death, my foot cut up from broken glass and breathing through a wet wool sock. Does that invoke sympathy? I'm just kidding. I'm not that bad off really. I'm reading by a candle I made of butter and a shoelace inside a Coke can. Pretty resourceful, eh? In any case, things suck right now . . ."

Things got worse.

Early in February, the stress got to Warden Al Stevenson and he booked off on sick leave on February 6. A new warden, Lou Kelly, moved in. He seemed to have a simpler game plan: he'd talk to the inmates about their issues, but he wasn't going to take any more crap from troublemakers.

Of course, he had to start from scratch. A national inquiry into the uprising that had cost one life, many injuries and one million dollars' worth of damage would later note that one of the major problems at Millhaven was a lack of communication among management, staff and inmates. J Unit, they found, had for years been treated like an SHU, and there had been little or no constructive dialogue between the cons and the coppers. So whenever trouble arose, there were no lines of communication for peaceful solutions.

Kelly had to do something to correct that, but they weren't going to make it easy for him. He was, according to the word of the senior citizens of J Unit, "a real dog." Which, in the circumstances, was probably just what the joint needed.

10.

LETTER, FEBRUARY 7, 1997.

Dear Linden

Feb. 5 was J Unit's turn to get searched and since they don't have any empty cells over there, they placed the 27 residents of one range in three different common rooms, nine to each. Each unit is comprised of a central hub with three wings protruding outward, sort of like a peace sign. Each wing has two floors, each with a range on it, except for one of the wings where the downstairs is a servery.

In between these three protruding wings are common rooms. They are utilized for guys to play cards together. They used to be furnished with TVs and such but that was long ago. One wall of the room looks into the central security bubble which is protected with bullet proof glass and bars. There are gun ports in the bubble from which they can shoot bullets or tear gas. The opposing wall looks outside and the other two walls border the front of the range.

While inside these common rooms, the guys flipped out when they saw their TVs and belongings being carted away and broke up some heating and water pipes which they then used to smash through the walls to other ranges where guys were locked up in their cells.

They then proceeded to smash the cell windows and lights in those ranges. All in all they ended up chasing all the coppers out of the area and got onto three ranges where they smashed everything in sight.

I guess some members of the media were here at the time to follow up on the previous two weeks of incidents and were coincidentally on the scene for the uprising. Guys on two of the ranges that faced outside to the perimeter fences made up signs on bedsheets and displayed them out their cells for the cameras.

I I.

BECAUSE OF THE UPROAR ON J UNIT, there had been no food after an early-morning bag lunch on February 5. An emergency-response team broke up the disturbances in the common rooms, and eight suspected ring leaders were hauled off to segregation.

Early the next morning, sitting in his chilly cell, hungry and depressed, Ty was startled to see a strange face peering at him through the window in his cell door. It was a face that was familiar from newscasts and he could feel the stirring of some unconscious associations that were making him uneasy. Who was it?

Then the answer came in a flash of recognition: Art Hanger, justice critic for the Reform Party, "the asshole who'd like to see convicts in the dungeons, strung up by their toes." The politician was on a fact-finding tour, but Ty Conn realized it would be pointless to seek any sort of comfort from him. And he knew that any "facts" he might contribute would, in all likelihood, be used against them.

The joint settled down gradually. There were isolated incidents including fires and assaults, but on February 11 management identified fourteen people as principal trouble-makers and they were shipped out to the Quebec special handling unit in Ste. Anne des Plaines.

It required emergency reinforcements from Kingston, Collins Bay and the Joyceville Institution to help the Millhaven guards subdue the cons they'd singled out for transfer. The fourteen were forcibly removed from their ranges in handcuffs and shackles, had their clothing cut off (to avoid the necessity of removing the restraints), were searched and redressed, then strapped into body belts and carted away.

On February 18 an additional twenty-three designated troublemakers were bundled up and shipped out to the SHU in Saskatchewan. Improvements would be slow coming, however, and Millhaven remained locked down all through February and March.

1 2.

LETTER, MARCH 17, 1997.

Dear Theresa

Howdy. Happy St. Patrick's Day. With a name like Burke you very well might be Irish? Just had me a St. Pat's drink and a cigar to celebrate the occasion. Not bad for a guy in jail, eh? More ammo for those out there who would have us workin' on the chain gang.

We just had yard yesterday for the first time since January 20th and discovered that they have built a fence out in the yard that has effectively taken about 2/3 of our yard from us. Ironically they've taken most of the grassy area and left us with the concrete, asphalt and crushed stone. We also found out that from now on we will only be getting yard once a week.

I also saw the new cell plans and I'd have to say that I'm impressed. From the looks of it they are going to install steel on all four walls of our cells as opposed to the current two. It looks like they intend to weld some more shelves and clothing hooks on the wall. The plans said a removable desk but that contradicts what I've heard and doesn't make much sense as the cell desks were used during the various smash-ups. All in all though I don't mind a stationary desk as long as they give me more shelving space and a way of hanging up our clothes.

Hey. Have you heard of the guy who got shot by the cops last week in Toronto? Well, he's a friend of mine.

13.

BY APRIL, LIFE WAS STILL IN SUSPENSION and Ty was becoming disheartened: "I've always hated prison and this place in particular but I can't recall a time where I've felt so helpless to affect where and how I'm going to live my life within these fences. I've spent the better part of 12 years in these federal joints and I'm rapidly becoming aware of just how much I crave a regular routine. Not knowing what is going to happen is killing me. Usually you can rely on these types of situations resolving themselves within a month or so, but this thing seems to be going on and on . . ."

It had been going on, in fact, for nearly four months. And it would go on for many months to come. And in the course of the year his plans for rehabilitation would be effectively sabotaged. He was having trouble with his correspondence studies. The federal government kept threatening to withdraw financial support. His prison employment was constantly interrupted. At some point during the year he quietly gave up on his studies. By the summer of '97 he was so broke he couldn't afford postage stamps.

For all the uproar in late 1996 and the early months of 1997, Ty's record was remarkably clean. He'd helped other inmates smash through a concrete wall and broken cell windows a couple of times. On one occasion he was verbally abusive to guards. The usually unforgiving institutional record noted that his behaviour was "assessed as being part of a larger range action." They imposed substantial fines, but Warden Kelly indicated they'd reconsider enforcing collection, depending on his future conduct.

By mid-summer he was fervently hopeful that the disturbances were finally over. His long-term goal, a parole hearing before the year 2000, was becoming more remote as
each fruitless day passed. Never a deep sleeper, he'd lie
awake at night fighting panic at the dreadful thought that he
was stuck in Millhaven permanently. To prevent slipping into
another perilous depression, he decided to ask his case
officer to explore avenues for a transfer out of Millhaven. It
was a long shot, but better than just sitting there.

Collins Bay would be perfect. He told her he was anxious
to prove to them that, notwithstanding his two previous
escapes from there, he deserved another chance. He admitted that he hated Collins Bay when he was there, but that
was a long time ago. He didn't realize then that prison could
be a lot worse than "the Bay." And, in any case, if he was to
maintain any realistic hope of getting parole any time in the
reasonable future, he was going to have to get into a
medium-security institution *somewhere* and into some useful
personal development programs.

14.

LETTER, JULY 24, 1997.
Dear Theresa

I had a dynamite PFV [personal family visit] with my
kid brother and my Ma. He came in on Friday and my
Ma came in the next morning. He brought me this
Cuban cigar that has to be the best thing I ever
smoked. Really smooth and mild and nothing like

what I've had access to in here since I started smoking the damn things. I'm what you could call a recreational smoker. I hadn't smoked one in over three months when he brought me this Cuban cigar. Eat your hearts out America! Serves them right, harassing Cuba for the last 40 years.

Things might be returning to normal sometime soon. They just called out about 20 guys and gave them work assignments to begin next week. I won't mind getting paid again but I have $40 in fines to pay yet and I have two more charges, each of which is serious and capable of hitting me with $50 more. Hopefully this fine shit will cease. I rarely get into trouble myself and fines have been a rarity for me, but all these range/joint actions where everybody does something have been hitting me hard in the last six months.

I've just made a musical discovery which might seem slightly insane. I watched Much Music the other night. They often do this thing called Intimate and Interactive where an artist comes in and plays for a small audience. It's usually pretty laid back and the audience and viewers can ask questions etc. Well, I normally don't watch it unless it's somebody I like. The other night I had nothing to do and I gave it my attention. Sarah McLachlan was featured and I really haven't been exposed to much of her music at all and . . . well, was I ever surprised. I loved this woman . . . have you heard her? I know she's Canadian and all but I haven't really listened to her before.

15.

ON SUNDAY, AUGUST 10, WHICH WAS ironically Prisoners' Justice Day, there was another run-in with guards, and the cons were convinced that the staff were attempting to prolong tension and the extreme conditions in the joint out of self-interest. They were making a lot of money in overtime pay, and generally their jobs were simpler when the place was locked down and the inmates deprived of their scanty rights.

There was limited access to the yard that day, five prisoners at a time. During one exchange, an inmate who had an empty plastic bag in his hand snapped it in a guard's direction, startling him. According to Ty's account of the incident, about ten guards promptly jumped on the offender and, after roughly subduing him, dragged him away. Then the remaining cons were taken in one at a time, strip searched and escorted to their cells individually by five officers.

That night, probably to celebrate justice day, several inmates on one of the J Unit ranges got drunk on brew, and the emergency-response team, which presents an awesome physical spectacle in any circumstances, arrived to "subdue" them. The result was a bloody melee.

On August 12, Ty told Theresa Burke that they had been scheduled to end the lockdown officially the day before, August 11, just after justice day. From the inmates' viewpoint, it was more than a coincidence that everything went to hell at the last minute.

"Whenever we act up, it's very much like a lottery [for the guards]," he observed. "They rake in thousands of dollars in overtime."

It would be September before Millhaven returned to a routine that resembled normalcy. In addition to the periodic confrontations, there were major changes underway. Repairs and alterations to the facilities would cost $4.5 million before they finished. They were also revamping the food-delivery system, soon to resume using the kitchen at the Bath Institution next door. Starting in Mid-October, meals would come from there in hot-carts. There was even talk of fundamental change in the role of Millhaven in the corrections system, including rumours that the hated reception unit would be moved to another institution, probably KP.

None of this mattered much to Ty Conn. They could put hot tubs in the cells for all he cared. He was becoming desperate to get out of Millhaven and he was only comforted by the fact that his case officer had finally started to see the situation his way. She agreed that he was going nowhere in maximum security and she was promising that she'd help get him an improved security classification. Then the CSC promoted her and he got a new case officer and had to start all over again, convincing somebody anew that he wasn't as bad as the files made him out to be.

He started working in the Millhaven library in September and that improved his morale somewhat. It got him out of his cell, his responsibilities weren't onerous, and he was almost joyful at being set loose among twenty thousand books.

And there was an unexpected bonus. His computer, then three years old, needed upgrading, but he knew he'd never be able to afford a new one. One day the librarian sent him on an errand to a storage room, and he discovered a treasure trove of discarded computers there. They were headed for the scrap heap anyway so it wasn't really stealing. He swiftly took one apart and removed whatever memory chips he needed to significantly increase the RAM in his own machine.

16.

LETTER, DECEMBER 14, 1997.

Dear Linden

I just came out of the trailer with my Ma and kid brother. I had a good time and it's the closest we've ever been in the trailer to Christmas time so it had a special feel to it. I brought out some chocolate bars with which we made fudge and my kid brother brought me a couple of Cuban cigars. I didn't have the heart to tell him about a *Marketplace* show I saw recently on the subject of Cuban cigars. It appears that they've become victims of their own success and as many as 75 per cent of Cuban cigars in Canada are likely fakes!

Last Tuesday they threw a guy in the hole for not doing his job and the range below me decided to smash up. The instrument with which they smashed up was a fancy new metallic food cart that we got about three months ago. They cost approximately $16,000 a piece. And, remember, we have five of them. This thing was so sturdy and tough that they smashed through the front steel barrier at the head of the range as well as the rear door.

After that they managed to open doors on either side of the stairway at the back of the ranges and gained access to outside areas as well as the cloister areas [small open outdoor spaces between the buildings]. Anyways, the guards went kind of nuts and I saw at least 10 of them with AR-15s [rifles] making sure none of them got outside. Outside means just outside, but with two fences between them and freedom. But in that area, they could have gotten to where there were several vehicles belonging to contractors who are repairing the ranges. We're supposed to move into those ranges this coming week. After about three hours and about eight shots of tear gas, they were all taken to the hole.

17.

IN JANUARY 1998, TY WENT SO FAR AS to draft a letter to the institutional preventive security officers (IPSO) at Collins Bay requesting forgiveness for his past sins against the establishment.

"I was in the SHU for 31 months," he wrote, "and during my time there I decided that it would be better to give up any escape related activities as they seemed to be all consuming and caused me no small amount of frustration and grief.

"Escape was a particularly brief respite from any prison term I was attempting to obtain relief from, and the only result seemed to be many more years of imprisonment. Thanks to escape I turned a seven year sentence into a 47 year sentence.

"It was clear to me that if I wished to rescue any substantial part of my life from imprisonment, the only way to do so was to obtain a parole."

His case officer, after reading his letter and making some inquiries at Collins Bay, advised against mailing it. It really wouldn't be worth the stamp.

In February he wrote to a senior official in Corrections Canada in which he pointed out that the system for assigning security ratings inadvertently discriminated against him. There were three criteria in the system: public safety, escape risk and institutional adjustment. He rated "high" on all three.

He accepted the fact that he scored high as an escape risk and hoped to get a better (moderate or low) rating eventually. But it wasn't really fair that he also had high ratings for the other two factors. Armed robbery is, by definition, a violent crime, he agreed. But actually physically harming another person was "a line I could never cross.

"I understand that my Public Safety is still 'high' because of an offhand comment made by a judge in 1991. She made a comment about how it was a miracle that I *hadn't* ever harmed anyone and wondered if I'd care if I did.

"I understand that this may well be taken into account, but I'm puzzled as to why I should be condemned as a high public safety concern because of someone's comment or opinion on how I *hadn't* hurt anyone.

"Shouldn't the fact that I haven't hurt anyone be a positive slant on my public safety instead of a negative point?"

It was a valid argument. In the system of classification, he accepted the likelihood that he'd be rated a high-escape risk for a considerable period of time. But to also have a high rating as a public-safety risk effectively disqualified him from medium-security status indefinitely. In practical terms, an offhand and ill-considered aside by a judge had blocked off any possibility of rehabilitation and parole. It was as if he had, without any of the due process, achieved the status of a dangerous offender.

"My situation is currently Catch-22. Since my ratings are high, I have to address them in some fashion, yet I'm not being provided with any such options . . .

"I know I cannot obtain any parole from a max so I have to get into a medium for several years, develop some plans and perhaps then I'll have a chance.

"Instead of being provided with an opportunity to prove myself, I'm basically being punished. It's been over five years since I've been involved in any escape related activity, yet it seems that I'm bound to continue being punished for it for many more years. I currently have no hope so how can I ever envision getting out and rescuing what's left of my life?"

His appeals in early 1998 fell on deaf ears.

At some point in the spring of that year he realized that nobody was going to help him get out of Millhaven and into a more constructive prison setting. As always, it seemed that he was going to have to make his own opportunities for progress.

He didn't have to wait long for such an opportunity to arise, but it would force him to make agonizing and perilous choices.

18.

THE SAME FACTOR THAT STOOD IN the way of his parole—
his history as an escaper—eventually became the springboard
from which he departed Millhaven, never to return.

At some point in the spring of 1998 a representative
from a small group of hardcore maximum-security inmates
in the unit approached him with a proposal. They were cooking up an escape plan and they wanted him to help by providing advice based on his own experience. In return, they'd
make arrangements for his freedom once they were on the
outside. Regardless of how he felt about it, it was an offer
that he couldn't refuse without putting himself in danger.
Just mentioning it to him made him a part of it, whether or
not he wanted to participate.

The authors' knowledge of the details of the scheme is
based on Ty's telling of it, and, because the escape never happened, his account cannot be definitively confirmed. But
corrections officials have verified key elements of his story.
There is no doubt at all that there was a plot and that he was
involved in it. Senior officials at Millhaven have also verified
details of how the scheme fell apart and how it ultimately
changed Ty Conn's life forevermore.

The essence of the plan, as he explained it, was a
bizarre ploy to gain admission to a civilian hospital in the
area. Two of the plotters planned to swallow small frag-
ments of a razor blade which, while causing real damage to
their digestive systems, would also present symptoms that
would suggest a crisis far too serious for the Millhaven
health centre.

A third inmate, who was about to be paroled, would somehow deliver guns to the hospital and help effect the escape by overwhelming what would inevitably be a formidable police guard. They were prepared to shoot their way out of the place if that's what it would take, and there was no doubt in Ty Conn's mind that such an escape would require exactly that.

Ty couldn't believe what they were suggesting. A gunfight in a hospital carried with it the probability of a lot of collateral damage to doctors and nurses and other innocent bystanders. But he wasn't about to express his reservations to the plotters. Being "solid" meant being cool with any inmate initiative, no matter how bizarre or dangerous it seemed.

In later conversations with the authors, Ty said he agonized over his situation for days. There was a part of him that was ready to abandon the difficult path to "rehabilitation" through the unhelpful programs available in the corrections system. Once again he was on the edge of that dark place where a desperate action could be justified by the remote prospect of success, or the sure promise of the oblivion that would follow failure.

But this time it was different. His commitment to legitimacy was genuine. And his aversion to real violence was a permanent part of his character. No matter how dispirited and pissed off he got, he didn't have it in him to participate in an escapade that could lead to a bloodbath. And in a hospital!

Then he concluded that he had arrived at a crucial juncture in his life. He had to choose between two mutually exclusive systems of morality. Based on the cons' code there could be no betrayal of a brother inmate, no matter what his personal objections might be. In that rigid system, his only option was to see it through and keep his lip buttoned.

But fourteen years of fidelity to the inmates' code had earned him a life he no longer wanted. The alternative was to think like a citizen: expose the conspiracy and perhaps save a lot of innocent people from a lot of grief.

And then comes the selfish question: What's in it for me?

There was no easy answer for that. For certain there was a huge physical risk. For certain he would have to live with a lot of guilt and self-loathing no matter what happened. He was steeped in the values of a criminal subculture. He was a bank robber and an escaper, and there is no more respectable category of offender in a prison. And there is nothing lower than a rat. An informer. And that was how he would see himself and eventually be seen by other convicts for the rest of his life. And, handled the wrong way, it might not be a very long life. But the alternative was to go along with something that could easily turn into murder.

Finally he went to see the institutional protective security officers. The IPSOS, Jane Korosi and Yves Deslaurier, weren't much help. They couldn't make deals. It was up to him to "do the right thing." The right thing, from their point of view, was to continue monitoring the escape plans and to keep them abreast of developments. He had to become a spy.

The first phase of the plan clicked neatly into place. The inmate whose job was to supply guns went out on schedule and was making arrangements to complete his part of the project. Then, without warning, the Ontario Provincial Police arrested him . . . prematurely, and apparently without solid legal grounds for doing so.

In the aftermath, through legal bungling and bad luck, Ty Conn discovered in early May that the escape plotters were aware that someone in the institution had betrayed them. By late May he had solid reasons to believe that by a process of elimination they suspected him. Just before the end of May, believing that his life was in danger, he approached IPSO Deslaurier and asked to be admitted to a cell in dissociation—known officially as the ECA (environmental control area), but to Millhaven inmates as "the back hole."

It is an unimaginably depressing place, designed for the confinement of desperate and uncontrollable people. There are sixteen cells in dissociation, each secured by a solid steel door. On each door there is a small window, usually blocked by a sliding shutter, and a slot, usually locked, through which food, medication or documents can be passed to the inside. It is a place of harsh light and bland, grimy pastels of green and grey and tan. It is for people who have reached rock bottom in the human condition, the total absence of liberty. And it was to this place, on May 28, 1998, that guards escorted Ty Conn in order to save his life.

The next day they locked down the entire institution, spirited him into a prison truck and drove him to Kingston Penitentiary, Canada's oldest and most disreputable prison.

He had unofficial assurances that he wouldn't be there long. Without actually making any promises, Millhaven management and security officers had eventually encouraged him to believe that his bravery would not go unrecognized, even while they privately held the view (expressed to the authors long afterward) that his action had been significantly motivated out of self-interest.

Perhaps it was. But the self-interest is hard to fault. Inertia and lack of imagination in the corrections bureaucracy left him in a position where he was likely to grow old in prison, watching people who were guilty of far more serious crimes, including rape and murder, arrive, serve their time and leave. The choice he made was morally and socially responsible and it demonstrated that in spite of all his years in confinement with criminals and in spite of all the education he got from them, he still had a conventional sense of what was right and what was wrong. When the chips were down, he did what was right. And, like most people, he expected to get a little bit of recognition for it. So what.

It wasn't as if, driving to Kingston that day in May, 1998, he was congratulating himself for having weaseled his way out of prison. It wasn't like in the U.S. where ratting out an escape was virtually guaranteed to get you down to minimum.

He was, in fact, scared to death. He was on his way to the worst prison in Canada. It was worse than Millhaven because it was ancient and because of the stigma that went along with being there. And the best he could hope for was another, less awful prison after that one. Warkworth, with its population of skinners and diddlers. And if people there, or in KP, ever found out what had happened in Millhaven, he'd be dead. And yet, it would be better than being stuck in Millhaven. And if he survived, at least he could now start doing something constructive to improve his miserable lot in life.

His only consolation was in thinking that he had somehow demonstrated to "the system" that he was not the grave threat to public safety that the cops and the judges and the bureaucrats said he was. And that soon he'd get on track toward eventual freedom.

So who could fault him, other than someone who was, as he had been for so long, deformed by the twisting and twisted values of the damned? He didn't belong in a maximum-security joint by then. His confinement there was of absolutely no value to him or society. He needed the encouragement and programs that were only available in a medium-security institution. And here he was on his way to Kingston, to old KP which, by most standards of comparison, made Millhaven look good.

At Millhaven, they'd indicated with a wink and a nudge that he wouldn't be in Kingston for long. A few months maybe. October at the outside. From the depths of his terrified soul he prayed that they were telling him the truth.

CHAPTER TWELVE

Fishing Trip '99

I can't seem to get a break from these people. It seems I'm doomed to pay for past mistakes forever. . . I'm going to put some thought into changing tactics.

Ty Conn, March 29, 1999

I.

TY CONN LOOKED FORWARD TO FAMILY visits the way a starving man looks forward to food scraps. Family visits gave him access to at least a representation of the real world. For an entire weekend he could pretend that he was in a home with normal people, talking to someone who was not an "offender" about the challenges of living on the outside where each day started as a mystery. In prison only the outbursts of demons lurking in the souls of the condemned broke the rigid routines. Sometimes you even welcomed the dangerous excitement they could cause.

This is not to say the visits were always easy or unadulterated fun. There was a lot of heavy work going on in those trailers in the early days, digging through the past, moving obstacles that could have blocked relationships with Ma and his half-brother, Max. These were people who, overnight, had arrived in his life as a fully formed family, and he hadn't ever known people like them before.

Growing up with the Conns, you wouldn't have had much contact with people like Max and Marion, down-to-earth folks who lacked the artifice that seems to go with social status. These were people who liked to get things out in the open and deal with issues and personal baggage before they grew into unmanageable problems. They lacked the formalities and the social conventions that sometimes let problems fester and make private lives miserable behind façades of public success.

On top of that there was the surprising discovery he'd made in the early trailer visits that just sharing space with people came hard to him. This was unexpected. He'd lived from the age of fourteen in close quarters, involuntarily locked up with people who were not family and not of his choosing. You'd think he'd be fully conditioned to other people in any circumstances. But the trailer visits were different.

Living in an institution, privacy becomes a virtue, and private space is sacred. A cell is an estate, secured by the conventions of the prison world with the same rigour as the fences and electronic devices that protect the property of the rich. One violates the privacy and the property of a prison inmate at great personal risk.

Ty took a long time getting used to those shared weekends with his mother and, occasionally, with his brother. Ma presented particular problems because of her gender and her age. He suspected at least once that she snooped in his stuff, a perfectly normal thing for a mom to do, but there had never been much in his world that was perfectly normal. Even little things bugged him sometimes. He wasn't accustomed to talking to people first thing in the morning. It was irritating when she'd change the channel on the TV. All small things, but they could get to you.

Marion, therefore, learned to expect mood changes and sulks and even the occasional outburst, and she just let them pass. She knew they weren't connected to anything substantial. They just reflected the large cultural differences between them. Which is probably why she missed a lot near the end.

She remembers a Sunday evening, as they watched a segment on *60 Minutes* about Jack Kevorkian, the American doctor who has made euthanasia his professional specialty. Ty seemed unusually focused on the piece and when it ended he turned to her and told her that "if anything should ever happen," he didn't want to be artificially revived or sustained on life support.

It seemed like a particularly grim subject to raise, but she knew him well enough by then not to be surprised by the morbid streak that appeared from time to time.

Then he added that if he should die before her, he wanted his body to be cremated and the ashes to be scattered where they would disperse. He didn't want what remained of him to turn some patch of the earth into a place of sorrowful remembering. He emphatically didn't want to end up in an urn on someone's mantelpiece.

She also remembers that he was unusually restless during that particular visit. She'd learned that he was a light sleeper at the best of times and probably an insomniac. He'd casually mention programs that he'd seen on television at strange hours and she'd be wondering what on earth he'd been doing awake at that hour anyway. And there were nights she suspected that he'd been up practically until dawn reading. But on this visit, she saw him during the dead hours after midnight just staring out a window.

Inside the walls of Kingston Penitentiary there isn't much to look at, day or night, except walls. He told her he was watching the dog patrols. Dog patrols? Yes, he said. At night they make periodic rounds with guard dogs in case somebody should be attempting to escape.

Escape? From Kingston Pen? Nobody ever escaped from Kingston Pen. You wouldn't even try.

And during that trailer visit they talked about making plans for their next Christmas, wherever he might be by then. Christmas Day was going to fall on a Saturday in 1999. They were going to try to arrange a trailer visit for that weekend. It was still months away, but it was nice to think ahead to when they'd all gather as a family, celebrating together for the first time in years.

This all happened in the last quiet moments they would ever have together. It was on the weekend of April 25, 1999. He had been in Kingston Pen for almost a year by then.

2.
———

IF, AT AN EARLIER STAGE OF HIS incarceration, somebody had told Ty Conn that he'd one day be a long-term resident of Kingston Pen, he'd have laughed . . . or punched him out, as any self-respecting con would do. KP was one place he never expected to be. The closest he came was a brief spell in the Regional Treatment Centre, which was technically within the walls of the Pen. An inmate at KP? Ty Conn? No way. Maybe he'd have made a joke: I'll be in the House of Commons before I'm in KP. Ty Conn was a solid con and solid cons avoided KP like the plague.

But on Friday night, May 29, 1998, that's exactly where he was, and he was having a lot of misgivings about the circumstances that got him there. And he was wondering just how he could survive. He was desperately hoping somebody would get him out of there in fairly short order.

Just being in Kingston was dangerous. It creates a stigma that the inmate never shakes. Kingston is reserved for people who need special protection from other inmates or who need special management so they don't harm others. People who go to KP voluntarily are immediately suspect.

Perhaps that's why people rarely tried to escape from Kingston. It wasn't that Kingston was any more secure than Collins Bay or Millhaven. It was just that the type of inmate who went to Kingston usually wasn't inclined to run away, there being very few safe places that he could run to.

Clint Suzack, who befriended Ty Conn at Kingston, used to say, "If you opened the door in front of a dozen of them, eleven would stay inside."

Suzack is a convicted cop killer and, from the point of view of the system, a hard case. People like Clint sometimes find themselves being sent to Kingston for attitude adjustment. Now in a medium-security institution, he always carries the documents that prove he was in KP only because he was forced to go there.

The comment "I hear you're just out of KP" can be the prologue to a lot of unpleasantness. . . even for a tough guy like Suzack.

Inmates confined in Kingston Pen are, in the words of one writer, "the detritus of the Ontario federal prison population . . . the flotsam and jetsam of the system."

In his book, *Canada's Big House: The Dark History of Kingston Penitentiary,* Peter H. Hennessey argues that Kingston Penitentiary is a paradoxical result of an effort in the system to classify prisoners according to their crimes and their potential for improvement. Classification was designed to hasten the process of rehabilitation. But in any effort to classify inmates there will always be the hopeless cases, and there has to be a special place reserved for them so they don't infect others with their hopelessness.

He compares the system to the grading of students in school: people who rate as As, Bs or Cs get priority in passing through the system. Those below get Kingston.

"After nearly 175 years, it houses the Ds and the Fs of the Canadian prison population: the 'worst' of the sex offenders and murderers, the least educable, the least reconcilable, the most godforsaken, the most hated."

Tyrone Conn was neither a murderer nor a sex offender. He had an IQ far above the average inside or outside the prison world. He always got along well with people, whether con or copper, and he wanted nothing more from life than a chance to become a productive citizen. At the end of May 1998, he became a part of "the detritus . . . of the system."

The best he could hope for was that it wouldn't be for long and that he'd be off to Warkworth before becoming tainted by the Kingston syndrome. A short stay there wouldn't be the end of the world. But it was really important to him that he get out of KP before too many people discovered that he was in there.

Millhaven wasn't making any promises. But there were implied assurances that he would, in fact, be moving on after no more than a few months. And he had outside friends and a Toronto lawyer keeping an eye on the situation.

Dan Brodsky had become familiar with Ty Conn's case a year earlier. Ty, back in 1997, was interested in cutting a deal with the justice system to clear up a number of unsolved robberies from his early criminal days. Where he was responsible—and there were about ten of them outstanding—he was willing to admit it. But it was a complex process. He wanted to plead guilty to the crimes, but he didn't want to get any more time added to his already massive sentence of forty-seven years plus.

Brodsky thought he could stickhandle a deal because he knew police officers and prosecutors are always keen to close the files on unsolved crimes, even if it means leniency for the perpetrator. In Ty Conn's case he figured most would agree that he was already facing penalties enough to satisfy the most stringent standards of punishment. The project fizzled when he went to Kingston, but Brodsky still had a file on the young robber and was monitoring the move. And he was still prepared to represent him free of charge.

With concerned friends and an aggressive lawyer, Ty felt certain that he'd be out of KP and into medium security by the end of the summer.

And, in fact, all signs were suggesting that this was exactly what was going to happen. The Millhaven IPSOS,

Korosi and Deslaurier, had given a fair and positive account of his actions there during the spring. Millhaven management agreed that Conn deserved their trust and a bit of their goodwill. They were already reviewing his security classification as he was settling in at Kingston.

By the middle of August his parole officer at Millhaven, Beverley Pitcher, was recommending reclassification to medium security, and the rest of the case-management team there agreed with her. Of course by then he'd been in Kingston Pen for nearly three months.

There were two hurdles left. The transfer to medium wasn't entirely up to Millhaven. Kingston Pen also had to classify him as a medium and Warkworth Institution had to agree to let him go there.

3.

AUGUST WAS A GOOD MONTH. HE was pleasantly surprised by Kingston. In a way it was a big improvement on the awkwardness of Millhaven, with its volatile mix of hard cases on J Unit and untouchables in reception. It was easier to move around in KP and there seemed to be more social life.

While Kingston is a protective-custody institution, the five different layers of security there function independently of one another. The different groups don't mix. At the low end of the food chain there are people like Paul Bernardo, the notorious sex murderer from St. Catharines. He lives in almost total isolation from the other inmates, as did Clifford Olson when he was in Kingston.

Then there are the slightly less disreputable cases, the police informers or former cops, and people who are there because of gambling debts incurred in prison. They mix only with one another, and even then, warily.

And then there's the crowd on Upper G, many of them murderers and heroin addicts who are in Kingston because other institutions can't handle them.

Ty eventually moved onto Upper G, to Number 3 range, and in spite of the fact that he wasn't a druggie and he wasn't violent, he fit right in with the killers and the junkies. Ty's cell neighbours were Clint Suzack and Mike Larrabie. Mike was also doing time for murder.

Paulo Teixiera was an addict who claimed to have AIDS and was considered by many to be a little bit crazy. He'd threatened to bite a guard at Millhaven, so they hog-tied him and sent him to the Regional Treatment Centre, then into the Kingston population.

Wally Pitt and Bear and Big Kenny were all hard men with violent criminal records, people whom Ty might have found too frightening for friendship on the outside. But in prison you don't make judgments about people. There are reasons for everything. Extenuating circumstances. Shit happens. Do your time, don't be a judge, don't whine and don't discuss. Clint, in particular, was a good friend, and he became a strong influence. While getting to know Clint and Wally, Ty discovered that they, like him, had been adopted into dysfunctional situations when they were children. That biographical detail became a bond.

Clint and Mike Larrabie were both partly of First Nations heritage and they were active in the Native Brotherhood group at Kingston Pen. Eventually, they invited Ty to participate in some of their activities.

Ty had never been very religious and he'd seen a lot of spiritual hypocrisy in his time, but there was something about the simple sincerity of the native ceremonies that appealed to him. The sweat lodges and the sweet grass gave him a rare feeling of well-being.

On August 8 there was a special ceremony to mark the change of seasons. A lot of friends and special guests from the outside attended, along with native elders and dancers from as far away as Brantford. There was a healing circle and prayers that really sounded like they meant them, prayers addressed to the goodness in old souls. In the smoke of the open fires with the rich aromas of cooking food, your skin drenched in sunshine and the cool cobalt sky above, you could almost forget where you were. At least for a few hours.

He was almost wistful that day at the likelihood that he'd be leaving there soon. It was rare, in prison, to be part of a tight and solid group that wasn't a gang. He was even beginning to think of the group on Upper G as his family. He was really getting something out of the native stuff, even though he didn't have a single aboriginal gene in his whole body. He liked a lot of the guys in the brotherhood. They were solid and serious and their spirituality seemed to give them an aura of personal power. And sadly, in a way, it was all going to end for him when he moved on. Any day now, he was saying. October at the very latest.

On August 21, true to their cautious assurances, Millhaven formally lowered his security classification. All he needed at that point was a similar rating at Kingston and a green light from Warkworth and he'd be on his way.

In the euphoria of the summer and the new friendships and the native spirituality and the prospects of moving into a process that would put him on the long pathway to parole, it was easy for Ty Conn to forget a lot of the past. He was in a forward-looking frame of mind. Or maybe, with seventeen years of incarceration behind him, he actually dared to hope that in four or five more years, Justice would finally feel appeased and Society forgiving.

Looking back from a less hopeful place in the near future, that native ceremony on August 8 to mark the change of seasons would have ominous significance for Ty Conn. Summer was surely ending and he was heading straight into the winter of his life.

4.

IN PRISON TERMINOLOGY "AN INCOMPATIBLE" is somebody who doesn't like you. Everybody has incompatibles somewhere, but in the vivid world of prison, emotions become exaggerated and personal incompatibility can easily become institutional instability. Prison administrators have enough to deal with, so if they can see a new problem coming, they usually exercise their options to prevent it.

At some point during the summer of '98, Ty Conn was told the reason he wasn't moving to Warkworth right away was because there was an incompatible there. This was a big surprise. In all his years in training schools and jails and the pen, he wasn't aware of having made a single enemy.

Eventually, he heard a name, and after struggling to recall an identity, it still didn't mean anything to him. Maybe there had been a boyhood fracas in a reform school, but it would have been so minor that there would have been no reason for hard feelings immediately after the incident, let alone all these years later. But that was the explanation. There was an incompatible. The good news was that, whoever he was, the other inmate's sentence would be up soon and he'd be moving on in October. Ty was hoping to be gone from Kingston before that, but he didn't have a lot of choice. He'd wait and stay busy to keep his spirits up.

Jeremy Conway arrived from Warkworth in October, shipped to Kingston for a serious drug offence. He couldn't enlighten Ty much about the so-called incompatible there. Warkworth is a big place. The most populous pen in the country, with over six hundred inmates. Incompatible? Jeremy was skeptical.

Jeremy was a sad case. He was young and pleasant in appearance and was doing serious time because he'd been with a group of young thugs, all stoned on LSD, who beat an old disabled man to death for a few dollars. He'd avoided a life sentence because of reduced responsibility, due to the drugs. But Jeremy, while in prison, had developed a serious heroin habit and was having a hard time breaking it. He and Ty became good friends. Jeremy, with his youthful face, long blond hair and Club Monaco T-shirts, could have been Ty Conn's brother by the look of him.

How Jeremy got into heroin is a story all by itself, and it says a lot about how the corrections system can end up providing the opposite of rehabilitation. Because drugs figured prominently in his criminal profile, they made him go to a narc-anon program. It was supposed to be aversion therapy. He was supposed to be frightened and turned off, listening to the stories of addicts and their ruined lives. But it didn't work out that way. Jeremy became fascinated listening to junkies describe their experiences with heroin and the highs they got from it. It sounded like the perfect escape from the torments of a guilty conscience and the daily agonies of survival in the dark world of corrections. Soon he was into it himself and it wasn't long before he was hooked.

Jeremy was a follower. In Clint Suzack's opinion, "He's a junkie because he's around junkies . . . when he hung out with me for a few weeks he spent all his time working out in the gym."

Ty, who expected to be leaving any day, knew from his own experience just how vulnerable Jeremy was, so he got hold of some copper pipe and a grinder and he fashioned an excellent shank for him. The handle was of tubing and the blade could be screwed off and reversed and stored inside the handle.

"It was elegant," Jeremy later recalled. "It was threaded on one end so you could put the pick in the tube and hoop [insert in the anal canal] the whole thing."

Jeremy had a wife and a baby, and Ty, based on his experience inside, was able to give him advice on how to handle the little conflicts and crises that inevitably arise due to the separation that comes with incarceration. He kept reminding him how lucky he was to have a family and a real chance of getting out in a few years.

It was difficult, in October, to remain upbeat. Life was chugging along all around him. His brother, Max, and his wife were having a baby. Theresa Burke had arrived at the August 8 native social immensely pregnant. Even Jeremy Conway, for cripes sake, had a family.

5.

AT SOME POINT IN NOVEMBER THE paperwork from Millhaven finally arrived in Kingston with the positive recommendation that his security classification be marked down to medium because of improvements in his institutional adjustment and diminished escape risk. They were still considering him, unlikely though it seemed, a high risk to public safety.

But that should have been a small technicality. With two of the three security factors rated as medium by Millhaven, it was almost taken for granted that Kingston would follow suit. After all, Millhaven knew him best, and his case managers there were in the best position to make an assessment of the risks he posed and of what he needed.

He'd never been an inmate in Kingston before this episode. But there were people in Kingston who knew him and remembered some of his past escapades, and one of them, by unfortunate coincidence, was the manager of the prison unit that included Upper G range. His name was Rob Clarke, formerly Ty Conn's case manager in Collins Bay. Clarke was there when Ty took off in 1989.

After a prisoner arrives at an institution, the people who will be in charge of his life have a placement meeting. It's not unlike a hiring board, except the applicant isn't there. Parole officers and supervisors and program-delivery people sit around a table and discuss the inmate's file and decide just how he will be managed during his stay. The chairman of Ty's board was Rob Clarke.

Clarke knew Ty well in Collins Bay and considered him to be a model inmate. He had actually escorted Ty on three passes to the outside world. They'd gone to lunch and to the parks and walked along the Kingston waterfront looking at the boats. On one of the outings Marion had been with them, and they took a train ride and visited Kingston's steam museum.

Then, on a fourth escorted pass with someone else, Ty ruined everything by running away. Rob Clarke never forgot that, and it was very much on his mind as he reviewed the files from Millhaven.

"I know that there was a desire at Millhaven Institution to reduce his security level to medium based on the circumstances that were going on over there . . . and they would forward it over to us for ratification, which they did," Clarke remembers.

It was, he also recalls, a long and difficult board. Both parole officers, from Millhaven and Kingston, were recommending that Ty get medium status and move on to Warkworth as soon as that institution was ready to receive him. But Rob Clarke didn't agree with them.

"I did take it upon myself," Clarke admits, "to express concerns about Tyrone as an escape risk based on what I knew of the case and his previous escapes and the fact that when he did escape there was generally an escalation in the offence cycle."

Clarke, in short, had the last word on what Ty Conn's security classification would be. After listening to the arguments of the parole officers in favour of a medium-security status, he overruled them.

"I was not compelled at that point to make his escape risk any lower than high, although I did rate him as low institutional adjustment because he was such a model inmate. I guess to be quite frank . . . I had still [the belief] and to this day believe that Ty really liked the excitement. I always had the feeling over the years that I knew him that if I was to just open the door and give him a suitcase and say, good luck, but you can't be involved in crime any more, he would find that less stimulating than the cloak-and-dagger kind of activity that he ended up involving himself in. That's just a personal observation."

It was a personal observation that was based on knowledge that was then eleven years old. It was a personal observation that failed to take account of the possibility that people sometimes change between the ages of twenty and thirty-one. In fact, most people change as they mature. It was an observation that ran directly counter to the opinion of the parole officers who knew Ty Conn at that point a lot better than Rob Clarke did. And they believed that the inmate had changed and that his determination to go straight was sincere. And if there had been any lingering doubt that there had been a transformation in his thinking during his time in the SHU, it should have been dispelled by the choice he made in Millhaven. But Rob Clarke, the unit manager at Kingston, had the last word.

6.
———

OCTOBER HAD BEEN A KIND OF psychological end point. It wasn't that he hated Kingston any more than Millhaven. It was just that he had a plan for his future and he wanted to get on with it. He'd invested a lot of moral capital in that plan and he needed a payoff or he was likely to find himself in some serious difficulty. He had put his fate in the hands of the corrections system and he needed some assurance by October that he hadn't made a big mistake.

As October slipped by with no word of a transfer to Warkworth, the demons of depression returned with a vengeance. His friends on Upper G recall that they could tell that there was something seriously wrong. Clint Suzack, who lived in the next cell, was one of the first to notice. Ty would skip his meals. Some days, if he ate anything at all, it was only because Clint brought a tray for him. If somebody asked him what was wrong, he'd just mumble that his asthma was acting up. Clint, who lost a lung in the shootout that killed a policeman and put him in the pen for life, found it a strange excuse.

"Sometimes I have trouble breathing too," he said. "But it doesn't make me want to stay in bed all day."

Wally Pitt figured it was a sign of depression. Wally knew the symptoms well. He felt for the guy, and in a misguided fit of compassion he went to some people in the joint and scrounged up an antidote for the despair. Enough heroin for a couple of lines. He wouldn't let him shoot it, he insisted in an interview as a guard sat impassively beside him. Shooting up was too dangerous. Too many people got AIDS that way. Instead, he made Ty snort the powder and, not surprisingly, it made him feel better. For a while.

He became an occasional user. He could probably have gone on like that for a long time before becoming hooked, because he didn't have an addictive personality. He'd never seriously smoked tobacco or used alcohol. He had too much respect for his mind to cloud and distort his thinking by using drugs. But this despair that caught up to him in the autumn of 1998 seems to have grabbed on more fiercely than any he'd known for a long time.

Then he got in trouble. The sequence of events is unclear, but at one point the institutional security people checked his computer and found a couple of things they didn't like. He had a CD-ROM that he had purchased for fifty dollars from a departing inmate. Because it wasn't on the manifest of approved personal possessions, they took it away from him. And scrolling through the files in his hard drive, they spotted one entitled "hostage taking."

What was that about? Nothing really. He wanted to write a thriller and he was collecting information and stealing ideas from established writers so that he'd be able to create a credible fiction—since he had no personal experience in the field, etc. And did they really think that if he were planning to take some of them hostage, he'd open a file called "hostage taking"?

They didn't seem to believe his protests. Well, to hell with them, he thought. Why should he care? He was on one side of the line and they were on the other.

Then there was the "bullet-proof vest" incident. The way he told it in one of his frequent telephone calls during this period, a serious bodybuilder wanted a canvas vest with front and back pockets that were large enough to carry weights when he was working out and jogging. Ty was working in the canvas repair shop, and there were lots of scraps of material around and a big sewing machine, and he said sure. No problem. He'd make one.

The guards found the vest and concluded that it wasn't for physical fitness at all. With weights in the pockets, they pointed out, it would be bullet-proof. What did he want a bullet-proof vest for? He must be planning something. He protested strenuously and he figured for a while that he was in real trouble. As he put it at the time, he thought he was "about to lose everything." He didn't seem to know yet that he already had.

The drug use hadn't become a problem, but there were danger signs. During one binge, he made himself sick, and his friend Clint Suzack went to him with an ultimatum. Leave the heroin alone or consider the friendship ended, Clint told him. Clint despised the stuff. It turned good people into thieves. It was turning the joint into a snake pit in which you couldn't trust anybody and it was killing a lot of people.

Ty listened. Clint was right. But he needed something to beat the despair that was threatening to close in and smother him. And that was when he revisited the fantasy world where he had found so much distraction and comfort in the past. He started dreaming up an escape.

7.

PEOPLE WHO KNEW HIM WELL, including senior corrections officers, still believe that it was largely an academic exercise. It was like the novels and the screenplays he never wrote, a creative exercise in his head.

Lou Kelly, the warden at Millhaven, remembers a friend in his university days who was always plotting the perfect bank robbery.

"It was like an intellectual exercise for him. He was never going to do it. He just loved thinking about it and planning it. He was always casing banks. I think Ty Conn was like that. Always scheming. Except he'd occasionally act impulsively on a scheme."

The most dangerous thing about Ty Conn, according to Lou Kelly, was that "impulsivity."

Ty Conn was aware that one of the big problems at KP was a history of sour management-labour relations that went back long before his time. Even early in his stay there, in the summer of '98, he knew there was a lot of friction between staff and management. In October he'd been amused to read a series of features in *The Toronto Sun* that were obviously based on the guards' grievances.

The stories, by Michael Harris, who is an author and was then a *Sun* columnist, were dripping with sarcasm and reflected staff animosity toward the new warden at KP, Monty Bourke. The way they presented the facts, Bourke was handing the joint over to the cons at the expense of the guards' safety. He'd been mollycoddling inmates and letting them get away with intimidating and abusing staff.

Harris was scathing about how the CSC had allowed lapses in security at KP. Among other things, there was no electronic warning system for the top of the wall, and one of the guard towers, on the southeast corner, wasn't even staffed on the graveyard shift, from 11 p.m. until seven in the morning. Ty made a mental note of that.

It wasn't that he was planning anything specific. It was just that after a while certain responses become reflexive. The famous old bank robber Edwin Alonzo Boyd made the same observation once in a private conversation many decades after he'd become a law-abiding citizen. He said even as an octogenarian, whenever he'd walk into a bank, he'd instinctively seek out the defences, and his mind would automatically make note of weaknesses and vulnerabilities. Even though he was long past robbing banks, he liked the mental exercise.

"Being a bank robber or an escaper," Ty Conn said once, "is a lot like being a typist. When you spread your hands over the keys you just can't help but feel out where the letters are for the words you're thinking."

And so, just as one would stoop and scoop and pocket a coin seen lying on the ground, Ty scooped and filed away the fascinating intelligence provided by Michael Harris in that tribune of law and order, *The Toronto Sun*. And just as the coin would inevitably be spent, the intelligence would one day be put to use.

It was during a prolonged period of punishment in the hole—Kingston Pen's dreary segregation unit—that the fantasies took on the potential for reality.

8.

ONE LOOK AT TY CONN ON JANUARY 30, 1999, which was a Saturday, told a disturbing story. He was puffy and pasty and a little bit scruffy. Visiting a prison inmate over any extended period of time will reveal a variety of moods, all the way from elation to grumpiness to cold cynical anger. Ty's mood that day was unusual for him. He seemed to find it difficult to sustain a conversation. When he wasn't distracted, he was bitter.

One suspected, but didn't know for sure until much later, that he'd been fighting a nearly suicidal depression by taking drugs. He was buying anti-psychotic medication from mentally disturbed inmates in segregation. It had been a bad month. Two suicides in the joint, and just that week—just as he was supposed to get out of the hole and return to his cell—there was a serious incident on Upper G.

On the Tuesday, January 26, Alfie Martin went bananas on the range, and a couple of the guys there finally had to kill him to stop him from hurting somebody. That made Upper G a crime scene, and everybody had to leave temporarily. Ty was already in segregation and this meant he wasn't going to get back to his cell and his computer and his TV and his stuff until the coppers finished their investigation. Which could take a long time.

In the meantime they'd moved him into the segregation range where Paul Bernardo lived. He was just two cells away from the son of a bitch.

So what's he like?

Who?

Bernardo.

He's a nobody.

It was like that for much of the visit. Conversation was like pulling teeth. And then he loosened up a bit and related how he liked to torment Bernardo, telling him that he was having a camera smuggled in and was going to take photographs of him and sell them to the tabloids for millions.

For Ty Conn the murder of Alfie Martin would mean that his time in segregation would extend to a full six weeks. And it had all started because of a letter and an act of carelessness by one of his acquaintances on the range, Paulo Teixiera.

People who knew Ty Conn would later spend a lot of time trying to figure out why he ever trusted a guy like Paulo in the first place. He hardly knew him. They had nothing at all in common. You just had to look at Paulo and he'd make you nervous, and yet Ty put his life in Paulo's hands. Not once, but twice.

In December Ty heard that Paulo was going out on statutory release. This was unusual. People hardly ever go from KP to the street. An inmate would normally pass out through medium- and minimum-security institutions and programs. Paulo was going straight to a halfway house back where he came from, in the world of small-time hoods and drug dealers in the west end of Toronto.

Ty asked him if he'd do a favour. Would he mail a letter to a trusted contact when he got out? He wanted the letter to bypass the usual institutional scrutiny. Letters mailed from inside have to be handed in unsealed. The contents of letters can be monitored, and the contents of this one were sensitive. Paulo would have known that the letter was dangerous for both of them. Ty was instructing someone outside to obtain a city map of Kingston and how to smuggle it in for him.

Nobody knows for certain what he wanted the map for. He already knew the city from having spent time there when he was fourteen, just before he went to Brookside. And if he were planning a breakout, would he really want to spend much time wandering around Kingston? He emphatically denied to the authors that he was actively planning an escape at any time in December. But whatever he had in mind, a bit of bad luck made it moot.

Paulo lost the letter. The coppers found it. Ty went to the hole for six weeks. Paulo went home. And then, on January 30, Ty was saying he was stuck there because of Alfie Martin.

The murder on the range was an illustration of one of
the things he hated most about the place. The atmosphere
was bad enough just because of the age of the joint and the
clientele. But on top of that there was the ongoing friction
between management and the union, and the inmates were
getting caught in the crossfire.

The killing of Alfie Martin, he said, was classic. It shouldn't
have had to happen. Alfie was a well-known discipline problem. He was routinely flipping out, especially when he'd get
into booze or drugs. He was psycho, Ty said, and everybody
knew it.

You could see trouble coming a mile away on the 26th.
Alfie was out of control again. But the scary thing this time
was that the coppers didn't seem to give a damn. Even when
Alfie spit in one copper's face, the guy just wiped it off and
turned away. Normally an inmate who spits on an officer is
taken down hard. It means instant segregation and worse. But
not this time. The officer just sent Alfie back to the range.

Sooner or later somebody on the range was going to have
to deal with him if the guards didn't. Bob Simpson, who was
doing eleven years for manslaughter, and Donald LaKing,
who was serving three life sentences, eventually did. They
admitted, afterwards, that after ducking and dodging Martin
for what seemed like most of the afternoon, they finally
shanked him. And that was that. They couldn't figure out,
though, why the guards let it happen.

Simpson told a *Toronto Star* reporter afterwards it was like
"putting a bunch of pit bulls in there and watching them fight.

"That's madness," he said. "I have the right to self-preser-
vation. I have the right to defend my own life. It doesn't
matter if I'm in there for eating people. I have the right not
to be murdered like a dog."

9.

IT WAS DURING THIS EXTENDED STAY in seg that Ty heard the news that Warkworth had formally turned down his request for a transfer there. He would later admit to his friend Theresa Burke that this was when he went over the edge. Screw it, he decided. He was going to get out *his* way. No more waiting for this sclerotic system to deliver what he felt he deserved—a chance at freedom. He was going to go for the whole thing in one big gamble. Win or lose, it didn't matter any more.

By the time he returned to the range in mid-February he had the project neatly analyzed and broken down into manageable components.

To get out of any prison requires planning for three escapes: from the cell, from the enclosed interior space and from the perimeter of the institution itself.

The cell is most difficult because it is small and sealed and under almost constant scrutiny. Even if he did escape the cell, movement inside the institution was tightly controlled by impenetrable doors, guard posts and cameras. And if he managed to get beyond the two inner circles of confinement, the perimeter was a high wall monitored by cameras, armed guards in towers and foot patrols.

Obviously, the hard part would be getting to the wall. Once there, he figured, the task would be straightforward. Just a matter of climbing. And that would be where institutional vigilance was weakest. The wall. Nobody ever expected the inmate to get that far because the first two levels of security were so daunting.

Escapes, like magic tricks, depend on the creation of illusions. Getting out of a cell is easy. The coppers *let* you out every day. The challenge was to figure out how to avoid going back into it once they'd let him out. That's where the illusion came in. He had to make them think he was in the cell when he really wasn't.

And so, for months, he worked on the illusion. First he got permission to put his bulletin board at the end of the upper bunk that was closest to the front of the cell. It would block a clear view of his head and shoulders when he was sleeping. But the guards said it would be okay since they'd still be able to see the rest of him.

He didn't sleep much anyway, so it wasn't difficult for him to maintain a fairly consistent position in the bunk when the guards were making their rounds. He'd adopt a pose that they would notice and remember and, eventually, come to anticipate. He slept in sweat pants, often with his running shoes on, one leg crooked and partly hanging over the side.

Sometimes a guard would speak to him as he passed. This could be a problem. So he found an unused radio and took it apart. Then he built a speaker that he modified by various muffling and filtering materials until it would perfectly transmit a human voice. When the time came to complete the illusion, he'd run hidden wires to another cell. That way, even if a guard spoke to the dummy, he'd get a sleepy response.

The solidarity of the little "family" unit on Upper G was remarkable. He needed help at every stage of the project, and it seems there was no lack of it. What was really amazing was that in all the time and effort the plan required, nobody betrayed him.

Ty Conn had an unusual amount of freedom to move around within the institution. He was always active on committees and in the social life of the joint. He was a familiar figure, hurrying about delivering canteen orders and organizing activities, always presenting a cheerful and chatty demeanor to cops and cons alike. He always had an interesting interpretation of whatever was current in the news or the gossip mill, or a bit of advice, or just a minute to stand and listen to somebody's beef. You'd never know looking at him or listening that he was incubating a wild and perilous plan.

In early March he was organizing the Native Brotherhood's food drive "because nobody else would do it."

In his travels he would inevitably spot scraps of debris and junk in corners and forgotten storage rooms, and he'd helpfully pick things up and reorder them and even relocate them to more convenient storage places. He was especially fastidious about long pieces of metal used for constructing bookshelves. Ty Conn, everybody noted, was always busy at something.

Working in the canvas shop, he complained one day about the pigeons that seemed to fly in whenever they wanted to and roost there and make a mess of the place. They were coming through a loading-dock entrance. It was a second-floor doorway, about twenty feet off the ground. The doors opened from the inside. For extra security there was a heavy padlocked grille just beyond the doors. When the doors and the grille were open during the day, the pigeons just took over the place. He persuaded the shop foreman to hang a large piece of canvas in the opening to stop the pigeons.

The canvas baffle became a permanent fixture, hanging there between the door and the grille. The pigeon problem went away. You had to hand it to that young Ty Conn. He had a solution for just about everything.

The shop was in a room that was much larger than the space they needed for the work they did there. But in a joint as old as Kingston, you used whatever space was available, whether there was too little or too much. Function followed form. The shop, with its generous dimensions, was a perfect place to stash the materials he needed without raising suspicion. Already stashed there was an ancient stepladder.

Sometime in March he discovered that he was once again classified as a maximum-security inmate. There had been a review of his security status in February and he was formally confirmed at maximum. And at about that time, while helping out in the canteen one day, he saw a name stitched on the pocket of a customer's shirt, and a chill ran straight through his gut. It was the "incompatible" inmate who had blocked his access to Warkworth the previous autumn. The face meant nothing to him.

He asked the guy if he knew about the situation. The guy seemed to know something, but he denied that he was responsible for keeping Ty out of Warkworth. In any case, he'd been gone from there since October and this was March and there must be some other explanation.

So what was he doing in KP? Simple. Like so many who go out on statutory release, he'd screwed up and was back in the system again. Just passing through Kingston. In there for assessment. Paperwork. On his way to medium. Blah blah blah.

Ty just felt cold. Wherever this loser went he'd still be considered an incompatible and Ty would consequently be excluded from that place. And there were damned few options available to him. Collins Bay wouldn't have him because of his past. Warkworth had already turned him down. Which left Joyceville Institution. What if this asshole went to Joyceville? (Which he later did!) Ty Conn suddenly realized that his chances of ever getting out of Kingston were in the same zone of probability as Paul Bernardo's.

Obviously the fury and the frustration showed in his face. There was a copper standing nearby listening to the exchange. Half joking, he remarked "for a pack of smokes I'll go for a walk and you guys can sort this out privately." Nobody laughed.

Mr. Incompatible scurried away then. Ty watched him go. To hell with him. To hell with the guard and his flip advice. To hell with Warkworth and Collins Bay and Joyceville and the whole pathetic system. If there was any lingering doubt about what he had to do, it evaporated at that moment.

10.

LETTER, MARCH 29, 1999.

Dear Theresa

I haven't been writing, running or anything lately. I've been in a blue mood for most of the last six weeks since I got out of seg. That's got to change soon.

I'm writing to a woman at the local detention center, in Napanee, who's in on a very controversial charge. (I'll explain later.)

Aside from that, nothing new is happening. I've basically spent the last three months feeling sorry for

myself and questioning my judgment in ever co-oper-
ating with these people. I can't seem to stop myself,
however. I just took part in something where I edu-
cated a guy on the risks of bringing a gun into the
institution. Essentially I dissuaded him from doing so.

I can't seem to get a break or a chance from these
people. It seems I'm doomed to pay for past mistakes
forever with these people and they can't be convinced
that I just want to get out of jail legally. I'm going to
put some thought into changing tactics.

11.

OBVIOUSLY HE COULDN'T DISCLOSE that he'd already put
a lot of thought into changing tactics. And he was equally
noncommittal during a personal visit on April 1. He looked
worn and tired but seemed to be healthy and in good spirits.
Nobody noted at the time that it would have been the sixtieth
birthday of his birth father, Jack Hayes, if he'd been alive.

After the visit Ty followed up with a telephone call a few
days later. There were a few things he hadn't wanted to say
in front of Theresa.

"You know what I mean, Linden?"

Maybe!

He was always careful around Theresa, out of some
quaint sense that she, being female, was of a more delicate
sensibility than the guys he knew. The woman he was writing to in Napanee was Louise Reynolds, who had been
charged with murdering her child. It was, he was convinced,

358 ❖ Who Killed Ty Conn?

a bum rap and she'd eventually prove it. But he was worried that Theresa, who had a baby of her own, would disapprove of his correspondence with someone suspected of killing a kid.

What do you think?

No chance of that happening, Ty. Theresa is tougher than she looks.

Yeah, but. You never know.

Another thing. He wanted to apologize because he'd been kind of stoned during the visit. Did anybody notice?

No.

Good. These are bad times in the joint.

Yes, but they'll get better . . . hang in, Ty.

Yeah. I guess.

The other thing that he wanted to disclose could be misunderstood and he hoped it wouldn't be. It was just that when Theresa hugged him before he left, he was almost overwhelmed by a wave of panic. Never felt anything like it before. Pure fear. Couldn't imagine what it meant. What do you think?

Probably nothing. Everything is going to be okay, Ty.

You're probably right.

12.

JUST BEFORE NOON ON MAY 6 HE ate lunch in his cell. He then left to help out in the canteen. He paused at the entrance to the cell of one of the people who would help cover his absence that night, and they just stared at each other for a few moments. Then he said simply: "My life is in your hands, my friend."

He stayed at the canteen longer than he had to so that when he finally arrived at the canvas shop for his regular job, he was able to slip in without being noticed. Most important, the foreman had completed his count before Ty had arrived. He was not officially there.

Back on G 3, while a couple of inmates created a series of minor distractions, some others assembled a dummy for his bunk and connected the speaker wires to a makeshift microphone in a cell farther down the range. The dummy was pretty elementary: a stuffed T-shirt, sweat pants and running shoes. The bulletin board conveniently obscured where the head would be. From time to time that day and night, the dummy would be moved and even dismantled and assembled again so not to raise suspicion.

The dummy fooled them during the 4:30 p.m. count. Ty was hiding in the deserted canvas shop by then. At four o'clock the shop foreman had counted everybody out and then locked up. Ty hadn't been there for the count just after noon and so the foreman's numbers tallied. As his fellow shop workers straggled off toward their cells, Ty Conn was hiding inside the wire cage where they stored the industrial sewing machine.

The cage had no ceiling, and when the joint settled down, according to a subsequent investigation, he simply climbed out of the storage cubicle. He covered the shop floor with canvas to muffle sound. Then he went to work on the centrepiece. He bolted shelving brackets to a small stepladder, extending it to a length of twenty-seven feet. The uprights came together at the top and he secured them with many extra layers of tape to prevent any telltale sounds when the metal touched the stone wall. Metal brackets from the mail-bags served as rungs.

In Collins Bay, back in '91, he'd been able to find pieces of wood for rungs and bolts to hold everything together. This time he had no wood and he had only a few bolts. Much of the ladder was being held together by tape, and because it was alarmingly flimsy he could only hope that it would last through the two climbs he had ahead of him: getting out of the second-storey canvas shop and scrambling to the top of the wall.

He worked quietly and efficiently in total darkness. Occasionally he'd put a small portable radio to his ear to check a local newscast to make sure his absence from the cell hadn't been noticed. In fact, that part of the plan had come off without a hitch. After the 11:30 count—the fifth since he'd left the range—his accomplice with the microphone breathed a sigh of relief, gave a gentle tug on the wires that led to Ty's cell and reeled them in, eliminating the evidence of his complicity.

In the canvas shop, Ty found himself ahead of schedule. He had his ladder. His rope was a forty-foot-long piece of canvas made from scraps that he'd sewn together. Working behind the canvas sheeting that had been installed to keep the pigeons out, he cut through the padlock that secured the grille just outside the loading doors. When he finished that, he had a nap.

Shortly after 2 a.m. he carefully wrapped the long canvas "rope" around his left forearm to provide protection in case he was attacked by a guard dog. He was carrying a sharpened spike in his right hand to attack the dog if that became necessary. He was wearing a weight belt, and attached to it was a fire extinguisher. If confronted by armed guards he figured he could gain a few seconds by releasing a cloud of CO_2. Which, if nothing else, would make it more difficult for them to shoot him.

Carefully he lowered the ladder to the ground and climbed down from the loading platform. Once on the ground it took ninety seconds to run to the wall, carrying his ladder and the rest of his paraphernalia.

The wall around Kingston Pen is built in sections. The height of the wall varies from place to place. The section of the wall he intended to climb was thirty-three feet high. He positioned the ladder almost where that part of the wall joined a higher part. Standing on the very tip of his ladder, he'd be able to easily climb over the top. But halfway up, the ladder slipped sideways, so that he was suddenly facing a higher section of the wall.

He didn't have time to go back to the ground to reposition the ladder. And he doubted that the flimsy device would actually survive another climb. So, balanced precariously on the very tip of it, stretching as far as he could reach, he got his home-made grappling hook over the edge. At that point he wished he'd spent more time in the weight pit and less time jogging. He couldn't imagine hauling his body weight up and over that distance. But he had no choice. So he did it.

The rest was easy. He slid down the long strip of canvas on the other side. Then he liberally sprinkled cayenne pepper on the ground to neutralize the tracking dogs. Then he discarded the weight belt and fire extinguisher and he started to run.

Actually, it felt like flying.

The night air was fresh and the sky clear, and it was as though he was the only human being alive. He had not been outside a prison in more than eight years, except on melancholy trips to court or between jails. He'd been jogging in the small spaces that were available on prison property for exercise, trudging through the repetitive loops, surrounded by the dreary grey of the KP walls or the menacing black mesh of the tall fences around Millhaven yard.

There is no colour inside prison, just the drab pastels of the painted concrete, stone and metal walls. Now it is 3 a.m. and he is out and the colours of the urban world are bedazzling and almost blinding him. Suddenly there are brilliant lights everywhere, reds and greens and ambers in the traffic signals, street lights, houses with their yellow porch lights on.

And he felt like he could run forever. He *would* run forever if running felt this good. With the lights glaring around him and the endorphins pumping pure ecstasy and his mind exulting at having just accomplished the impossible, he was higher than he'd ever been on any drug.

He ran seven miles to Highway 401, the familiar belt of superhighway that cinched the middle of his small world, Kingston to Cobourg. He crawled through a culvert to the north side of the highway. Just beyond the 401 there was a small and unfamiliar bedroom community. There, with the daylight oozing in around him, life was finally stirring.

A milkman's van appeared, and he ducked behind a small red pickup truck and crouched down out of sight. In his mind the world by now was buzzing with the news of his escape. Everyone, he thought, was looking for him. Even a milkman. And when the milkman had moved on he happened to look inside the little red truck and he noticed that the owner had carelessly left the ignition keys on the seat. Even God was on his side.

13.

THAT MORNING, MAY 7, MARION CHAMBERLAIN was stealing a few extra moments of quiet time before facing her day. It was a Friday. End of the week for most people. But she has jobs to go to almost every day. She needs all the work she can get just to stay ahead of the bills. One of her jobs is superintendent of the little apartment building she lives in. So she wasn't surprised to hear a knock on the door at about 7 a.m. A tenant looking for something, she thought.

Her husband had gone out already, so she headed toward the door wearing his bathrobe. She and Max had been separated for a while, but they'd recently reconciled and he'd moved into her place and brought a lot of his things with him. The place was so cluttered you could hardly move.

Peering through the peephole, she couldn't see anybody at first. Then she spotted someone moving near the head of the stairway and it looked just like Ty. She figured she must be seeing things. She'd just had a card from him the day before. Happy Grandmother's Day, it said. Mother's Day was two days away. He told her how much he'd enjoyed their trailer visit a couple of weeks earlier and asked her to say hello to so-and-so.

And then she realized that it really was Ty. And a completely irrational thought came to her mind: "The little bugger didn't tell me he was getting a pass to come and see me for Mother's Day."

A pass? From Kingston Pen? For Mother's Day? She could have been on her death bed and he wouldn't have got a pass from that place. She could have been the Governor General and they wouldn't let him visit her. But that's how it was in her mind at that moment. "All these stupid thoughts go through your head?"

The first thing he said when he walked in was: "What the hell happened here?"

He was looking in disbelief at all the unpacked boxes.

"I said, 'Absolutely nothing,'" she reported later. "'As long as I can find the bed and the fridge, I'm okay.'"

It was about then that she noticed that he was soaked in sweat and the panic struck her. This was serious. Where had he come from? How did he manage this?

"Stupid question, Mum," he said.

Quietly he told her that the less she knew, the better off she'd be. He just couldn't take any more of prison. No matter what the future brought, he wasn't going back. He needed some money and he needed some fresh, clean clothes. She dug out some clean shirts that belonged to Max and he changed and then prepared to leave.

"And I turned around and I thought . . . I wonder if I should say what I'm thinking. And so I did. I turned around and I said, 'I know that this might not mean a lot to you right now' because he was like, he was pumped. And I said: 'Your life is very valuable to me.'

"I don't know why I said it. Those thoughts must have been suppressed. Because, thinking back to what he had said to me a couple of weeks previous . . . that 'if anything ever happens to me'. . ."

Then he hugged her and he left. When he was gone she ran to her balcony window for a last look. But all she could see was the back end of a little red pickup truck disappearing around a corner.

And she couldn't help thinking of another day long before, in Picton, watching a strange vehicle driving by and a small boy inside waving. And of the car disappearing around the corner.

By midday the escape from Kingston Pen was on all the newscasts, and on Saturday it was in all the papers. It was the first time anybody had managed to get away from the place in more than forty years. They were reporting that he'd left a cryptic message in his cell. On his calendar, over the date May 6, he had written: "Fishing trip '99."

CHAPTER THIRTEEN

"Death of a Sinner"

Who desireth not the death of a sinner, but
Rather that he may turn from his wickedness
And live.

English Book of Common Prayer

I.

AFTER HE LEFT HIS MOTHER'S APARTMENT on May 7, he made one telephone call and then headed back up Sydney Street in Belleville toward Highway 401. Where he went from there is anybody's guess.

There was no further mention of the stolen red pickup truck in any of the official reports on his escape. He claimed that he dumped it, hoping by the way he parked it to leave the impression that he'd headed for Ottawa. Then he stayed with friends, probably in the vicinity of Stirling, northwest of Belleville, for eight days. He was practically in a state of paralysis. As usual, he'd devoted all his brain power to the immediate challenge of getting out. Now what?

He'd been surprised that the first two people he contacted on the outside, his mother and a media friend, hadn't already heard of his escape. He just assumed that the coppers would have noticed his absence during one of their counts during the night. But as it turned out, he had executed his escape plan with such finesse that he could have been in Toronto by the time they realized he was gone—if he'd planned ahead that far.

It was probably while he was visiting his mother that somebody noticed a long strip of canvas hanging from the exterior wall near the southeast tower of the penitentiary. Warden Monty Bourke recalls that when the phone call came advising him that somebody had obviously breached the wall, two names came instantly to mind. One of them was Tyrone Conn. He was one of the few people in the system with the motivation and the moxy to pull it off.

The story was slow breaking, but once out, it didn't take long before it acquired sensational momentum. Early reports had the sober law-'n'-order tone of official releases from Corrections Canada and the police. Age, description, first in forty years, past escapes, bank robber, armed and dangerous, etc.

Then, as people found out more about him, the tone of the story changed. Reporters were getting snippets of an unhappy childhood and relevant detail from his prison background—the astonishing length of his sentence, the absence of any physical violence in his record. And there was the undeniable intelligence and derring-do of the escape itself.

This was not your ordinary contemporary doped-up sociopathic street hood. He had the makings of one of those

folkloric crooks whose crimes were the result of social circumstances and real need. The media suddenly were grouping
him historically, with people like Edwin Alonzo Boyd, who
was decent, and Red Ryan, who was nasty but colourful. The
notorious Ty Conn was becoming famous overnight.

Whatever it might have done for his ego, he would later
complain that it screwed up his escape. Even a well-intended
profile published in *The Globe and Mail* on Monday, May 10,
pissed him off because it made an opaque reference to "criminals he once betrayed." That, he claimed, would have been
enough to seal off certain avenues of escape that he'd been
counting on. He didn't care if people knew that he was
intelligent and complex and non-violent. He just wanted to
disappear.

And then his picture was everywhere and his story was
the hottest thing on the news, and it became very difficult
for him to budge from where he was hiding for fear of being
recognized.

On Tuesday, May 11, Erin Andersson reported in *The
Globe and Mail* that Monty Bourke was making "an emotional
appeal" to him to come back. Bourke had reviewed the
inmate's file and was inspired by the absence of violence and
by a lot of other information that indicated the potential for
redemption.

Andersson reported the warden's pledge: "If Mr. Conn
voluntarily walks through the prison's gates, the warden will
personally help him get his life together for a future parole
date."

Mr. Conn, unfortunately, didn't see much of value in
what Mr. Bourke was offering. Even if Monty Bourke were
sincere, he later told Theresa Burke, the KP warden would

have no hope of delivering on the concessions that he was promising. The first thing that would happen to Ty, if he surrendered, would be a trip to a special handling unit for about five years. Warden Bourke would have no control over that.

And even if the warden were able to prevent a transfer to the SHU, where would they put him? Back in Millhaven, where he'd survive for maybe twelve minutes? Or in Kingston Pen where, with the status of warden's pet, he'd be persecuted by both inmates and staff—and, sooner or later, killed? It was a non-starter.

The response to Monty Bourke was thanks but no thanks. He didn't actually speak the words, but he conveyed the message in a manner that the warden could not have misinterpreted.

2.

WARDEN BOURKE ATTACHED A STRICT condition to his offer. There was a small window of opportunity, he had said. But it would close permanently the moment that the fugitive reoffended. One theft or robbery or act of violence, and the deal was off.

At some point on Saturday, May 15, Ty came out of hiding. And when he surfaced it was in a place with a name that resonated among the strongest memories of his childhood.

Oak Lake is a small cottage enclave just outside Stirling, about twelve miles northwest of Belleville. The Conn family once had a cottage at Oak Lake, and it was there that Dr. and

Mrs. Conn took Ty, aged three and a half, to meet their other three children in the summer of 1970. They had just picked him up at the Children's Aid Society offices in Picton. Oak Lake was where he started his life with the Conns.

He went back to Oak Lake on the night of May 15 to steal a car. The one he selected was parked near a cottage no more than 110 yards from the old Conn place. He was a better car thief than driver, however, and he promptly demolished the first one he managed to get started. He accidentally went over an embankment before he got more than a few metres.

Despite the racket he must have caused, he was able to steal a second vehicle and a can of gasoline and get away before anybody noticed.

Doreen Lovett, who worked as Dr. Bert Conn's secretary for eighteen years, lives at Oak Lake, and she found out about his nocturnal visit on the Sunday morning. She had known Ty well when he was a boy. He'd come to the office occasionally. Now and then she'd look after him and the other Conn kids. But she hadn't seen him since she'd left Dr. Conn's office, to be replaced by the secretary who would become the second Mrs. Conn.

She had fond memories of him, and knowing a lot about the domestic situation in which he'd grown up, she had a lot of sympathy for him—even though he was a notorious fugitive.

"He drove behind me and through my rock garden and through the wooden fence . . . and somehow or other, the car was demolished down by the corner.

"And then he picked up the Chrysler Intrepid I think it was . . . and [the people who owned it] didn't miss their car until they were going out to church."

Police investigators were soon on the scene and confirmed for her that the car thief was, in all likelihood, the little boy she remembered so well.

The policemen asked her what she'd do if he showed up again.

"I said: 'You know what? I've thought about that.' And this is what I told them: I said 'I'd bring him in. There's no doubt that he'd be hungry and I'd make him soup and sandwiches if it was lunchtime.' And of course they gave me a real bad going over about that attitude."

She wasn't the only one with sympathetic feelings for the young fugitive. A lawyer in the Belleville area confided that in the days just following his escape he left his garage door open day and night, just in case Ty Conn needed a place to rest. People all over southern and central Ontario were quietly rooting for him, to the great annoyance of bankers and police officers.

Then, unfortunately, Ty crossed the line that Warden Monty Bourke had drawn to mark the limits of his willingness to help.

That Sunday morning, at the wheel of the car he stole at Oak Lake, he drove to Trenton, and just before opening time at the local Canadian Tire store, he joined a small crowd waiting in front to be admitted. The store owner would later tell reporters that weekend openings are always chaotic. People rush in and plunge into their shopping while the staff are still only half organized for the day.

Once inside, Ty walked straight to sportswear and selected a long all-weather coat from the rack. Undetected, he removed the tags and put it on. Then he went to the hardware section and picked a sturdy bolt-cutter and concealed it underneath the coat.

The gun rack was conveniently located beside the back door and the bolt-cutter made quick work of the lock that was there to keep the weapons out of the hands of the curious and the larcenous and the psychopaths. According to a later statement by the owner, he selected a nine-hundred-dollar camouflaged turkey gun and two boxes of shotgun shells. Then he went out the back door and drove away. It all took ten minutes.

Later that day in Frankford, he ditched the Chrysler and stole another car. This one was a 1977 Buick Lesabre. It was bright yellow. Yes, he explained later, it was conspicuous, but he didn't have many options. He had to steal an older model. He'd been in jail for so long he was unfamiliar with the newer cars and he didn't have a clue how to circumvent or dismantle car alarms. And, even without the alarms, the more recent cars are harder to break into. The locks are more secure. Nobody trusts anybody any more.

On the afternoon of Tuesday, May 18, he drove the yellow Buick to Colborne, a little town halfway between Cobourg and Trenton. Colborne is famous locally for its apple blossom celebration near the end of May and, to travellers, for the giant red apple alongside the Highway 401 exit you take to get there.

Colborne is also famous for its bank. Once, back in 1951, Lennie Jackson and Steve Suchan, who later became notorious members of Edwin Alonzo Boyd's "gang," robbed it. Ty Conn robbed it twice.

Cindy Hickman has the dubious honour of having been there for both Ty Conn's visits. The first time, in November 1991, was terrifying. This one was worse because she couldn't help recalling that she had testified at his trial afterwards and identified him and helped put him away. This was a distressing thought to have in mind as you watched him robbing your bank again with a shotgun under his arm in May of 1999. She could only hope that his memory wasn't as clear as hers.

She needn't have worried. If there was going to be bloodshed that day, it would have started even before she noticed him and his shotgun. Walking in, he'd approached a lady who was at the bank machine in the lobby and ordered her inside. She sharply refused and then, when he insisted, she just marched away. And he just watched her go. Inside, when he announced that he was robbing the place, one of the customers grabbed a kid and ran outside. Again, he just watched them go.

Cindy Hickman remembers that this time he was wearing a mask. But she didn't notice much more than that because she was trying so hard to be invisible.

"I can't even remember what kind of a mask because this time I mostly kept my head down because I didn't want him to recognize me. So I kind of froze and I had a customer in front of me . . . but I did look up once when he was at the teller's and we actually made eye contact. which really scared me at the time. His eyes were very recognizable. Like his eyes just stood out because, from the first robbery, you have dreams afterwards and his face was always coming up in my dreams . . . nightmares. And he had, I don't know. His eyes were deep . . . deep eyes that you could study . . . the main feature of his face."

She also recalls that the tellers were so upset that they were throwing money into his bag. And he was telling them that "if you don't give me enough money today I'll be back tomorrow to blow your fuckin' head off." And they just kept piling it in until it was almost full. Then he headed for the back door, and she almost fainted because she knew he couldn't get out that way. In 1991 he'd just walked out the front door, but this time he was going to discover that his escape was blocked by a locked door and he could become angry and God knows what would happen then.

"And he was kicking it and getting very upset. And I knew that he had to come back past me to get out again," she said afterwards.

But eventually he was gone, out the front. They could see him hurrying around to the back, where his lurid yellow car was waiting.

He probably wouldn't have been surprised reading in the *Toronto Star*'s account of the robbery the next day that as he was going about his business in the bank, one of the escaped customers was next door in the Colborne Health Centre desperately trying to reach the police.

Pam Schick, a dental assistant, was frantically dialing 911 . . . and getting a busy signal. Then, after the fourth try, a skeptical dispatcher wanted to know how she could be so sure there was a robbery in progress. Robberies weren't very common in Colborne. She had to explain that a customer from the bank had just run in "pretty shook up" and there was no doubt about what was happening.

The delays were eating up seconds, but they were crucial seconds, because the nearest OPP officer was a fifteen-minute drive away.

By the time the police got to the crime scene, the holdup man was heading for Toronto and already looking forward to dumping the stolen yellow car. It wouldn't have been any more conspicuous if it had had flashing lights on the roof spelling out the words "Bank Robber."

He had survived the robbery, for the moment. But because of his own past experience and because he was an avid reader of crime history, he should have known that the bank in Colborne had visited very bad luck upon those who robbed it in the past. He was captured a few weeks after he robbed it in 1991, and that job was one of the factors contributing to his forty-seven-year prison sentence. Jackson and Suchan, who robbed the same bank in 1951, were subsequently caught and hanged for killing a Toronto police officer during a later gunfight.

And, of course, driving along the 401 with the towers of Metro Toronto looming in the haze, he fully realized that the window of opportunity that the warden at Kingston Pen had opened the week before had just closed with a resounding slam.

3·

HE LATER CLAIMED THAT HE HAD A plan in mind for when he got to Toronto, but nothing about the next two days would indicate any evidence of premeditation.

He needed identification and travel documents. But he'd later complain that the publicity had frightened the individual who had promised to supply them. He needed a place to lay low for as long as it took for the story to die down. He'd have preferred Halifax, but it was a bit too far away in the circumstances. Hanging around Hastings County or

Kingston wouldn't work—it would only be a matter of time before the cops would be on the doorstep of everyone he'd ever known.

Toronto was big and busy and full of transients and street people. He'd fit right in, he figured. The papers were publishing pictures of him, but most of them were from years earlier and showed him as a benign-looking teenager. Just to be on the safe side he shaved off his thick crop of sandy-coloured hair and bought some startling blue contact lenses.

Shaving his head would create one potential problem. A couple of years earlier, on a whim, he'd shaved his head and had a tattoo printed on the back of his skull. It was a "Celtic Trillium" design that would, he was told at the time, stand out like a red flag if he was ever on the run again. He just laughed and declared that such a possibility was highly unlikely.

So now he was a fugitive with this conspicuous artwork on his bald head, which meant his disguise would have to include a ballcap at all times.

Of course his old friend Ian recognized him right away, notwithstanding the ballcap and the piercing-blue contact lenses. He'd been expecting a phone call ever since he first heard of the escape. But here Ty was, on his doorstep. And he needed a place to stay. Ian couldn't bring himself to say no, clean and simple, and so that was when he invented the harmless lie—that the police had already been there asking about him.

He couldn't possibly have known, being a law-abiding citizen and businessman, that this deception would set off a chain reaction in Ty Conn's mind. If the cops had been there already, it meant that they were making a lot more progress in their manhunt than he'd anticipated. Sure they'd have been in touch with his mom and MacIntyre and Burke, and maybe some of his old acquaintances from past escapades.

But the only way they could have known about Ian was if they'd gone into the hard drive of his computer where he had a list of practically all his friends and pen pals. If they did that, there was absolutely nobody that he could safely approach. Well, almost nobody.

4.

THE FIRST THING TY SAID TO PAULO when he arrived was: "I'm Jeremy. Remember me?" He was carrying a gym bag. Paulo told him to come right in, then led him down into the dark and shabby basement apartment with walls the colour of masticated bubble gum.

Paulo remembered afterwards that "he just showed up at the door with a big bag of money." He also had his shotgun, sawed down on both ends so it would fit in the bag. Paulo says he asked Ty to unload the gun. He obliged. Sandy was watching the whole thing wide-eyed. Then they counted the loot from the Colborne robbery.

Sandy had never seen so much money before. There was at least thirteen thousand dollars. The money and the shotgun, she later gushed, were a major turn-on.

Ty wanted to go out on the town right away, but Paulo didn't think that was such a good idea. He offered to run any errands that were required. But Ty was adamant. He hadn't gone to all the trouble of breaking out of prison just to spend more time inside, especially inside a dive like the basement apartment at 101 Alberta Avenue.

Paulo had some business to transact and had arranged to meet some people at Remy's, an upscale restaurant and bar in Yorkville. So all three went there and had dinner while Paulo got the business out of the way. Then they went to Eaton Centre to shop.

He'd been there years before as a fourteen-year old runaway. It was all very thrilling back then, but now the traffic and the noise and the hurrying crowds of people were making his head spin. Life is so static in prison and, after so many years inside, a place like Yonge Street in Toronto becomes almost overwhelming. The street moved too quickly and inside the cavernous shopping centre it wasn't much better. People hurrying blank-eyed and bustling, jostling. People never jostle in the joint.

He bought some jeans and running shoes and a cell phone and gifts for Sandy and Paulo, and then he said he just had to get back to the house before his head exploded from all the big-city chaos.

Back at 101 Alberta Avenue he gave Paulo some money for drugs. Paulo disappeared for a while and when he returned he had a rock of crack cocaine. Ty tried to telephone some friends but couldn't make contact. Sandy and Paulo partied for most of the night. Paulo reported later that Ty didn't like crack, so like a good host, he went out in the early hours of the morning and found some bootleg liquor. But in Paulo's subsequent account of the evening, Ty didn't figure much in the activities. He remembered that particular night mostly because he and Sandy "had one of the best times we ever had in our relationship."

On Wednesday he went out a lot alone. Sandy and Paulo were partying again and Ty, between absences, was talking a lot about going to Nova Scotia. He'd been there back in '89 and had fond memories of the ocean and the historic waterfront and the sailboats. He felt safe in Halifax. Would Paulo go too? Sure, he said.

That night 101 Alberta Avenue was humming with activity. People coming and going. It was making him nervous, too many strangers and too many drugs. Too many slip-ups. People actually using his name out loud. It was getting ridiculous. He snorted a couple of lines of cocaine and it settled him down. Finally, at about 11 p.m., he took his cell phone and stepped outside and dialled Theresa Burke's telephone number.

She was half asleep when she heard the ring. By the time she got to the phone, the line was dead. Since May 7 she'd been expecting to hear from him and trying to imagine what she'd say to him. She had changed the message on her answering machine to instruct telephone operators that she accepted any and all collect calls. Standing there that night, May 19, with the dead telephone receiver in her hand, she somehow knew that the call had been from her friend.

Impulsively, she punched in the Bell Canada code for retrieving missed phone calls, *69. A woman answered immediately.

"Hi," Theresa said carefully. "I'm trying to get in contact with a friend."

Wordlessly, Sandy Beach handed the cell phone to Ty.

"Well," he said when he heard her voice. "The wonders of modern communications."

They talked for two hours. His greatest concern was that she might be feeling betrayed by what he'd done. He was anxious to assure her that the escape plan only became serious when he was locked up in segregation back in January. Prison was a form of living death at the best of times, he said. But in segregation it was worse. He scrounged drugs from the "bugs" who were on medication there and eventually decided to acquire a dosage that would be strong enough to kill him.

"I was planning to kill myself," he told her. "I just couldn't stay there any more. Then I decided, fuck it. I'm not going out that way. I'll take one last shot."

He explained some of the details of the escape. He talked about how he stole the shotgun and how he robbed the bank. She asked why he'd ignored the warden's offer, and he replied that the warden wouldn't have been able to deliver.

Theresa tried one more time to discuss the implications of voluntarily going back to prison, but he was adamant.

"I've thought about it. I was willing to pay for my crimes. But I've paid with eighteen years, and I can't go back there.

"Whatever happens," he said, near the end of their chat that night, "I'd rather go out a different way. I left a note on my computer. I really hope you get to see it, because it explains everything. It explains what I did and why. If anything happens to me, don't let them tell you anything else."

Whatever he had written in the note will remain a mystery. By the time she had a chance to look for it, the note was gone from the computer's memory.

5·

AFTER SPEAKING TO THERESA BURKE that night, Ty joined
the party inside 101 Alberta Avenue. By then it was past
midnight and into Thursday morning. The way Paulo
reported it later, Ty and Sandy Beach were doing heroin non-
stop for the rest of the night.

"He was really messed up on junk. I kept telling him
don't do so much, man, it's really good [potent]. But he
wouldn't listen. He just kept doing it. 'Okay,' I said. 'But
you're going to pay for it. You're going to be puking your
guts out.' But he didn't want to hear about it. He just
wanted to get as fucked up as possible."

And he did. But there would be a persuasive reason to
believe that it wasn't heroin that made him sick.

The weird thing about the way he felt on Thursday was
that nobody else seemed sick. Sandy and Paulo were just fine,
even though they had been far more heavily into the drugs
and the booze than he. He spent all day trying to shake it. But
it kept getting worse. You'd almost think he'd been poisoned.

And there was something else that he couldn't quite put
his finger on. There seemed to be a lot of tension in the air,
as if Paulo and Sandy were having some kind of a spat. And
as if it had something to do with him.

The bag with his gun and his money was in a closet, and
when he went to check and take some money out for later,
he realized that a lot of the loot was gone already. That was
depressing. It was time to get out of there. At this point it
was still early afternoon.

He walked up as far as St. Clair Avenue and found a pay telephone and called Ian's number. Ian answered. He explained that there seemed to be some domestic difficulty happening where he was staying and could he at least sleep in Ian's garage that night. Ian said no. Well, what about that friend up north, who used to have a boat. They stayed with him back in '89. No. That wouldn't be possible either. But there might be something else available, closer. He took down Ty's cell-phone number and promised to call him back.

By the time he finished on the phone, the nausea was worse. He was almost too sick to stand up. He had to get back to 101 Alberta Avenue.

Once there, he fell asleep. About mid-afternoon his phone rang and it was Ian reporting that he'd made arrangements for Ty to rent a room from a friend. The friend was an alcoholic and a bit of a loser, but he had no criminal record, and Ty would be safe and comfortable there. The friend, whose name was Todd, was expecting him . . . right away. Can you get over there now? We'll expect you in a couple of hours at the latest, Ian said.

Ty thanked him but he was just too damned sick to move.

6.
___

AT ABOUT 2 P.M. ON THAT THURSDAY Paulo and Sandy left the house and went downtown to take care of some business. At about 4 p.m. they checked into the Colony Hotel. Paulo later explained that he had a mysterious pre-monition that dangerous people were after him.

"I had some stuff of my own happening then and I had some problems and some shots fired and I wanted to get inside as fast as possible and I didn't want people to follow me to the house because I didn't want them to know where I lived. So I said let's get a hotel."

The Colony is a popular mid-scale hotel in the middle of downtown Toronto, a brief stroll from City Hall. Using Sandy Beach's real name (Cheryl Hamlyn) and old address (50 Raglan Street) they registered and settled into Room 950. Paulo claims they were only checking in for the night, but the hotel records show that he paid $250 cash up front for a room that only cost $149.

In fact, they stayed there for five nights, running up a bill of $1,045.64, all paid in cash instalments as the days went by.

Paulo also claims that because he'd been up almost non-stop for two days, using cocaine to stay conscious, he was nearly delirious with fatigue that Thursday afternoon and went straight to sleep. He doesn't remember much more than that until the next morning.

But, according to his hotel bill, somebody in the room was sufficiently awake to send out for pizza and order up a movie. And according to his upstairs neighbour at 101 Alberta Avenue, Pam Houston, Paulo phoned her at 8:30 that evening—presumably from downstairs—to warn her to take her kids and get out of there. The cops were on the way. Sandy Beach subsequently confirmed that she and Paulo had returned to the house in the evening to pick up some of their things.

Pam was frying up a package of fish sticks for the kids' supper when Paulo called, but there was something urgent about the way he was speaking when he told her to flee, so she immediately stopped what she was doing and left. On the way out, she passed Paulo's cryptic message to the lady who lived in the ground-floor flat, and on her way past the entrance to the basement apartment she called out Paulo's and Sandy's names, just to double check. But she got no answer.

Paulo and Sandy were already driving away in a taxi. The only person left inside was Ty Conn, who was too sick to answer her.

Pam and her kids were hurrying along Alberta Avenue on foot when she saw the cop car lurking in the shadows up near St. Clair Avenue. It was unmarked but "they were undercover cops. You can just tell."

Moments later the neighbourhood was crawling with about thirty of them, undercover and uniform, two teams from the emergency task force and the entire eight-member ROPE (repeat offender program enforcement) squad which had been tracking Ty Conn ever since he'd bailed out of Kingston, almost exactly two weeks earlier.

It seems that everybody in the neighbourhood could see them coming, or knew in advance that they were coming. Everyone, that is, but Ty Conn.

7.

HE WAS STILL PROSTRATE THERE WHEN, at about 9 p.m., the police arrived and shouted their standard ultimatum. He was caught. There was no point in prolonging the situation. He was to come out, unarmed, etc.

He shouted back that he had no intention of giving up and that he had a shotgun. If they tried to come in he'd use it—on himself. And to show he meant it, he cocked the weapon and pressed the barrel to his chest.

Fighting nausea and fear, he tried to assure them that it was not his intention to harm anyone, but that he would rather die than go back to prison. They talked about his options, but no matter how they tallied the choices available to him, the bottom line was always a big zero as far as he was concerned. After nearly an hour, negotiator Jim Bremner good-naturedly suggested that they should "just wrap this thing up so we can all go home."

Home? For Ty Conn the word was an abstraction and he bitterly corrected the policeman. "*You* can go home," he said.

It would have been difficult for him to avoid thinking back nearly eight years, to December 20, 1991, when he'd had a similar chat with an Ottawa policeman named Eric Hanson. In the hard days and months and years after that night he'd often regretted his decision to surrender then. He wasn't going to make the same mistake this time.

He asked for permission to get a drink. He was nearly dehydrated. Could he go to the kitchen for a drink of juice? Sure, they told him. Passing through the living room, he set the shotgun down while he continued on his way to the kitchen. He was barely at the refrigerator when there was a sudden commotion behind him, followed by a blinding flash and an explosion.

It was a stun grenade. It should have left him blinded, deaf and disabled. But Ty Conn was young and fit and he had the reflexes of an athlete. The police were startled to see him bounding through the smoke to where he'd left his weapon. This is probably when the police shot two rubber-ized projectiles into the room to either stop his progress toward the gun or to knock it out of his reach.

That didn't work either. He didn't seem to notice the rubber bullets any more than he'd been daunted by the violence of the grenade. And in a split second he had the gun again and the cops were desperately trying to restore their credibility and their control. They were back to a point somewhere south of square one.

Bremner was coaxing then, talking to Ty about his family and about the great reputation he had among all the people who knew him. Everybody liked him. He had everything to live for. Etc.

Finally running low on inspiration, Bremner asked him if there was anything he wanted. It was then he replied that, yes, there was. He'd like to speak to his friends, MacIntyre or Burke.

Theresa Burke was just arriving home at 11:55 P.M. when she noticed that there was a telephone message waiting for her. For two weeks she'd been on edge, watching for messages or waiting for a knock on the door. Then he'd surfaced just the night before. She hadn't really expected to hear from him again so soon.

This call, however, wasn't from Ty.

"This is Sgt. McAteer of the repeat offenders task force," the message said. "We have an emergency situation dealing with Tyrone Conn. Please call as soon as possible."

He left two telephone numbers.

It took a while to get through. First Bremner had to quiz her to make sure she was capable of having the conversation and perhaps even achieving something useful. Then the cell phones wouldn't work. Four times they had to send a cop to the window to hand in a telephone. And each time they did, a battery promptly died.

Finally she heard his voice and it was vastly changed from the night before.

They spoke for thirteen minutes. Their first conversation had been on a telephone, July 18, 1994. And now they had begun what would be their last. He seemed to know it. He was distraught. He sobbed as he tried to tell her that he'd stored a lot of information on a floppy disk. Everything she had to know about him was available from sources he'd provided on that disk, he said.

She tried to tell him that he was far more important than any disk or "journalism project." She cared about him. She wanted him alive and safe.

"It was primal," she would later recall. He was hovering close to a total emotional collapse. And then he'd pull himself together and warn the police to stay back, always emphasizing that he meant no harm to them. Only to himself. Cornered, the man who had for so long been classified as a high risk to public safety had taken himself as hostage.

His moods seemed profoundly contradictory, oscillating wildly between anger and fear and despair and irony. The cops were being decent, he told her. They always were when they wanted something. He broke down and wept again when she asked him if he knew how they'd found him. He implied that he'd been betrayed. He said, "It's always the same."

He was embarrassed, and he apologized when he had to stop talking long enough to vomit.

She told him that half the country was cheering for him and the other half were in love with him.

He said he never wanted that.

What did you want? she asked.

"Not to be treated like some fucking cartoon character," he answered, referring bitterly to a *Toronto Star* headline that had christened him "King Conn."

"I'm not a cartoon," he repeated.

The media coverage will work to your advantage, Theresa told him.

"It won't last," he replied.

He interrupted frequently to warn the police to stay back.

"You can't trust the coppers," he said wearily.

A rug in the next room was still smouldering where the stun grenade had landed.

Then he told her that there was a lot of static on his end of the conversation. He was missing much of what she was saying. He wanted to hear every word. He was going to try to change positions to improve reception. She could hear him ask someone if he was allowed to move, and she could hear a voice reply, "That's fine, Ty."

Thank God, she thought, they know enough to call him Ty.

He was yelling then: "I'm going to get up now . . . I'm crossing the room between the bedroom and the main room . . . I have to pass this chair . . . you'll see my legs first through the window."

He was moving carefully, the shotgun held to his chest with one hand, the cell phone in the other. The voice was steady. She believed that finally he had his emotions under control. The conversation had turned an important corner.

He wasn't only keeping the line of communication open, he was attempting to improve it.

He found a place to sit and he asked if she could hear him more clearly. She said she could. He seemed to be in the act of sitting down, settling in for a prolonged conversation.

He started another sentence, but never finished it.

He uttered two words and she tried hard afterwards to remember what they were. But the events that followed erased them from her mind.

She heard a muffled sound. A kind of soft pop. It could have been a shot or even a small explosion. Loud sounds are difficult to identify through a telephone receiver. Then she heard the cell phone striking something hard. The floor, perhaps. Everybody knows the sound of a dropped phone. And almost instantly there were voices and one of them distinctly said, "Get handcuffs."

But there would be no need for handcuffs. Ever again.

The police probably never knew how close they'd been to missing their chance to capture Canada's then most high-profile fugitive. Had he not been so ill he'd have been gone from 101 Alberta Avenue hours before they arrived. He'd have been safely settled in a rooming house arranged by his friend Ian. Whatever it was that made him so sick ultimately cost him his life.

As far as Paulo is concerned, he brought it on himself with the booze and drugs and the partying. Paulo warned him. It was high-quality heroin, and Ty should have known better than to overindulge.

That's how Paulo remembers it. But like a lot of what Paulo remembers from those two days, it's difficult to winnow the truth out of a lot of self-serving chaff. Ty Conn was cautious about booze and drugs and understood the importance of remaining clear-headed. Theresa Burke spoke with him at length late Wednesday night and into Thursday morning. She found him calm and lucid and sober. Would he have gone from that warm and hopeful chat into a heroin binge?

The truth about what caused his debilitating illness on Thursday, May 20, may well be a bit more sinister than the consequences of excessive partying. The toxicology report from his post-mortem revealed the surprising presence of the synthetic drug methadone in his system.

Paulo had been fighting heroin addiction for about a year and was on a methadone program at the time. Methadone blocks the high that addicts get from heroin. It's used by recovering addicts to numb the symptoms of withdrawal. It would not have been difficult to substitute some methadone for the cocaine and heroin that was available during the frantic socializing in the house on Wednesday night and early Thursday morning.

Ty Conn was not a recreational drug user, but in prison he had taken heroin to fight depression. He considered cocaine useful when he had to stay awake and alert. At 101 Alberta Avenue he'd unquestionably have felt the need to remain vigilant. There were traces of cocaine in his system, with the methadone.

Experts in the field of toxicology and narcotics say that methadone would cause extreme nausea in one who was not a heroin addict. This could explain why Ty Conn was so sick on the day he died that he lacked the strength and the will to move to a safer place when he had the chance.

And so, at 101 Alberta Avenue, his project failed. His escape was a long-shot gamble at getting a new start in life. It succeeded only in removing him from the living death that prison had become.

If he could speak, he'd probably insist that that was good enough.

TY'S MOTHER GOT THE NEWS AT about 1 a.m. on May 21. A Toronto reporter told her that her son was dead. He died in a stand-off with police in a basement apartment where he had taken refuge with some friends. The reporter implied that he had killed himself. She wanted to know if Marion had any comment to make. Later, a sympathetic Belleville policeman came by and told her what had really happened.

A single discharge from a shotgun into his chest from close range killed him quickly. Nobody was quite clear specifically how it had happened. But the Special Investigations Unit, an Ontario civilian agency responsible for overseeing police conduct in situations like this, would be looking into it. The police would be held accountable.

But who killed him? The Belleville policeman didn't know or wasn't prepared to say.

The shot that took Ty Conn's life came from the gun he was holding against his own chest. The initial investigation of his death revealed some suspicious circumstances. Two mysterious projectiles discovered in the room raised the possibility that the police had caused the gun to discharge by some ill-considered action to take him by surprise.

Theresa Burke was on the phone with him for the last thirteen minutes of his life and would probably have heard a secondary sound. She heard only one sudden and surprising interruption when the conversation ended.

Did he kill himself?

The subject of death was often on his mind, his life was so marginal and miserable. He often flirted with the idea of suicide. More than once he made half-hearted attempts. Part of the mental preparation for escapes inevitably included coming to terms with the possibility that he'd be killed trying. The prospect never daunted him. In fact, he always said that death would be a welcome alternative to capture.

But then, faced with the real prospect of oblivion, he always opted for survival. He was, by all accounts, closer to suicide on the evening of May 20 than he'd ever been before. He was physically ill. He was humiliated by the prospect of an ignominious failure in an unprecedented glare of publicity. He was profoundly distressed at the certain knowledge that once again someone had betrayed him. But did he commit suicide?

From what we know of him and all the evidence available, he didn't. All his actions indicate he wanted his conversation with Theresa Burke to continue. His relationship with her was deep and respectful and gallant. He could not have committed an act of obscene violence in her presence.

So who killed him?

Paulo Teixiera's sudden disappearance from 101 Alberta Avenue has raised disturbing questions. The coincidental timing of his flight to a downtown hotel on the afternoon of

May 20; his prophetic warning to Pam Houston, his upstairs neighbour, to get her kids out of the house minutes before the police arrived; Paulo's surprising failure to warn his friend Ty Conn, who was downstairs and who had more to fear from the police than any of them; the post-mortem analysis revealing strong traces of methadone in Ty Conn's system.

These are all circumstances that point accusing fingers in Paulo's direction.

But it is a long leap from there to the accusation that Paulo killed him. And it would be too simple. The circumstances of Ty Conn's death are so tightly interwoven with the fabric of his life that they cannot easily be separated.

Who killed Ty Conn? Everybody? Nobody?

These were questions that throbbed in Marion Chamberlain's mind as she drove toward Toronto just before dawn on May 21. Vast questions suddenly wrapped around her entire life.

When she was still a child, she gave birth to a child. And because she was still a child and lacked the means and the maturity to become an adult quickly, she had to let him go. She assumed that it was the best alternative available for both of them. Now, in the rosy dawn of a spring day nearly thirty years later, she wasn't so sure.

Her son was dead. But that wasn't the worst part. He had never really lived. Why? What went wrong? Whose fault? Big questions, no longer of specific relevance to the boy who became Tyrone, but perhaps important for other boys whose lives began as his did and weren't yet over.

It happens all the time. Individuals fail in their relationships and their responsibilities. It is so common that society has developed reflexes that react almost automatically to parental failure. There are mechanisms and procedures so often used that they are worn and smooth and silent. Child care. Child protection. Juvenile justice. They are supposed to compensate for personal failure, to protect the innocent. And yet they all failed the boy who was born Ernest Bruce Hayes and died Ty Conn.

If only she had known. About the adoption process. About his childhood. About his brushes with the juvenile justice system. She would have tried to intervene sooner. But she couldn't have known any of that. We cloak the lives of children like Ty Conn in secrecy for their protection. A writer on delinquency and crime once referred to "the veil of administrative decency." We don't want the early failures in a life to handicap the life for all time. But whom does the veil of decency really protect?

The secrecy that shrouds adoption and juvenile justice also conceals abuse and failure. Problems flourish in secrecy alongside the incompetence and wickedness that cause larger problems. Failure is not exclusive to the individual. Institutions fail too because, ultimately, institutions are composed of individuals. But isn't it odd that we are allowed to know so little about when and how the institutions fail our children?

How much did the social and professional status of Bert and Loris Conn influence the Picton Children's Aid Society when they approved the adoption of a small and needful child in 1970? Did social status exempt them from the scrutiny that is routinely and rigorously applied in adoptions? Did social status exempt the Conn family from the oversight of social agencies during the eight years that Ty lived with them? Did the "veil of administrative decency" conceal domestic troubles in the Conn home that could only have exacerbated nascent psychological problems that the little boy brought with him into the adoption?

Who killed him?

His death was a logical consequence of his life. To understand his death and why and how it happened would require a close examination of a life and all the factors that played upon it and shaped it into such a tragic waste of gifts and time. A year after the tragedy at 101 Alberta Avenue in Toronto there was no indication from any of the relevant authorities that there would be such a search for answers.

The official position seems to be: Ty Conn is dead; asking questions cannot bring him back; he's better off.

But Ty Conn would have wanted answers, and his family and his friends want them because they might explain a lot of other lives while there is still time to make them better.

The institutions that took responsibility for the little boy who grew into a troubled adult failed him at every stage of his life. For years nobody noticed him, then nobody cared enough or knew enough to deal with him. How many Ty Conns are there in our institutions and our systems? Who knows? The workings of the systems are purposely obscured by a protective scrim of secrecy. Protecting whom? Who cares?

Ty Conn spent fourteen years in federal prisons. People who knew him there unanimously describe him as a likeable, polite and respectful inmate whose only deviance from institutional order was an irrepressible desire to escape from prison. It made him popular among other inmates but a potential threat to how society perceives the penal system. If Ty Conn can break out, what about Bernardo? Or Olson? And, consequently, the system had to treat him as a risk to public confidence and peace of mind. This became the priority.

They insisted on classifying him as a high risk to public safety, not so much for the harm he'd do if he got out, but for the harm he'd do to public confidence in the people and the systems that were supposed to keep him in.

But what if he didn't really belong "in"? How difficult would it have been to rehabilitate Tyrone Conn? And if they couldn't rehabilitate him, what hope is there for anybody in the system of "corrections"?

When he was twenty-seven, incarcerated in the Special Handling Unit of the csc's western region, in Prince Albert, Saskatchewan, he decided to rehabilitate himself. He made dramatic progress in his thinking and his self-awareness and his maturity. He took responsibility. But the corrections system didn't notice.

Because the people who run the system didn't notice that he had changed essentially, nobody was prepared to make the special effort that he needed to help solve deep-rooted problems, problems so much a part of his childhood and infancy that he could not have solved them by himself.

He had the will to live and the intelligence and knowledge to penetrate the gloom if only he'd had a little bit more help. From the system of corrections. From his friends.

Maybe if the visits and the conversations with his mother had continued a bit longer, they'd have reached some answers and they'd have restored his faith in developing a better plan for getting out of prison.

We'll never know.

Driving toward Toronto in the pre-dawn gloom on May 21, 1999, Marion Chamberlain fell back on the primary and often only source of comfort available to grieving mothers since the dawn of time. She told herself: He's at peace now; he's in a better place; no more pain.

And that helped.

At 10 a.m. she and young Max met Robert Hughes of the Special Investigations Unit and his partner at the morgue on Grenville Street. The roar of the city washed like a sea around this odd little island of dramatic sorrow smack in the middle of Canada's largest city. It was sunny and warm, festive and Friday.

They went in together then, to the glinting room of stainless steel and tile and fluorescent light. Robert Hughes and his partner seemed at home in there. The woman who led them in was buoyantly professional, like the guide in the CN Tower who warns you that your ears might pop as the elevator rises quickly. You see rooms like this in movies and they seem bigger and more sinister. This was like a very tidy storage room in a large legal office, with drawers along one wall. Quite ordinary, except for the pungent antiseptic odours and the chill.

The stranger in the drawer with the sheet bunched tightly at his neck was bald and gaunt and angry-looking. Somehow Marion had expected to see a peaceful expression. Dead people sometimes look like they're asleep. Maybe she was hoping to see some evidence of victory, the look of one who has finally beaten all the systems. But there was no sign of triumph and no peace in his expression.

Marion stood very close to young Max who kept a sheltering arm around her shoulders. Max was like a rock.

Then someone gently but officially asked Mrs. Chamberlain: "Is that your son Ty?"

It was a larger question than he could have known. She could have spent all day answering it. But she only had a moment.

"Yes," she said.

In the week that followed Christmas of 1999 and just before the close of the old millennium, the question was still resounding in her mind. Was that her son Ty?

Of course she could never forget that day in 1967, on January 18, when she'd nearly lost her mind from the fear and the pain of delivering him. She had no doubt about the biological connection and how she felt when she brought him home thinking that he was then as grafted onto her life as he had been rooted in her body during those long months of pregnancy.

But then it became 1970, and all the important people in her life seemed to be saying he wasn't hers any more. Her mom and dad. Social workers. A judge. And Jack Hayes was saying nothing at all. Just waiting to get on with his life. And then in less time than it had taken to push him out of her body and into the world, he was severed from her. Gone into nothingness for fifteen years.

And then he was back again, reconnected to her life, and when they'd get together in the wretched prisons it was as if he'd never gone.

Surely he was her son. He called her Ma. He listed her as "next of kin" in his prison documents. The government of Ontario handed over his mortal remains for her to dispose of according to the instructions he'd conveyed to her. Monty Bourke, the warden of Kingston Pen, delivered Ty's computer and his few possessions to her. She arranged his funeral and for the disposal of his ashes. All according to his wishes.

And so she just assumed . . .

But according to that young lawyer Dan Brodsky, who had tried to help Ty at various times, it wasn't all that simple. When Dr. and Mrs. Conn adopted Ty, they became his legal parents. Giving him back to the Children's Aid Society didn't change that. It just relieved them of responsibility for him.

There were documents, he said, that Dr. Conn would have to sign before he finally gave up his parental status. In view of everything, it would surely be nothing more than a formality. Lawyers talking to lawyers. And then Brodsky told her maybe it would be simpler if she just looked after it herself. A parent talking to a parent. Two people who had shared Ty's life. Two people who, perhaps, shared a common sense of failure and of grief.

And so, just before the end of the year and the century, Marion parked her bus at the end of Dr. Conn's driveway in a fine neighbourhood in the east part of Belleville. And she knocked on his door.

She'd never been there before. She'd only met Dr. Conn a couple of times, and only on Ty's behalf. And only at his office. Ty was always trying to find out where he stood with the Conns, as if it weren't clear enough already. And Dr. Conn, to his credit, had never tried to mislead him. He was glad that Ty and his birth mother had been reunited. So now they should all just get on with their lives.

And they did, eventually. But there was this small formality.

Dr. Conn didn't really understand when she explained about the documents.

Standing in the doorway of his festive home that day, he replied that, as far as he was concerned, his parental role in Ty's life had ended in December of 1978 when he returned the boy to the Children's Aid Society.

Well, yes, she replied. But in the eyes of the law . . .

It was important to her, she said, that Ty belong to someone. She had given him up to the Crown in 1970 and so he wasn't really hers. And now Dr. Conn was telling her that he had given him up to the Crown in 1978 and so he wasn't really his either.

"I guess," she said sadly as she prepared to leave, "poor Ty was nobody's child."

Then Dr. Conn corrected her. That wasn't true.

The boy was "society's child."

They studied each other then for a few moments.

Finally she handed him the documents that she said would make Ty unambiguously hers. He should really belong to someone more particular than "society."

He said he'd study them and he bid her a good day and closed the door.

And she went home to wait.

A FOOTNOTE

TEN DAYS AFTER TY CONN's dramatic flight from Kingston Penitentiary the commissioner of the Correctional Service of Canada, Ole Ingstrup, launched a formal investigation to discover how and why it happened. Three of the four members of his board of inquiry were senior officials of the CSC. This was the first mistake. It asks a lot of human nature to expect people to objectively investigate their own shortcomings.

The second mistake was a corollary of the first: a myopic focus on the mechanics and administrative minutiae that helped make the escape possible. The preoccupation with jailhouse-keeping either caused or enabled the board to skip over a number of more troubling philosophical and policy issues that Ty Conn's story might have illuminated.

The board handed in its report on October 6, 1999. We requested a copy of it, under the Access to Information Act, on November 22. We received a heavily edited copy when the CSC released it publicly on May 17, 2000. It was hardly worth the wait.

Anybody who knew Tyrone Conn as something more than FPS 690154B, including a surprising number of people in the corrections system, were and remain convinced that the most important question raised by the escape was: Why was he still in Kingston Penitentiary on May 6, 1999, anyway?

The board of inquiry did not ignore that question. What they did, in our opinion, was worse. They constructed a retaining wall of half-truths, innuendo and distortion to support the flawed judgment and administrative fumbling that abandoned him there and destroyed the last traces of his trust in the system and its pious mission statements.

From the time he returned to Millhaven Institution from the Special Handling Unit in Saskatchewan near the end of 1995 until he went to Kingston in May of 1998, Ty Conn was determined to leave prison legitimately. His goal, stated repeatedly to anyone who would listen, was to work his way to parole and then to begin a normal and productive life. The first step in that direction was to earn a reclassification to medium-security status.

It was his misfortune to arrive at Millhaven as the place was falling apart in chaos through no fault of his and, arguably, because of a lot of mismanagement and confusion at senior levels of the corrections system. He was, indeed, being considered for reclassification to medium-security status but he never got it, mostly because of a lack of continuity in his case management at Millhaven. Other circumstances intervened, and when he became involved in a violent plan by several inmates to escape from Millhaven, he took a position of civic responsibility, severed himself from the inmate culture and its code of silence and helped put a stop to the scheme.

But here is how the csc's board of inquiry reports those awful months: "He returned to Millhaven Institution in 1995 and, after a period of adjustment, was being considered by his case management team for a transfer to medium security. Unfortunately Conn was unable to accept that he did not have any credibility and by 1997 he was once again implicated in the planning of an escape. Protective custody concerns arising from this escape attempt precipitated a transfer to Kingston Penitentiary even though he was still viewed as medium security."

This attempt to avoid the truth is an affront, not just to the English language, but in our view, it offends logic itself. It says (1) he returned to Millhaven where he (2) adjusted well enough to be (3) considered for medium-security status but (4) had no credibility, and when (5) he became involved in an escape plot, which he helped to foil, (6) he went to Kingston Pen for his own protection (7) as a credible candidate for a medium-security placement.

And this is construed to be evidence of his unreliability!

On the very next page reality reluctantly resurfaces in this paragraph: "There is reference to a conversation between the KP parole officer and the IPSO [institutional preventive security officer] from Millhaven Institution which apparently vindicates Conn from the 1997 escape plan from that institution. The report states that a written account of this information is available on the preventive security file, however, it was not found by board members when that file was reviewed."

The next paragraph comes closer to revealing the truth than any other statement in the long and generally incoherent report.

> Although Conn continued to be supported for a transfer to medium security by his parole officer when he

arrived at KP in May 1998, *managers did not feel he
should be transferred and so there was a delay in a firm decision being made* [italics added]. By October though,
Conn was once again involved in activities that suggested he was planning an escape.

The board might have wondered whether the "delay in a
firm decision being made" violated the CSC's own rules as
well as personal assurances given Ty Conn at the time he
moved to Kingston. He and the authors had clear indica-
tions that he would not be there for long—October at the
latest. By October he was nearing a state of despair, convinced that he had been betrayed and abandoned by his jail-
ers. He vigorously denied, to the authorities and to the
authors, that the "activities" in Kingston Pen in late 1998
had anything to do with an escape plan.

The alleged activities were, however, convenient to institutional officials who refused to accept that Ty Conn had
changed. They needed to justify their inability or reluctance
to make "a firm decision" to move him to a medium-security
institution where he would have recieved some real help in
his effort at rehabilitation.

Of course by February 1999, after he'd been in the KP
hellhole for nine months, he was making it easy for his case
managers to make a firm decision to reconfirm him as a maximum-security inmate. It would have been, for him, the end
of any remaining hope that he'd ever leave prison legitimately.

The failure of the board to examine the key issue of why
he was there in the first place is understandable and thus
unforgivable, because it helps the system avoid any real
commitment to improving itself. Repeatedly, the report

characterizes Ty Conn as a potentially dangerous offender who was constantly scheming to break out of prison to inflict more havoc on society. Why, it implies, should anybody be surprised that he'd find a way to break out of KP as he had before, at Collins Bay?

The fact that he'd never really had an opportunity to function normally in society was unworthy of consideration or comment. The fact that he was serving an aggregate sentence that was baffling even to hardened policemen deserved no comment. And yet the authors of the report found it important to demonize the inmate by including the completely unsubstantiated slander that "unbeknownst to inmates and the majority of staff Conn established himself as an informer in the institutions he was housed in."

If it was "unbeknownst" to inmates and the majority of staff, where did the board members find this inflammatory piece of intelligence?

Ty Conn shared the inmates' abhorrence of prison informers to the point where he never forgave the famous bank robber Edwin Alonzo Boyd, whom he otherwise admired, for having "ratted out" another inmate after the brutal and unprovoked murder of a prison guard in KP.

The official investigation of Ty Conn's escape avoided other key issues that may well have contributed to his flight and its tragic aftermath. Labour-management relations at Kingston Penitentiary were abysmal before and during the time in question. Ty Conn knew about the weaknesses in prison security because staff members leaked the information to a columnist at *The Toronto Sun* who used it for an assault on the supposedly "liberal" Warden Monty Bourke and his boss, Commissioner Ingstrup. No mention was made of the malicious note Ty supposedly wrote to Justice Minister Anne McLellan when he was on the run, mocking her and Warden Bourke. It was a forgery, probably originating with disgruntled members of KP staff.

The board might have performed an important public service by examining the entire system of classifying prisoners and whether or not that system serves the purposes the CSC so nobly espouses—the "effective, safe reintegration" of reformed criminals to society.

Warehousing the worst of them in barren maximum-security institutions would seem to be in complete contradiction to the spirit of the corrections mission.

There is no more eloquent statement of the failure of that mission than the sinister walls of Kingston Penitentiary.

And there is no greater evidence of the emptiness of the words of the mission statement than the story of Tyrone Conn, whose needs his jailors couldn't meet and whose potential they couldn't see.

ACKNOWLEDGEMENTS

MANY ASPECTS OF TY CONN'S LIFE read as if lifted from fiction. Because it is a true story, it is more difficult to tell than fiction. Telling it would not have been possible without the generous assistance and trust of people who shared the authors' belief that there are important lessons to be learned from his unhappy experience. We are grateful for that assistance and for that trust. We have made the story as complete and accurate as possible. Where there are blank spots it is because some of the people and institutions who shared parts of his life found the experience too sensitive or painful to revisit. We respect their judgment. We have tried to be scrupulous in avoiding error, but it would be rash to presume we have entirely succeeded. Where we failed, we beg the readers' pardon. We have struggled to avoid untruth.

Among the scores of individuals who made it possible to complete this undertaking, a few deserve special mention. Many officials in the Correctional Service of Canada were generous with their time and resources. We are especially grateful for the assistance of Monty Bourke, warden at Kingston Penitentiary, and Lou Kelly, warden at Millhaven

Institution, as well as the deputy warden at Millhaven, Paul Snyder. Jacques Belanger, of csc headquarters in Ottawa, and David St. Onge, curator and archivist at the csc museum in Kingston, were particularly helpful. Bruce Jefferson was generous with his time and expertise at Collins Bay Institution.

Dave Gundy of the Brookside youth training facility in Cobourg provided important insight and context regarding youth corrections in the province of Ontario.

The staff at the Lion's Club Home for the Deaf in Foxboro, Ontario, were kind enough to permit us to visit Ty Conn's childhood home.

Among our colleagues at the cbc, we are grateful for the forbearance of our executive producer, David Studer, and senior producer of *the fifth estate,* Susan Teskey. Diana Redegeld was able to offer invaluable help with her knowledge of Hastings and Prince Edward counties, and with the infinite resources of cyberspace. Neil Docherty provided his enriching friendship and support throughout, as well as a valuable response to the early manuscript.

Special thanks to Daniel Brodsky who generously provided legal advice and personal support to Ty Conn at crucial moments when he was still in Millhaven Institution and later, when he was in Kingston Penitentiary. He provided sensitive and valuable assistance to Ty Conn's family in the difficult months after Ty's death. Clayton Ruby provided invaluable support to Ty Conn's friends and family during the crisis that unfolded at 101 Alberta Avenue on the night of May 20–21, 1999, and in the difficult days following.

We are also grateful to Carol Off, who was drawn into the tragic circumstances of Ty Conn's life and death and responded with courage and compassion, and to Rick

Salutin, whose writings about Ty Conn and his plight revealed deep insight and generosity of spirit.

Robert Hughes of the Special Investigations Unit of the Ministry of the Attorney General of Ontario, while constrained by his professional obligations, provided important guidance and advice.

Ty Conn spent most of his life after the age of fourteen incarcerated, but he acquired many friends and supporters in the community of citizens at large, in various parts of Canada as well as in Germany and Israel. We owe special thanks to Heather Atkins, who shared letters she received from Ty when he was much younger than the earnest and hopeful inmate that we got to know after 1994. Many thanks also to friends and acquaintances within the inmate populations who openly and honestly provided invaluable details concerning Ty Conn's life within the prison walls, and his escape from them.

The story could not have been told without the trust and candour of members of his family, notably his brother, Max Chamberlain, stepfather Max Chamberlain Sr., and his mother, Marion Chamberlain, to whom we have dedicated this book.

And finally, though of paramount importance, we must gratefully acknowledge the involvement of four of the many people who dedicated their skills to making this project a reality out of a principled awareness of its importance as a public document: Suzanne Depoe, Don Sedgwick, Cynthia Good and Mary Adachi.

INDEX